The
END OF
NORMAL

The Great Crisis and the Future of Growth

JAMES K. GALBRAITH

SIMON & SCHUSTER

New York London Toronto Sydney New Delhi

Simon & Schuster
1230 Avenue of the Americas
New York, NY 10020

First Simon & Schuster hardcover edition September 2014

SIMON & SCHUSTER and colophon are registered trademarks of
Simon & Schuster, Inc.

For information about special discounts for bulk purchases,
please contact Simon & Schuster Special Sales at 1-866-506-1949
or business@simonandschuster.com.

The Simon & Schuster Speakers Bureau can bring authors to your live event.
For more information or to book an event contact the Simon & Schuster Speakers
Bureau at 1-866-248-3049 or visit our website at www.simonspeakers.com.

Interior design by Aline Pace

Manufactured in the United States of America

10 9 8 7 6 5 4 3 2 1

Library of Congress Cataloging-in-Publication Data

Galbraith, James K.
  The end of normal : the great crisis and the future of growth / James K. Galbraith.
    pages cm
1. Global Financial Crisis, 2008–2009. 2. Europe—Economic conditions—20th
century. 3. Europe—Economic policy—20th century. 4. United States—Economic
conditions—20th century. 5. United States Economic policy—20th century. I. Title.
  HB37172008.G337 2014
  330.9'0511—dc23   2014012308

ISBN 978-1-4516-4492-0
ISBN 978-1-4516-4494-4 (ebook)

For Bruce Bartlett
A brave and honored friend

Politics is not the art of the possible. It consists in choosing between the disastrous and the unpalatable.

—*John Kenneth Galbraith*

Contents

Contents

The
END OF
NORMAL

Prologue

A Contest of One-Note Narratives

In 1930 John Maynard Keynes wrote, "The world has been slow to realize that we are living this year in the shadow of one of the greatest economic catastrophes of modern history." No such hesitation attended the tumult of September 2008, as the financial world collapsed into the arms of the US government. Nor were scribblers and analysts slow to react. Because of the Depression, the New Deal, and World War II, no history of the Great Crash emerged until a slim volume, written over a summer by my father, appeared in 1954. But today, barely a half decade since the Great Crisis, we have the benefit of many books by journalists and economists, a growing number of political memoirs, and a shelf of official reports. The problem is what to make of them.

A first round, including David Wessel's *In Fed We Trust* and Andrew Ross Sorkin's *Too Big to Fail*, focused on the top bankers and on the George W. Bush administration; later Ron Suskind's *Confidence Men* and Noam Scheiber's *The Escape Artists* did similar service for the

Obama team. Political memoirs (so far) by former treasury secretary Henry Paulson, by former special inspector general for the Troubled Asset Relief Program (TARP) Neil Barofsky, and by former chair of the Federal Deposit Insurance Corporation Sheila Bair tell the story of the crisis mainly in human and political terms—of the strengths and failings of the men and women who were caught in the storm.

The political and personal accounts usually do not describe the practices that produced the debacle. This is the domain of business reporters, a few law professors, and official investigations. For these, the essence of crisis lies in the behavior of the entities that provided housing finance in America in that time. Major efforts include *All the Devils Are Here* by Bethany McLean and Joseph Nocera, *Griftopia* by Matt Taibbi, *The Subprime Virus* by Kathleen Engel and Patricia McCoy, and *Anatomy of a Financial Crisis* by Marc Jarsulic. *The Big Short*, by Michael Lewis, stands a bit apart as an account of speculators who bet profitably against a doomed system. Official investigations have been led by the Financial Crisis Inquiry Commission (chaired by Phil Angelides), the Congressional Oversight Panel (chaired by Elizabeth Warren), the Senate Permanent Subcommittee on Investigations (chaired by Carl Levin), and by the Office of the Special Inspector General for the Troubled Asset Relief Program (SIGTARP). These investigations have between them marshalled evidence. Some of their accounts are mesmerizing, like a good horror movie. But they are narratives of fact and not, generally, of explanation.

To take an example, the majority report of the Financial Crisis Inquiry Commission presents a detailed, well-documented history of misfeasance both in government and in the banking sector. (For a government document, it is also very well written.) It establishes that what happened did so in plain view. But to what end? What's the theory that comports with the facts? Even a powerful story line does not by itself explain *why* the circumstances were such. Nor can it lead effectively toward a safer, more stable economic and financial world. The facts are vital for establishing whether individual and business conduct met standards of ethics and law. But even if these matters are fully disclosed, and even if they were fully acted upon by competent authority (which has not been the case), by themselves they do not guide us to what *we* should do to repair the damage and to prevent such things from happening again.

Then we come to the stage when writers turn from *what* happened to *why*. This is the economist's task. The economist in these matters is an interpretive artist, placing facts within a framework that can convey understanding and (where necessary) motivate action. It is an important role; without it, the personal and business histories remain barren. Economists take this role seriously, guarding with some jealousy their professional hold over this niche in the discourse. And so a small shelf of interpretations, by authors ranging from Nassim Taleb (*The Black Swan*), to Nouriel Roubini (*Crisis Economics*), to Raghuram Rajan (*Fault Lines*), to Joseph Stiglitz (*Freefall*), to Paul Krugman (*End This Depression Now!*), has appeared.

But so far no common understanding has emerged. On the contrary, each economist brings to the job a distinctive vision, set apart from that of anyone else, reflecting that economist's place in the larger constellation of the profession. These visions then compete in a marketplace of ideas and a contest of marketing. What it takes to win acceptance is not entirely settled, but passion, political allies, and a prominent platform for promoting book sales all play their roles. And so does simplicity: the power of what is easy to grasp. It is far easier to sell a simple idea, even if that means that the conflicts with other ideas must go unresolved.

For the most part, what the economists have delivered so far are efforts to interpret the crisis as the instance of a theme. The themes vary. Black Swans. Fat Tails. Bubbles. Big Government. Inequality. The Liquidity Trap. Some are simple metaphors; others more developed. Some are conservative; others liberal. Some comport with the dominant views in academic economics; others dissent. A few are mainly misinformation, political, opportunistic, even arguably corrupt; others contain large elements of truth. Yet all are incomplete. There has been not much effort to weigh these arguments against one another, and no common framework seems to exist to set the rules for doing so. The situation brings to mind what child psychologists call "parallel play."

A brief survey can help bring this situation into focus.

Black Swans

The "Black Swan" view is perhaps the simplest possible explanation of the Great Crisis; it holds that there is nothing, necessarily, to be explained. Like black swans, crises are rare. The failure to predict an event that happens rarely is unfortunate, but it is not a sign of scientific failing. A model can be a good one, even if rare events that it did not expect do sometimes occur. The Black Swan view calls our attention to the predictive limits of even the best theoretical apparatus. It can be used to defend the contention that "no one could have foreseen" the oncoming disaster of 2008—even though some people *did* foresee it. It may even be that the best available forecast beforehand was "no crisis," and that those who claimed otherwise were alarmists who on this occasion merely happened, like the proverbial stopped clock, to have been right.

One problem with applying this particular point of view to financial crises, though, is that, viewed globally, they are not especially rare. To ordinary citizens of the United States and Germany, a full-scale financial meltdown may be a novelty. But they are a stock-in-trade of international investors and currency speculators, and the citizens of less stable lands deal with them as a matter of course. Just since the mid-1990s, we have seen financial crises in Latin America, Africa, Mexico, Russia, Iceland, most of Asia, Japan, the United States, and the Eurozone.* The notion that

---

* Moreover, the history of financial crises goes back at least eight hundred years, a history that Carmen Reinhart and Kenneth Rogoff celebrate in their famous book, *This Time Is Different*.

financial crises are scarce is a mirage, reflecting the fact that they don't generally happen at short intervals to precisely the same people, and less in the richest countries than in poorer ones.

Fat Tails

The "Fat Tails" view deflates the notion of Black Swans. It admits that extreme events are not rare. As a matter of habit and mathematical convenience, modelers typically assume that this distribution of errors is "normal" (or Gaussian), so that the relative frequency of extreme events is known. It is a feature of normality, in this statistical meaning, that extreme events happen rarely. Generally speaking for events measured on human timescales, the eponymous "Six Sigma" deviation from the average outcome should not happen but once in thousands of years. But crises may happen much more often than, from the statistical point of view, they "should." In the real world, the distribution of events about the mean expectation may not be Gaussian. In that case, extreme events will happen much more frequently than assumed. It is not even possible, under this view, to say just how frequently to expect a disaster. The essence of Fat Tails is that you cannot measure this; you know only that disasters do happen, and that the risk cannot safely be assessed by calculating the area under a normal curve.

And yet, even in a world of Fat Tails, the model that doesn't predict a crisis need not be wrong. The average view, which is also a model's "best" expectation at any time, may still be that things will go on as before. The message is that in this unpleasant and difficult world, one should be prepared in general terms for ugly surprises, in the certainty that they will occur but with no hope of predicting them in real time. One cannot even anticipate the direction the deviations-from-normal will take—there may be a boom, and there may be a bust. Fat-tailed distributions are mathematical monstrosities just as much as they are harsh features of the real world. They are hard on forecasters, rough on speculators, and hell on people who have to live with the disasters that they imply will occur.

Bubbles

The word *bubble* conveys something that seems to be a bit more specific. A bubble is a quasi-mechanical process—a physical phenomenon with certain properties. It inflates slowly. It pops quickly. These traits impart an apparent completeness to the concept of bubbles that, together with repetition, has made it a very popular term for describing financial dynamics. The concept almost seems to be a *theory*, in the sense of providing explanation and guidance. Many people, including many economists, use the term as though it were founded in a well-understood economics, so that one need only identify a bubble in progress in order to know that disaster awaits. This is not the case. "Bubble" is simply a compelling image, a metaphor, made familiar by long usage in the history of disasters.

The bubble metaphor conveys inevitability. Bubbles always pop. Once one is in a bubble, there is no way out. One can speak, with forlorn hope, of lancing the bubble so that it deflates gently, or of a "soft landing"—but these are mixed metaphors: the obvious artifacts of wishful thought. Bubbles are not boils, and they are not spacecraft.

Then again, the nature of a bubble is that it is insubstantial. Bubbles are epiphenomenal. They operate on the surface of a deeper reality. After a bubble collapses, according to the metaphor, fundamentals rule again. Things revert to the state of the world before the bubble happened. And if we follow the metaphor faithfully, on average the world is not worse or better off than if the bubble had never occurred. For this reason, the "Greenspan doctrine" upheld in the time of Federal Reserve chairman Alan Greenspan was intellectually consistent, or at least metaphorically unmixed, in holding that the authorities should not try to predict, identify, prevent, or deflate bubbles. It should be sufficient, the doctrine claimed, to clean up after they burst.

Finally, the word hints at a certain innocence of intent. Bubbles are playful. They are fascinating to children. Their behavior may be distracting. It may be disruptive. But in the longer run, the image conveys the notion that they are harmless. Bubbles are not shells or bombs; when they pop, they do not kill. In the nature of the metaphor, the mess left by a bursting bubble is not very large.

A common feature of these three themes—Black Swans, Fat Tails, and bubbles—is that they depict the economic system as having a normal, noncrisis steady state. Normality is interrupted but not predictably so. Crises are therefore inherently beyond the reach of preventive measures. Indeed, they can be explained only after the fact, and there is no guarantee that a fix will be effective in preventing the next one. These themes entail a certain fatalism. They work to reconcile the laissez-faire approach to regulation with a world in which terrible things happen from time to time. And they reinforce an even more dangerous notion, which is that when the crisis is over, the conditions previously thought to be normal will return.

The claim of normality on the imagination of economists is very strong—so strong as to be practically subconscious. Consider how Lawrence Summers, President Obama's chief economic adviser in 2009 and 2010, introduced an essay in the *Financial Times* in early 2012:

> On even a pessimistic reading of the [American] economy's potential, *un-employment remains 2 percentage points below* normal *levels, employment remains 5m jobs below* potential *levels and gross domestic product remains close to $1tn short of its* potential. *Even if the economy creates 300,000 jobs a month and grows at 4 per cent, it would take several years to restore* normal *conditions. So a lurch back this year towards the kind of policies that are appropriate in* normal *times would be quite premature.*

Notice the triple repetition of the words *normal* and *potential*. (I added the emphasis.) The repetition signifies a belief that Summers shared with many economists; a belief that is also built in to official US government forecasts, coloring the worldview of legislators and presidents.* The belief is that the market system tends naturally toward an end state of full production and high employment. The economy can be displaced from its normal condition by a shock or a crisis—and if the shock is great, the displacement may be severe. But when the shock passes, recovery begins, and once "recovery" is under way, progress toward "full recovery" is inexorable—unless some new shock or policy error gets in the way.

The next themes on my little list—government and inequality—run against this idea. That is, they are not merely metaphors or statements about the probability of displacement from a normal state. Rather, they are words rooted in economic theory. They describe specific and, in principle, measurable conditions that might stand as a barrier, or structural obstacle, to a return to normal. The barrier can, in principle, be long-standing or even permanent. It can derive from the ideas of the right or those of the left—and I have chosen one from each camp. In each case, the description of a barrier is an attempt to assert a causal sequence through a recognizable process, and thus to distinguish cause from effect. In this way, the argument challenges complacency and motivates changes in public policy. If you believe any of these theories, and if you want to change things, then something must be done.

Big Government

A conservative argument holds that US government housing policy was responsible for the Great Crisis. Exhibit A in this argument is the Com-

---

* Summers has since changed his view, taking up the theme of "secular stagnation" in the language proposed by Alvin Hansen in the 1930s.

munity Reinvestment Act of 1977, which requires banks to make loans in the communities where they collect deposits.* Exhibits B and C are Fannie Mae and Freddie Mac, the government-sponsored (though long-ago privatized) enterprises established to purchase mortgages from the private market, thus pooling the risk and refinancing the lenders. The argument, echoed notably by Gretchen Morgenson and Joshua Rosner in *Reckless Endangerment,* holds that these companies fostered "moral hazard" (undue reward for risky behavior) and "adverse selection" (the seeking out of unsuitable borrowers) because of the implicit public guarantee against loss. Peter Wallison's dissent in *The Financial Crisis Inquiry Report* puts it this way:

> *[I]f the government had not been directing money into the mortgage markets in order to foster growth in home ownership, NTMs [nontraditional mortgages] in the bubble would have begun to default relatively soon after they were originated. The continuous inflow of government or government-backed funds, however, kept the bubble growing—not only in size but over time—and this tended to suppress the significant delinquencies and defaults that had brought previous bubbles to an end in only three or four years. (FCIC 2011, 472)*

To this, some have added that both federal deposit insurance and the doctrine of "too big to fail" encouraged risk taking by providing an implicit public backstop to private lending decisions. They argue that if government had made clear that it would tolerate the failure of the largest banks, then market discipline would have prevailed, the banks would have been more cautious, and the crisis might not have occurred. Richard Fisher,

---

* Peter J. Wallison's dissenting view in the Final Report of the National Commission on the Causes of the Financial and Economic Crisis in the United States, submitted in January 2011, places responsibility not on the original 1977 CRA but on certain 1995 amendments.

president of the Federal Reserve Bank of Dallas, is a prominent and elegant exponent of this view.*

One may disagree with this argument and not despise it. The theory in which it is rooted is the textbook standard, under which markets and institutions give efficient results unless traduced by distortions—usually introduced by government (though sometimes by private monopolies or trade unions) and usually in the pursuit of some larger social goal. The theory has a complex structure. It posits a world of competitive, profit-maximizing business enterprises interacting with rational, goal-oriented individuals. It expects that business judgments would ordinarily minimize the losses associated with excessive risk. Business judgment, in other words, is ordinarily sound. From this assumption, it follows that public policy runs, at the least, the chance of upsetting the controlling force of sound business judgment. There is behind this the thought that if bureaucrats were as smart as business leaders, they would be business leaders rather than bureaucrats.

There is plain evidence that government *did* intervene in housing markets to encourage home purchasing by low-income families. Fannie Mae and Freddie Mac exist. They did branch out from their traditional mission of supporting prime mortgages, to fund the nontraditional mortgages that, when they defaulted, wrecked the system. If one feels a need for more evidence, there are ample clear statements of public purpose in home ownership in the housing statutes and other official documents. On this foundation of clear-cut theory and prominent fact, the Republican members of the Financial Crisis Inquiry Commission drafted their critiques of that commission's majority report. Wallison's long (and much derided) argument on these matters is, in this respect, meticulous.

---

* See Richard Fisher, "Paradise Lost: Addressing 'Too Big to Fail,'" a speech given November 19, 2009, at the Cato Institute. Fisher makes use of John Milton, Charles Mackay, Charles Dickens, and Walter Bagehot in these remarks.

Inequality

Did increasing inequality cause the financial crisis? The roots of an argument along these lines are quite old. A version may be attributed to Karl Marx, who foresaw a *crisis of realization* associated with aggressive wage reductions—the proletarianization of labor—accompanied by an increasing capital intensity of machine production. Put simply, there would be too many goods and too little income to buy them. Inequality of incomes would lead to a general glut, or a crisis of underconsumption. The consequence would be mass unemployment, unless or until capitalists found external markets that could absorb their goods. Marx (and later Lenin and the German communist Rosa Luxemburg) saw in this imperative the drive of the European bourgeoisie for empires in India and Africa and for forcing open the markets of Japan and China.

Versions of the same story were frequently offered as part of the explanation of the Great Depression—following the ideas of the late-nineteenth-century British economist J. A. Hobson. In more recent times, my father, John Kenneth Galbraith, made casual reference to the "bad income distribution" as a factor behind the Great Crash.[*] To provide a stable source of total demand for product by giving stable incomes to the elderly was part of the reasoning behind the creation of the Social Security system in the 1930s. The early New Deal lawyer Jerome Frank wrote in a 1938 book titled *Save America First*: "The total national income is bound to shrink alarmingly unless a large enough number of citizens receive some fair share of it. The fate of those Americans who receive relatively high incomes is therefore inextricably bound up with that of those who receive low incomes. The former cannot prosper unless the latter do."[†]

---

[*] *The Great Crash, 1929*, 177.

[†] I am grateful to Professor Allen Kamp of John Marshall Law School for this quote (Frank 1938, 235).

In the wake of the Great Crisis, economists seeking its source in inequality have recast the old arguments about underconsumption in terms of desires rather than needs. They also introduce the element of household debt—which was not an especially big factor in the run-up to the Great Depression of the 1930s, in a world where most households were renters and most purchases were for cash. Thus the argument has shifted, over the decades, from concern with the inability to meet basic necessities from current income, to a concern over the inability to meet the interest payments on inessential purchases from future income.

Following the great early-twentieth-century economist Thorstein Veblen (from afar), as well as the 1950s "relative income hypothesis" of the Harvard University consumption theorist James Duesenberry, the new inequality theories hold that an essential social consequence of the gap between the middle classes and the rich is *envy*: desire for the lifestyle of the rich. Some of that lifestyle is easily imagined in terms of goods: sports cars, boats, flat-screen televisions. Some is better measured in positional terms: neighborhoods with cleaner air, less crime, better schools. And there is the not-trivial status question of the college or university at which one's children may enroll. The observations especially of Robert Frank, author of *Luxury Fever* and a leading specialist in the economics of flash and bling, document these preoccupations.

This argument has been advanced by Raghuram Rajan in a book called *Fault Lines*. In Rajan's telling, the problem of growing inequality begins with stagnant wages in the working population. Wage stagnation leads to frustration, as living standards do not improve. And then, as people observe the rising incomes of the few—of the 1 percent, say—their envy gets worse. Since the thirst cannot be slaked from growing income (because of stagnant wages), it is met with debt—something that became possible for the first time with the postwar willingness of banks to lend to private households, mostly against the equity in their homes. Thus (private) debt and debt service rise in relation to income, particularly for those lower on the income scale. And the crisis breaks into the open when debts incurred for this purpose cannot be repaid.

This story is articulated mainly by moderate conservatives—a description that probably fits Rajan—but it is also well attuned to the preconceptions of a certain part of the political Left: for example, the "structural Keynesianism" view of the crisis advanced by economist Thomas Palley. The message is that median wages (and therefore family incomes) *should have risen* in proportion to the incomes of the wealthy. This would have kept inequality in check. Then, it is supposed, greed and envy would also have been contained. People would not then be tempted into debt in order to boost their consumption, financial stability would have been maintained, and crises would not occur.

Like the CRA-Fannie-Freddie account, this story is lent plausibility for the United States by a certain amount of surface evidence. One bit of such evidence is that, if one takes the working population as a whole, median wages *were* stagnant in real terms for most of the generation that followed the early 1970s, rising only for a brief period in the late 1990s. A second is the statistical fact that measured income inequality rose to a peak before the Great Crash of 1929 and again just before the Nasdaq bust of 2000. At least at this level of simple time-series association, there does *appear* to be a connection between wage stagnation, the rise of inequality, and the emergence of financial crisis—just as there appears to be an association between public statements about expanding home ownership (the "ownership society," as it was called for a little while) and private banking decisions to extend credit to home owners who ordinarily would not have qualified for loans.

But again: Is the tale persuasive?

To answer that question, in this case, it helps to consider questions of logic. First, is it necessarily true that a stagnant median wage implies that the incomes of individual workers are not rising, leading to the alleged frustration with the growth of living standards? Second, even if the incomes of individual workers *were* rising, would they necessarily be *less*

13

envious of those above them, and so less prone to competitive consumption fueled by adding debt to debt?

A moment's thought should convince the reader to be wary. Is it true that a stagnant median wage necessarily corresponds to stagnant wages for individual workers? Answer: no, it is not *necessarily* true. Consider a workforce where every wage, every year, for every job and experience level, was exactly the same as it had been the year before—and where there was no population growth or decline. In this world, the only thing that happens is that individual workers get a fixed raise each year, reflecting their seniority on the job, until the day they retire. Each year, a new group of high school and college graduates enters the workforce at the bottom, and an aging group of senior workers retires. In this world, the median wage will never change. Nevertheless, every single worker has a rising income every single year! Every worker will therefore have a higher living standard every year than he or she did before. It is an error, in other words, to confuse a stagnant median wage with wage stagnation for individual workers. A stagnant median wage is perfectly compatible (in principle, not necessarily in actual experience) with rising wages all around.

Now consider what happens when the labor force changes—as more women, young people, minorities, and immigrants come in, and as older white men are flushed out by age or industrial change. New workers, young workers, immigrants, and workers from disadvantaged groups almost always have below-median wages. So the overall median falls. In this situation, the median wage (which is the wage of the worker in the exact middle of the distribution at any given time) is pulled *downward, just because there are more workers below the previous median.* And yet every *new* worker is better off holding a job than she or he was beforehand, when she or he did not yet hold a job. And every worker continues to get a rising wage and income, every year, until the dreadful day when the plant closes, the job is offshored, or he is forced to retire. Over time, in this situation, the overall structure of employment does shift toward less-well-paid jobs. It may be, for example, that the new jobs are mainly in mundane and poorly paid services, while well-paid, unionized manufacturing jobs decline as a share of total employment. But only some individual workers experience that shift as a personal loss, so long as they remain in the workforce. For the majority, the year-to-year experience remains one of modest gains, with age and experience and occasional promotions.

Is this a plausible picture of what has happened in America? Of course it is. Over the past forty years, the share of white men in the active workforce has declined by about 11 percentage points, mostly (though not always) as older workers stopped working. The share of manufacturing workers in employment has dropped by at least half. And if one looks at the median incomes *within* the non-white-male ethnic and gender groups in the workforce, you find that they largely rose through the end of the 1990s, even though the overall median was stagnant.* Thus there is no strong reason to believe that individual workers were more frustrated, or more afflicted by envy, leading them into debt, than was true at other times in the past. Yes, many of them started out poorer, in relative terms, than was true of the generation before. Yes, the entire structure of the working population shifted toward less-well-paid employments. But from the individual point of view, what of it? Relative to their own past position, low-wage workers were (in many cases) making gains. And it is their own past position that matters to the idea that wage stagnation produces envy-fueled and debt-driven consumption.

The second part of the story implies that if wages *had* risen instead of stagnated, then workers would have been happier with their rising living standards and would not have accepted excessive debts in order to catch up with those higher than themselves on the consumption ladder. But why should this be true? Even if the pay of the working poor is rising quickly, it will always be far below the earnings of the landed and entitled rich. If

---

* An exception is the Hispanic group, which is constantly augmented by new immigrants, at the bottom of the wage scale. I am grateful to Olivier Giovannoni of Bard College for sharing his work on this point.

the *gap* drives debt, there is no reason why it should matter what the rate of wage growth is. The gap is there in good times and in bad, and (given the premise of desire driven by envy) so is the compulsion to spend ahead of income. What will matter, instead, is the willingness of lenders to make the loans.

Yet this factor is missing. Consider how the story that "rising economic inequality caused the crisis" treats the banks and shadow banks who made the loans. They aren't there. They play no active role. The theory assumes that loans are available to those who want them, for whatever purposes they may choose. In this peculiar world, rich people lend to poor people. Banks are merely go-betweens, shifting funds from those who have more than they need to those who need more than they have. Everything is in the demand for loans, nothing in the supply.

Having airbrushed the bankers from his picture, Rajan focuses on the source of rising demand for loans, with a very special view of why American incomes have become so unequal over the past thirty years. He roots the change in "indifferent nutrition, socialization, and learning in early childhood, and in dysfunctional primary and secondary schools that leave too many Americans unprepared for college" (Rajan 2010, 8). These have led, in his telling, to a widening of "the 90/50 differential" in wages, or the gap between wealthy Americans and those in the middle. In an efficient labor market, in other words, dumb people just get paid less. And this induced a "political response," which was to "expand lending to households, especially low-income ones. The benefits—growing consumption and more jobs—were immediate, whereas paying the inevitable bill could be postponed into the future. Cynical as it may seem, easy credit has been used as a palliative throughout history by governments that are unable to address the deeper anxieties of the middle class" (Rajan 2010, 9). Dumb people got loans to keep them happy.

Thus: at the deepest level, in this telling, the financial meltdown was caused by *malnutrition*, by *the inadequacy of Head Start*, and by *the failures of the public schools*. These failures—which are largely failures of

16

government—produced rising inequality, and in the end precipitated a response *by government* to make loans available, which leave an "inevitable bill." *Cynical as it may seem*, banks play practically no role in this story. Though Rajan states they are "sophisticated, competitive, and amoral," they bear no responsibility and might as well be bystanders in his tale.

If it is true, as this story alleges, that a prior process of rising wage inequality caused the crisis, then the entire postcrisis reinvigoration of bank regulation and supervision, and investigation into malfeasance was, logically, beside the point. The banks, after all, were only passive. The active agents were those middle- and lower-income households who held stubbornly to consumption aspirations that their wage rates did not entitle them to afford. Suddenly the morality tale takes on a different hue. Where the "conservative" interpretation is one under which public policies misdirected bank decisions, under the "inequality-did-it" narrative, banks do not make decisions, and the question of bank decision making does not arise at all. One has to wonder: Can this really be the "progressive" alternative to the conservative view?

Of course, it cannot be. Let us therefore suspend the search for one-note narratives. We need to take a different approach. The story, let me suggest, begins usefully with the economic world our parents and grandparents created, in the wake of the Second World War.

Part One

The Optimists' Garden

One

Growth Now and Forever

To begin to understand why the Great Financial Crisis broke over an astonished world, one needs to venture into the mentality of the guardians of expectation—the leadership of the academic economics profession—in the years before the crisis. Most of today's leading economists received their formation from the late 1960s through the 1980s. But theirs is a mentality that goes back further: to the dawn of the postwar era and the Cold War in the United States, largely as seen from the cockpits of Cambridge, Massachusetts, and Chicago, Illinois. It was then, and from there, that the modern and still-dominant doctrines of American economics emerged.

To put it most briefly, these doctrines introduced the concept of economic growth and succeeded, over several decades, to condition most Americans to the belief that growth was not only desirable but also normal, perpetual, and expected. Growth became the solution to most (if not quite all) of the ordinary economic problems, especially poverty and unemployment. We lived in a culture of growth; to question it was, well, countercultural. The role of government was to facilitate and promote growth, and perhaps to moderate the cycles that might, from time to time, be superimposed over the underlying trend. A failure of growth became unimaginable. Occasional downturns would occur—they would now be called *recessions*—but recessions would be followed by recovery and an eventual return to the long-term trend. That trend was defined as the *potential* output, the long-term trend at high employment, which thus became the standard.

To see what was new about this, it's useful to distinguish this period both from the nineteenth-century Victorian mentality described by Karl Marx in *Capital* or John Maynard Keynes in *The Economic Consequences of the Peace*, and from the common experience in the first half of the twentieth century.

To the Victorians, the ultimate goal of society was not economic growth as we understand it. It was, rather, investment or capital accumulation. Marx put it in a phrase: "Accumulate, accumulate! That is Moses and the Prophets!" Keynes wrote: "Europe was so organized socially and economically as to secure the maximum accumulation of capital . . . Here, in fact, lay the main justification of the capitalist system. If the rich had spent their new wealth on their own enjoyments, the world would have long ago found such a régime intolerable. But like bees they saved and accumulated" (Keynes 1920, 11).

But accumulate for what? *In principle*, accumulation was for profits and for power, even for survival. It was what capitalists felt obliged to do by their economic and social positions. The purpose of accumulation was *not* to serve the larger interest of the national community. It was *not* to secure a general improvement in living standards. The economists of the nineteenth century did not hold out great hopes for the progress of living standards. The Malthusian trap (population outrunning resources) and the iron law of wages were dominant themes. These held that in the nature of things, wages could not exceed subsistence for very long. And even as resources became increasingly abundant, the Marxian dynamic—the extraction of surplus value by the owners of capital—reinforced the message that workers should expect no sustained gains. Competition between capitalists, including the introduction of machinery, would keep the demand for labor and the value of wages down. Marx again:

> *"Like every other increase in the productiveness of labour, machinery is intended to cheapen commodities, and, by shortening that portion of the working-day, in which the labourer works for himself, to lengthen the other portion that he gives, without an equivalent, to the capitalist. In short, it is a means for producing surplus-value."* (Marx 1974, vol. 1, ch. 15, 351)

Yet living standards did improve. That they did so—however slowly, as Keynes later noted—was a mystery for economists at the time. The improvement might be attributed to the growth of empires and the opening of new territories to agriculture and mining, hence the importance of colonies in that era. But in the nineteenth century, economics taught that such gains could only be transitory. Fairly soon population growth and the pressure of capitalist competition on wages would drive wages down again. Even a prosperous society would ultimately have low wages, and its working people would be poor. This grim fatalism, at odds though it was with the facts in Europe and America, was the reason that economics was known as the "dismal science."

Then came the two great wars of the twentieth century, along with the Russian Revolution and the Great Depression. Human and technical capabilities surged, and (thanks to the arrival of the age of oil) resource constraints fell away. But while these transformations were under way, and apart from the brief boom of the 1920s, material conditions of civilian life in most of the industrial countries declined, or were stagnant, or were constrained by the exigencies of wartime. The Great Depression, starting in the mid-1920s in the United Kingdom and after 1929 in the United States, appeared to signal the collapse of the Victorian accumulation regime—and with it, the end of the uneasy truce and symbiotic relationship between labor and capital that had graced the prewar years. Now the system itself was in peril.

For many, the question then became: could the state do the necessary accumulation instead? This was the challenge of communism, which in a parallel universe not far away showed its military power alongside its capacity to inspire the poor and to accelerate industrial development. In some noncommunist countries, democratic institutions became stronger—as they tend to do when governments need soldiers—giving voice to the economic aspirations of the whole population. For social democrats and socialists, *planning* was the new alternative—a prospect that horrified Friedrich von Hayek, who argued in 1944 that planning and totalitarianism were the same.

By the 1950s, communism ruled almost half the world. In the noncommunist part, it could no longer be a question of building things up for a distant, better future. Entire populations felt entitled to a share of the prosperity that was at hand—for instance, to college educations, to automobiles, and to homes. To deny them would have been dangerous. Yet the future also could not be neglected, and (especially given the communist threat) no one in the "free world" thought that the need for new investments and still greater technological progress was over. Therefore it was a matter of consuming and investing *in tandem*, so as to have *both* increased personal consumption now and the capacity for still greater consumption later on. This was the new intellectual challenge, and the charm, and the usefulness to Cold Warriors, of the theory of economic growth.

The Golden Years

From 1945 to 1970, the United States enjoyed a growing and generally stable economy and also dominance in world affairs. Forty years later, this period seems brief and distant, but at the time it seemed to Americans the

24

natural culmination of national success. It was the start of a new history, justified by victory in war and sustained in resistance to communism. That there *was* a communist challenge imparted both a certain no-nonsense pragmatism to policy, empowering the Cold War liberals of the Massachusetts Institute of Technology (MIT) and the RAND Corporation, while driving the free-market romantics of Chicago (notably Milton Friedman) to the sidelines. Yet few seriously doubted that challenge could or should be met. The United States was the strongest country, the most advanced, the undamaged victor in world war, the leader of world manufacturing, the home of the great industrial corporation, and the linchpin of a new, permanent, stable architecture of international finance. These were facts, not simply talking points, and it took a brave and even self-marginalizing economist, willing to risk professional isolation in the mold of Paul Baran and Paul Sweezy, to deny them.

Nor were optimism and self-confidence the preserve of elites. Ordinary citizens agreed, and to keep them in fear of communism under the circumstances required major investments in propaganda. Energy was cheap. Food was cheap, with (thanks to price supports) staples such as milk and corn and wheat in great oversupply. Interest rates were low and credit was available to those who qualified, and so housing, though modest by later standards, was cheap enough for whites. Jobs were often unionized, and their wages rose with average productivity gains. Good jobs were not widely open to women, but the men who held them had enough, by the standards of the time, for family life. As wages rose, so did taxes, and the country could and did invest in long-distance roads and suburbs. There were big advances in childhood health, notably against polio but also measles, mumps, rubella, tuberculosis, vitamin deficiencies, bad teeth, and much else besides. In many states, higher education was tuition-free in public universities with good reputations. Though working-class white America was much poorer than today and much more likely to die poor, there had never been a better time to have children. And there never would be again. Over the eighteen years of the baby boom, from 1946 to

1964, the fruits of growth were matched by a rapidly rising population to enjoy them.

It was in this spirit that, in the 1950s, economists invented the theory of economic growth. The theory set out to explain why things were good and how the trajectory might be maintained. Few economists in the depression-ridden and desperate 1930s would have considered wasting time on such questions, but now they seemed critical: What did growth depend on? What were the conditions required for growth to be sustained? How much investment could you have without choking off consumption and demand? How much consumption could you have without starving the future? The economists' answer would be that, *in the long run*, economic growth depended on three factors: population growth, technological change, and saving.

It was not a very deep analysis, and its principal authors did not claim that it was. In the version offered by Robert Solow, the rate of population growth was simply assumed. It would be whatever it happened to be—rising as death rates came under control, and then falling again, later on, as fertility rates also declined, thanks to urban living and birth control. Thomas Robert Malthus, the English parson who in 1798 had written that population would always rise, so as to force wages back down to subsistence, was now forgotten. How could his theory possibly be relevant in so rich a world?

Technology was represented as the pure product of science and invention, available more or less freely to all as it emerged. This second great simplification enabled economists to duck the question of where new machinery and techniques came from. In real life, of course, new products and processes bubbled up from places like Los Alamos and Bell Labs and were mostly built into production via capital investment and protected by patents and secrecy. Big government gave us the atom bomb and the nuclear power plant; big business gave us the transistor. Working together, the two gave us jets, integrated circuits, and other wonders, but the textbooks celebrated James Watt and Thomas Edison and other boy geniuses and garage tinkerers, just as they would continue to do in the age of Bill Gates and

Steve Jobs, whose products would be just as much the offshoots of the work of government and corporate labs.

With both population and technology flowing from the outside, the growth models were designed to solve for just one variable, and that was the rate of saving (and investment). If saving could be done at the right rate, the broad lesson of the growth model was that good times could go on. There was what the model called a "steady-state expansion path," and the trick to staying on it was to match personal savings with the stock of capital, the growth of the workforce, and the pace of progress. Too much saving, and an economy would slip back into overcapacity and unemployment. Too little, and capital—and therefore growth—would dry up. But with just the right amount, the economy could grow steadily and indefinitely, with a stable internal distribution of income. The task for policy, therefore, was only to induce the right amount of saving. This was not a simple calculation: economists made their reputations working out what the right value (the "golden rule") for the saving rate should be. But the problem was not impossibly complex either, and it was only dimly realized (if at all) that its seeming manageability was made possible by assuming away certain difficulties.

The idea that unlimited growth and improvement were possible, with each generation destined to live better than the one before, was well suited to a successful and optimistic people. It was also what their leaders wanted them to believe; indeed, it was a sustaining premise of the postwar American vision. Moreover, there was an idea that this growth did not come necessarily at the expense of others; it was the product of the right sort of behavior and not of privilege and power. Tracts such as Walt W. Rostow's *Stages of Economic Growth* spread the message worldwide: *everyone* could eventually go through "take-off" and reach the plateau of high mass consumption.* Capitalism, suitably tamed by social democracy and the welfare

---

* Part of the appeal of my father's 1958 book *The Affluent Society* stemmed from the rebellion it spurred against this emerging consensus.

state, could deliver everything communism promised, and more. And it could do it without commissars or labor camps.

A curiosity of the models was the many things they left out. The "factors of production" were "labor" and "capital." Labor was just a measure of time worked, limited only by the size of the labor force and expected to grow exponentially with the human population. Capital (a controversial construct, subject to intense debate in the 1950s) was to be thought of as machinery, made from labor, measured essentially as the amalgam of the past human effort required to build the machines. As every textbook would put it, if Y is output, K is capital, and L is labor, then:

$$Y = f(K, L)$$

This simple equation said only that output was a function of two inputs: capital and labor. Note that, in this equation, resources and resource costs did not appear.*

The notion of production, therefore, was one of immaculate conception: an interaction of machinery with human hands but operating on nothing. Economists (Milton Friedman, notably) sometimes expressed this model as one in which the only goods produced were, actually, services—an economy of barbershops and massage parlors, so to speak. How this fiction passed from hand to hand without embarrassment seems, in deep retrospect, a mystery. The fact that in the physical world, one cannot actually produce anything without resources passed substantially unremarked, or covered by the assumption that resources are drawn freely from the environment and then disposed of equally freely when no longer needed. Resources were quite cheap and readily available—and as the theory emerged, the problem of pollution only came slowly into focus. Climate

---

* And would not, until Solow modified his model in the 1970s. But even then, the refinement was superficial; resources now entered only as another "factor of production." The fact that they are nonrenewable played no special role.

change, though already known to scientists, did not reach economics at all. It would have been one thing to build a theory that acknowledged abundance and then allowed for the possibility that it might not always hold. It was quite another to build up a theory in which resources did not figure.

Even the rudimentary and catch-all classical category "land" and its pecuniary accompaniment, rent, were now dropped. There were no more landlords in the models and no more awkward questions about their role in economic life. This simplification helped make it possible for enlightened economists to favor land reform in other countries, while ignoring the "absentee owners" at home, to whom a previous, cynical generation had called attention. Keynes had ended his *The General Theory of Employment, Interest, and Money* in 1936 with the thought that rentiers might be "euthanized." Now they were forgotten; theory focused simply on the division of income between labor and capital, wages and profits.

Government played no explicit role in the theory of growth. It was usually acknowledged as necessary in real life, notably for the provision of "public goods" such as military defense, education, and transport networks. But since the problem of depressions had been cured—supposedly—there was no longer any need for Keynes's program of deficit-financed expenditure on public works or jobs programs; at least not for the purpose of providing mass employment. Fiscal and monetary policies were available, though, for the purpose of keeping growth "on track"—a concept referred to as "fine-tuning" or "countercyclical stabilization." Regulation could be invoked as needed to cope with troublesome questions of pollution and monopoly (such as price-fixing by Big Steel), but the purpose of that was to make the system resemble as much as possible the economists' competitive dream world. Beyond those needs, regulation was accordingly a burden, a drag on efficiency, to be accepted where necessary but minimized.

The models supported the system in two complementary ways. They portrayed a world of steady growth and also of fundamental fairness. Both labor and capital were said to be paid in line with their contributions (at

29

the margin) to total output. This required the special assumption that returns to scale were constant. If you doubled all inputs, you'd get twice the output. While the omnipresent real-world situations of "diminishing returns" (in farming) and "increasing returns" (in industry) lived on and could still be captured in the mathematics, most economists presented them as special cases and, for the most part, more trouble than they were worth. (This author's teacher, Nicholas Kaldor of the University of Cambridge, was an exception.) As for inequality, while the basic theory posited a stable distribution, Simon Kuznets—who was not a romantic—offered a more realistic but still reassuring analysis based on the history of industrial development in the United States and Great Britain. Inequality would rise in the transition from agriculture to industry, but it would then decline with the rise to power of an industrial working class and middle class and the social democratic welfare state.

That these assumptions became the foundations of a new system of economic thought was truly remarkable, considering that less than twenty years had elapsed since the Great Depression, with its financial chaos, impoverishment, mass unemployment, and the threat of revolution. It seemed a world made new. Both history and the history of economics (known as classical political economy) became largely irrelevant. A certain style of thinking, adorned with algebra, would substitute. Curiosity about those earlier matters was discouraged, and pessimism, which had earlier been the hallmark of the establishment, became a radical trait.

Other issues that had seemed emergent in the 1930s were now left out. One of them was the role of monopoly power. In the new models, all prices were assumed to be set in free competitive markets, so that the inconvenient properties of monopoly, monopsony, oligopoly, and so forth, so much discussed in the 1930s, did not have to be dealt with. Along with Keynes, his disciple Joan Robinson and her work on imperfect competition were shunted to one side. So was the Austrian economist Joseph Schumpeter, an archconservative who had nevertheless pointed out the unbreakable link between technical change and monopoly power. The study of industrial organization—the field within economics that analyzes market power—was drained of its political and policy content, to be colonized by theorists of games.

Another inconvenient fact was even more aggressively ignored: that even in capitalist systems, certain key prices were simply controlled. They were (and are) set by fiat, just as they would have been under "central planning." This was true first and foremost of industrial wages, which were set largely in collective contracts led by the major industrial unions in autos, steel, rubber, railroads, and other key sectors. It was true of service wages, largely governed by the standards set by the minimum wage. It was true of public wages, set by government. And it was true of construction wages, which largely followed standards set in the public sector. All of these bargains imparted stability to the cost structure, making planning by business much easier than it would have been otherwise.

But not only were wages fixed. So were American oil prices, which were set to a good first approximation in Austin, Texas, by the Texas Railroad Commission, which could impose a quota (as a percent of capacity) on all wells in Texas. These measures ensured against a sudden, price-collapsing glut. This simple and effective system, supported by the depletion allowance in the tax code, gave America a robust oil industry that could and did reinvest at home. It was a strategy of "drain America first"—protecting the US balance of payments and the world monetary system from imported oil—but for the moment, there was no shortage of oil. And since the price of oil was under control, all prices that incorporated oil as a cost had an element of control and stability built in. So oblique and effective was this system of control over resource pricing that it played no acknowledged role in the economics of the time. Apart from a few specialists, economists didn't discuss it.

The new growth models also had no place for the monetary system—neither domestic nor international. Banks did not appear, nor did messy details of the real world such as bank loans, credit markets, underwriting, or insurance. Monetary and credit institutions were perceived as mere "intermediaries": a form of market standing between ultimate lenders (the household sector, as the source of saving) and ultimate borrowers (the business sector, the fount of investment). Banks were not important in themselves. Bankers were not important people. The nature of credit—as a contract binding the parties to financial commitments in an uncertain world—was not considered, and economists came to think of financial assets based on credit contracts as simple commodities, as tradable as apples or fish.

The role of law, which had been fundamental to the institutionalist economists of the previous generation, disappeared from view. The assumption was made that developed societies enforced "property rights," thus giving all producers and all consumers fair, efficient, and costless access to the enforcement of contracts. In such a world, crime would be met with punishment, and mere exposure would be met with catastrophic loss of reputation. Since businesses were assumed to maximize their profits over a long period of time, they would act so as to avoid such a calamity. Probity in conduct would result from market pressures. So argued the subdiscipline of "law and economics," which rose to great and convenient influence.

Government had no essential role in the credit system, and if it ran unbalanced books, they would only get in the way. There was a single pool of resources, to be divided between consumption and saving. The part that was saved could be taken by government, but only at the cost of reducing what would be available for investment and new capital in the next generation. This tendency was called "crowding out." It became a standard feature of public finance models and even of the budget forecasts made by the government itself.

The interest rate is a parameter that relates present to future time, and it could not be left out of a growth model. On this topic, elaborate and conflicting theories enthralled and perplexed a generation of students, with notions ranging from the "marginal product of capital,"* to "loanable funds," to "liquidity preference." In growth models, the dominant view related interest to the physical productivity of capital, which (since the capital stock cannot be measured in physical terms) meant that the dominant model of interest rates remained a textbook abstraction; something students were taught to believe without ever being able to gauge the performance of the theory against fact.

Here, for once, the theory made reality seem *more* complex and difficult than it was. In fact, interest rates were based on another controlled price. The rate of return on overnight bank loans (the federal funds rate) was set by the Federal Open Market Committee, an entity of the Federal Reserve System. Then as now, the FOMC met every six weeks in Washington for this purpose. There was a bit of camouflage, which has since disappeared: both operational secrecy and implementation of the interest rate target by buying and selling government bonds through primary dealers. But the reality was, the core interest rate for the United States was a price fixed by the government. As it is now.†

---

* In the marginal-productivity theory, the interest rate (or rate of profit on capital) was supposed to be an outcome of the model. Capital was paid according to its marginal contribution to output. If interest rates were low, that was the result of a mature economy having exhausted the easy investment opportunities. Capital would therefore flow out to developing countries where the returns were greater. However by the mid-1950s, economists already knew (or should have known) that, as a logical matter, this explanation could not hold. Since interest and profit could not be derived from the productivity of the capital stock, it was not meaningful to say that industries in rich countries were more "capital intensive" than in poor ones. Indeed, industrial studies suggested the opposite, a point that was called the "Leontief paradox." The intractability of the concept of an aggregate capital stock would be debated heavily, acknowledged in the middle 1960s, and then ignored.

† In Britain and for much of the financial world, the comparable reference rate is the London Interbank Offered Rate (Libor), which, as we have learned, is a rate set by a cartel of global banks—and susceptible to manipulation in their own interest, as we have also learned.

Other interest rates, such as how much savers could earn on deposits and how much they could be charged for mortgages and other loans, would depend in various ways on the core interest rate and the market power of banks and other financial institutions, but also on government regulation. Regulations prohibited the payment of interest on checking accounts, and gave savings and loans a small rate advantage over commercial banks. Later these regulations would disappear, and interest rates facing consumers would largely become a cartel-driven markup over the cost of funds.

Similarly, the international monetary system had no role in the theory. This was odd, because the actual system in place in those years was a human creation, built in 1945 largely by economists (in some cases, the close colleagues of the growth theorists) in response to the blatant failures of the world monetary system only a few years before. The new system was administered by two agencies of the United Nations—the IMF and the World Bank—newly created institutions with many jobs for economists. These institutions were headquartered in Washington and dominated largely by the United States, which was now the world's dominant financial power, thanks to the outcome of World War II. In the global balancing mechanism known as Bretton Woods, the world tied its currencies to the dollar, and the dollar tied itself—for the purpose of official settlement of trade imbalances—to gold at the price of $35 per ounce.* Here was another fixed price in a system where the role of price-fixing had to be overlooked lest people realize that perhaps they did not actually live under the benign sovereignty of the "free market."

It was all a fool's garden, and into it the 1960s dropped an apple and a snake.

---

* In this way, if the United States imported more than it exported, other countries built up reserves in dollars rather than gold—and the economic growth of the United States was therefore not tightly constrained by the limited physical stocks of gold.

The apple was called the New Economics, a postwar and post-Keynes reassertion of government's responsibility to promote full employment. Keynes's ideas had been tested, to a degree, in the New Deal and in World War II. The Depression had proved that a lack of management was intolerable. The New Deal, in its helter-skelter way, and especially the war had proved that economic management could work, at least under extreme and emergency conditions. Some of this spirit had been embodied in the Employment Act of 1946, but during the Dwight Eisenhower years nothing happened to suggest that the mandate of that act was practical policy. The new American version of Keynesianism did not dominate policy until the election of John F. Kennedy in 1960. At that time, for the first time in peacetime, a president would proclaim that the economy was a managed system. By so doing, he placed the managers in charge and declared that the performance of the economy—defined as the achievement of economic growth—was a permanent function of the state.

Even though the theory of growth, invented by Kennedy's own advisers, had no special role for government, from that point forward government was to be held responsible for economic performance. Depressions were out of the question. Now the question was control of *recessions*—a much milder term that connoted a temporary decline in GDP and deviation from steady growth. Tax cuts could be deployed to support growth, as they were in 1962 and 1964, setting the precedent later taken up by the Republicans under President Ronald Reagan. Given the belief that depression, recession, and unemployment could all be overcome, the president had to be engaged, even in charge, for he would be held personally to account. Speaking at Yale University in 1962, Kennedy bit the apple of responsibility:

> *"What is at stake in our economic decisions today is not some grand warfare of rival ideologies which will sweep the country with passion but the practical management of a modern economy . . . The national interest lies*

*in high employment and steady expansion of output, in stable prices, and
a strong dollar. The declaration of such an objective is easy . . . To attain
[it], we require not some automatic response but hard thought."*

As it happened, this apple was decorated with a peculiar empirical
assertion called the "Phillips curve," also invented by Kennedy's own
advisers, Paul Samuelson and Robert Solow, in 1960. The Phillips curve
appeared to show that there were choices—trade-offs—to be made. You
could have a little bit more employment, but only if you were willing to tolerate a little more inflation. The president would have to make that choice.
And sometimes outside forces might make it for him.

The snake that came into this garden was, as all agreed, the Vietnam
War. Economically, the war itself was not such a big thing. Compared
with World War II, it was almost negligible. But Vietnam happened in a
different time, as Europe and Japan emerged from reconstruction, and the
United States was no longer running chronic surpluses in international
trade and no longer quite the dominant manufacturing power. Never again
would the country's judgment and leadership go unquestioned. Vietnam
tipped America toward higher inflation and into trade deficits, and its principal economic consequence was to destabilize, undermine, and ultimately
unravel the monetary agreement forged at Bretton Woods.

Deficits and inflation meant that dollars were losing purchasing power
even as the United States was expecting its trading partners to hold more
of them, roping them into complicity in a war that many strongly opposed.
So countries impatient with the "exorbitant privilege" they had granted
by holding the excess dollars with which they were paid for real goods—
notably France under President Charles de Gaulle, but also Britain under
Prime Minister Harold Wilson—began to press for repayment in gold, to
which they were entitled under the charter of the International Monetary
Fund (IMF).

The system could not hold against that pressure. Once the gold stocks
were depleted, what would back the dollar? And why should the United

States forgo vital national priorities—whether Lyndon Johnson's Great Society or the fight against communism in Asia—just so that de Gaulle (and Wilson) could have the gold in Fort Knox for $35 an ounce? By the end of the 1960s, close observers could already see that the "steady-state growth model" was a myth. The economic problem had not been solved. The permanent world system of 1945 would not be around for much longer.

Two

A Decade of Disruption

In 1970, more snakes appeared in the growth garden. They prefigured a decade of challenge to the complacency of the fifties and sixties. That challenge overturned Keynesianism as it had come to be understood: namely, that the government could manage the business cycle and preserve high employment at reasonable rates of inflation. But efforts to reexamine the doctrine of growth itself were not successful. After the decade ended, the presumption and expectation of growth were even more firmly established in America than ever before. The difference was that in the 1960s, leading economists argued that the processes of growth could and should be managed. In the 1980s, the dominant view was that the best route to growth required the government to get out of the way. Neither view dealt effectively with the events that had caused the trouble.

The first new snake was what we now call "domestic peak oil": the achievement of maximum crude petroleum production in the lower forty-eight states. This peak had been predicted in 1955 by the geologist M. King Hubbert, using a technique that related production to discoveries, and relying on the fact that the big domestic onshore oil fields had mostly been discovered in the 1930s. Hubbert made a projection based on an assumption that oil production would decline roughly as it rose, following a bell curve. He predicted that the peak of production would come in 1970. In a triumph of geophysical forecasting, he was not merely right but exactly so: the peak occurred in the year he said it would.*

Yet peak oil was an event little noted by economists, and why should it have been? Resources weren't in the models. To economists, preoccupied at the time with the economic consequences of the Vietnam War, oil was just another commodity. In the national accounts, oil was not a large part of economic activity, even though it might be difficult to find activities that did not depend on it to some degree. In particular, economists—partly because they had a commitment to an unreal world of market-determined rather than controlled and administered prices—continued to overlook the tiny detail that peaking production would mean losing control over price.

Achieving peak domestic production did not mean that the United States was short of oil. It did not mean that oil was likely to be scarce in any near future. It meant only that roughly half of what could be extracted *by conventional means* in the familiar places was gone, and from now on, production from those sources would decline. There was more oil to be found in Alaska, more in the waters of the Gulf of Mexico, more to be

---

* The story of Hubbert's peak is told in Kenneth S. Deffeyes's *Hubbert's Peak: The Impending World Oil Shortage*. To be precise, Hubbert correctly predicted the peak, but afterward total production following the peak did not fall as rapidly as he expected. This point is made effectively (but somewhat misleadingly) by oil optimists, including Daniel Yergin. It is true that increasing investment and new technologies can and have increased the recoverable share of oil in known fields. It does not follow that total production of conventional oil can be expanded indefinitely or even brought up past the previous peak.

extracted by unconventional means—and much, much more available in the vast fields of the Middle East, in Mexico, in Africa, in Venezuela, and ultimately in Canada's Alberta tar sands and in the deep sea. The United States would have access to much of that.

Still, with onshore, conventional production in decline, a larger and larger share of US consumption would now come from abroad. The price could no longer be controlled by a public authority inside the United States. Foreign oil would have to be paid for at a price set somewhere else; the rental income associated with a price higher than the cost of production would flow overseas. Rental income makes a difference: it's part of the foundation of total global demand, and when it flows elsewhere or is hoarded, total employment, profitability, and business investment suffer. We began to discover this just a bit later in the 1970s; when oil prices surged, purchasing power drained from the industrial West, plunging the oil consumers into recession. The locus of global economic growth shifted to the oil-producing countries and to those developing countries (especially in Latin America) that were willing to borrow heavily from the commercial banks. This was a taste of the long-term future, and, at the time, some economists and national leaders said so. But even that premonition would be set aside soon enough.

The second new snake was a recession. In 1970 there was an actual downturn—an interruption in the continuous chain of economic growth—for the first time in more than a decade. It was not directly connected to peak domestic oil. Rather, the apparent cause was a contractionary policy. As Vietnam War spending slowed, fiscal policy became less expansionary, and the US federal budget went into surplus, in 1969, for the last time in thirty years. Meanwhile, interest rates were raised to combat the inflation of that moment, and perhaps for a less-stated reason, of interest to central banks: to curtail imports so as to stabilize the trade deficit and stop the gold outflow, which threatened the value of the dollar. Economic output declined, and unemployment rose.

By later standards, the 1970 recession was mild, but politically it was

41

traumatic. It hit certain sectors (textiles, notably) and certain parts of the country (the Northeast) hard. Moreover, the recession did not bring down inflation, contradicting the Phillips curve. The New Economics had held that something called "balanced growth" was a practical possibility, that the business cycle downturn was a thing of the past, and that inflation and unemployment could be traded against each other. All of this was thrown into doubt.

Yet from a political point of view, doubt was not acceptable. In the minds of voters, the New Economics had taken hold. By the lights of the New Economics, the recession was avoidable, a policy blunder. President Richard Nixon himself was committed to this expansive view of presidential power and accountability. This meant that when presidents made mistakes, as measured by bad economic performance, they could legitimately be punished. So it could be said—and it was said—that the events were Nixon's fault. In 1970, for the first time in the era of the theory of growth, a president faced the risk of electoral defeat for failing to measure up to the new standards of satisfactory economic performance.

What to do? Nixon's solution was to act as if there were a war emergency, even though, fairly clearly, there was not. His move came on August 15, 1971. It included a big ramp-up of civilian public spending and, with the help of a Federal Reserve under Arthur F. Burns, a big cut in interest rates. In a dramatic gesture, wage and price controls were imposed. And Nixon closed the gold window, devalued the dollar, slapped export controls over soybeans and other price-sensitive crops. In so doing, he set the stage for a big increase in exports of machinery and other finished goods, and also in armaments that were peddled to our then allies around the world, notably the Shah of Iran. In early 1972 Nixon also let Congress increase Social Security benefits, an increase that took effect—with favorable political consequences—just before the election.

Nixon's program worked—for the narrow purposes and the short time required. Growth revived, as did employment, while inflation remained under control. Or so it seemed. Nixon's moves told the world that American

42

politics came first, even over our role as leader of the world system. And the world took note. At this time the project of European integration began to accelerate and the Eurodollar market began to evolve, placing dollar accounts outside the control or reach of the United States. For Japan, sharp increases in food costs dictated the start of a new security strategy, which would have vast consequences in later years for the Argentine pampas and the Brazilian hinterland. For foreign oil producers, the problem was that oil was priced in dollars, so a devalued dollar meant that oil was even cheaper than normal outside the United States. The producers chafed.

The producers' oil problem could be remedied, in principle, with higher prices; all it required was a cartel to take over the now-abandoned function of the Texas Railroad Commission. In 1973, on the impulse of the Yom Kippur War (and US support for Israel in that conflict) the Organization of Petroleum Exporting Countries (OPEC) acted. OPEC set a new price, four times the previous one, and enforced it by imposing first an embargo and then a quota. There were shortages, lines, and hoarding. Americans got a first taste of what it means to be import dependent.

Economists dubbed this event the "oil shock." In using this term, they made a snap judgment of great importance. The term *shock* conveyed, peremptorily, that the economics of oil and energy had not changed in any fundamental way. A shock was something that could happen to anyone, almost at any time. Economists attributed this one (for the most part) to the Arab-Israeli war—and not to the changing geophysics of oil supply and the breakdown of Bretton Woods. So they expected that the shock would be transitory, as shocks are. Economic analysis of OPEC focused on the unstable dynamics of running a cartel. The profession largely predicted that the managed oil price would collapse (as eventually it did, though only under a powerful kick from American policy). The economy would then return to normal, output and employment to potential, and growth would pick up where it left off.

Soon enough, the notion that oil was a commodity of particular strategic significance faded away. That there had been an underlying and irreversible shift in the resource base was not seen clearly. And yet, as the 1970s progressed, the problem of reviving and sustaining economic growth did not go away. Economists noted a slowdown in "productivity growth," which they never could quite explain. Politicians and the public noted the stubborn persistence of inflation alongside unemployment ("stagflation") and the tendency of economic expansions to be interrupted by new shocks stemming from trade deficits and, in the new world of floating exchange rates, from a bidding down of the dollar. There were problems; they would have to be dealt with, somehow.

Given this reality, the 1970s became a decade of debates over economics. The control that mainstream Keynesians had enjoyed over the high ground of policy setting came under challenge from the more interventionist left and from the laissez-faire right, both of which spoke of operating on the "supply side" of the economy. There were, in principle, four different ways to proceed, and the 1970s saw brief, partial implementation of three of them.

First, we could have devalued the dollar, suppressed wage gains with incomes policy, ramped up the competitiveness of our industry, expanded our exports, and covered the import bill with tariffs and quotas alongside ingenuity and hard work. This would have been the classical mercantilist strategy, well known since the eighteenth century, with variations pursued by both Germany and the United States in the nineteenth century as well as by Japan after 1945. And this strategy would be the one followed later by China, another oil importer, in the 1980s and 1990s. But while the "Nixon shocks" of 1971 had elements of this, including devaluation and wage controls, to sustain the effort for a long time was impractical. It was incompatible with the living standards that America had achieved, with wage arrangements workers considered normal, with free trade, and with the rising power and position of the US financial sector already chafing against the regulatory straitjackets imposed in the 1930s. And whether for political or ideological reasons, leading policy economists of both parties were strongly opposed to this "pop internationalism," as Paul Krugman later called it in an excoriating book of that title. After Watergate and Nixon's fall in 1974, this line of strategy was dead, even though it continued to attract adherents and advocates for more than a decade, including on the Democratic left, and even among a few Reagan-era officials—Clyde Prestowitz, notably—who had to deal with the Japanese in the 1980s.*

A second line of thinking was to bind the oil producers to the United States, to accept their high prices and to recycle the revenues through arms sales and private commercial bank lending. US secretary of state Henry Kissinger advanced this strategy in the Nixon and Gerald Ford years, supported by the oil industry and the banks, and implemented it mainly through alliances and partnerships rather than with a large US military presence in the Persian Gulf. But it was a strategy with political and military limits, and it took a sharp blow in 1979 from the Iranian revolution, and thereafter from the unreliability of Iraq's Saddam Hussein as a client. Apart from clandestine wars in Angola and elsewhere, the confidence to intervene directly in the oil countries would not return until the 1990s, with the first Gulf War, after which the illusion of US superpower status would hold, in elite imaginations, for another fifteen years.

A third possible approach for the United States was to tackle the issue of oil imports directly with a strategy of conservation and efficient use. America could have cut its consumption of oil, moved to alternative sources of energy (especially nuclear) and to new transportation systems, raised the consumption price of oil and gas by taxing, and lived as well as possible with fewer hydrocarbons. The Europeans would emphasize this path, for the most part, given Europe's limited military options and the limits to a competitiveness strategy imposed by the rise of Asia. Nuclear power, mass transportation, and compact cities would loom large in Europe, as would natural gas imported (over American objections) by

---

* The concept of "industrial policy" was a narrower and more targeted version of the same idea. It always had advocates among those directly tied to the industries under threat—and among their congressmen, for whom this author did some occasional work.

pipeline from Russia. Although President Jimmy Carter initially favored a similar approach, politics and lobbies stood powerfully in the way, as did (at a very inopportune moment) a partial meltdown at the Three Mile Island nuclear power plant in 1979.

But the United States, being the United States, had a fourth option. It was to figure out a way to get the oil *without* actually paying for it; that is, to work out a system that would permit America to import physical product for cash, and ultimately for dollar-denominated debt, that cost nothing, in immediate resource (or as economists say, "real") terms, to produce. The fourth option, in other words, was to put the oil on a credit card that would never be paid. This solution was, of course, ideal from every political point of view. And it would become the dominant solution to the problem from the early 1980s onward—the secret of the Age of Reagan.

Thus three US presidents—Richard Nixon, Gerald Ford, and Jimmy Carter—had wrestled with the energy-resource-competitiveness-dollar problem and failed to resolve it. After breaking the link to gold in 1971, Nixon floated the dollar in 1973, and the greenback declined against the yen and the deutschemark for the rest of the decade. Goods in America became more expensive, real wages stalled out, and inflation became a chronic worry. The Federal Reserve reacted to inflation by raising interest rates in 1974–75, provoking a deep recession that helped cost President Ford the White House. Nixon's strategy of alliances proved to be at best unstable. The market for arms prospered, but there was no way that arms sales could begin to pay for oil purchases. The market for recycled petro-dollars boomed, but the recycling went to Latin America and other developing countries and did not support a return to growth in the United States. Carter's energy policies were ineffective, and soon enough he found himself up against a trade deficit, a declining dollar, and rising inflation—the traditional limits of Keynesianism in economies open to the world. Carter reverted to budget retrenchment, high interest rates, and credit controls, which produced a short but politically fatal recession in 1980. In a sense, he too was the victim of the high standards of the New Economics.

Having failed to cope with the policy complexity introduced by the oil-based instabilities of the 1970s, the New Economics was doomed. Among academic economists, the notion that unemployment could be traded for inflation fell into disrepute. Evidently the inflation risk was much larger than the Keynesians had believed, given the instability of resource costs, which they had ignored. But this would not necessarily be fatal to the Keynesian program. Shocks are by nature both unpredictable and transitory. So long as they could be blamed on sheikhs, they could not *also* be the fault of bad policy.

For this reason, the Keynesians had a vested interest in speaking of OPEC. But the anti-Keynesians of the day also saw their opportunity, which was to bury the Keynesianism of the 1960s altogether. They needed to reinterpret the inflation, to give it a *domestic policy* explanation—something for which the very application of Keynesian ideas might be blamed.

Milton Friedman's monetarism met this challenge. The monetarists asserted that inflation was "always and everywhere a monetary phenomenon"—something that happened only because of bad central banking and never without it. Inflation was therefore *national*. In the monetarist view, it was the one variable over which national public policy, and specifically the central bank, could exercise complete control. Unemployment, on the other hand, was reinvented, to be understood hereafter not as a failure of the market system but as a market-driven phenomenon with a "natural" value given by the balance between supply and demand for labor. This was then estimated, with typical values set at around 7 percent. The unemployment rate would gravitate toward the "natural rate" with whatever inflation resulted from money management—or mismanagement. In this way, the Chicago economists created a mental world in which government was responsible for inflation but not for unemployment.

By the 1980s, the counterrevolution in economic thinking was largely complete. The word *Keynesian* had become a term of opprobrium. Perhaps just as important in the long run, the acronym OPEC was rarely heard from economists anymore.

Curiously, the assault on economic management did not impair underlying confidence in the prospects for growth. Instead, it opened the door to
a new theory of fluctuations: to the "real business cycle" theory that rests
on waves in the advance of technology—the internal combustion engine
or the computer—independent of public policy. Growth in the new models
became subject to upswings and downswings that policy makers could not
control. So long as adequate saving was provided for, however, the trend in
the long run was not left open to doubt. Keynesian interventions to support
growth, or to dampen cycles, were declared unnecessary, even likely to
do more harm than good. What mattered were the overall climate of price
stability (to be provided by the Federal Reserve) and the attitude of the
government toward the free functioning of the market.

A further innovation at this time was the *supply-side* concept that the
growth rate could be increased through tax incentives to work, save, and
invest, by shifting the burden of tax from saving to consumption. Public
finance economists adopted a language of "distortions," according to which
all taxes except for per capita direct taxes (poll taxes) have effects on economic behavior. The accepted policy now became to design taxes so as to
minimize interference with the private decision to save—to get as close to
a capitation or poll tax as possible in the modern world—forgetting perhaps that the purpose of the actual, historical poll tax was to prevent poor
black Americans in the South from voting. This tax-incentive economics
was the foundation of today's Club for Growth approach—and that of similar antiregulation organizations—under which growth in the long run is
the pure result of the impulse and incentive to save, and the only obstacles
to growth are inefficiencies and misallocations induced by taxation and
regulation.

Echoing the simple models of the 1950s, the issue of resources and
their costs once again disappeared from the economists' agendas. And this
opened a deep rift between the economists and all other types of systems
analysts and operations researchers. For these other disciplines, built
as they are on physics and engineering, the essence of a "system" is the

interaction between materials, tools, and the energy that powers them. Economics took another path entirely. It became a psychological subject, dematerialized. The parameters of prime interest to economists would henceforth be matters such as "credibility," "confidence," "expectations," and "incentives"—ultimately the discipline would become enthused about "behavior." But forces and materials cannot be discarded so easily by people trained as engineers.

Even before the oil shocks, there were some who did not think that the resource-free, constant-returns-to-scale worldview of the growth theorists could be right. A few scientists and operations researchers had already come together at the Lincean Academy in Rome in 1970 to discuss resource depletion and the eventual rising cost of raw materials, especially oil. The work of this group became famous, or infamous, as the Meadows Report of the Club of Rome on *Limits to Growth*. Hugely influential, yet primitive, flawed, and vulnerable, the *Limits to Growth* report made the argument that when a resource is fixed, supply will eventually decline, costs will rise, and ultimately there will be no more to be had. The Club of Rome modelers buttressed the case with computer simulations; in effect, they made the not very surprising point that when a process of exponential expansion meets a fixed barrier, a collision must occur. It was, for the time, a complex piece of work on a computer, but it was also mechanical. As must be the case with a computer simulation, the grim outcome was programmed into the assumptions.

The economists brushed off the challenge. The computer modelers had forgotten the power of new reserves, new technology, and resource substitution. Discovery, invention, and substitution had always worked in the past, in transitions from wood and water to coal, coal to oil, and oil to nuclear and natural gas. The history of natural resources was littered with predictions of depletion that, for some reason, had never quite come true. The economists argued that therefore they never would. Historical induction triumphed over the computer—something quite rare in economic reasoning. The *Limits to Growth* argument was demolished, and to this day, it remains a touchstone for economists who wish to repudiate fear and scaremongering about resources.*

And so, as the Carter presidency's flirtation with an energy strategy faded in memory, the economic viewpoint would dominate for another thirty years. The mantra of sustained (and therefore unlimited) economic growth, subject now only to the possibility that government intervention might get in the way, became ever more deeply entrenched. This was not good for the relationship between economists and physical scientists, as the latter became ever more alarmed by the limitations imposed by the rising cost of obtaining physical resources and the ultimate threat of climate change. Yet apart from certain specialized spots (such as the Santa Fe Institute, where complexity theories were batted back and forth between economists and physicists, to uncertain effect) communication between the economists and those who studied energy, ecology, climate, and physical systems in general—communication that had never been entirely easy—broke down.

Despite rising concerns about resources and then about climate change, this communication has never been restored. "Environmental economists" do exist, but they are a subgroup within the profession, removed from substantial control over academic resources (especially appointments) and very far removed from the broader economic policy discussion. Resource and environmental economists are not integrated into the discussions of financial matters or macroeconomic performance; they have no substantial say about the nature of economic growth or the desirability of pursuing it. The dominant voices in economics, even on the left-liberal side of the mainstream, still echo the nostrums of the 1950s. Technical innovation and private saving remain, for most economists, the path to a prosperous future, provided that well-meaning meddlers do not screw it up.

---

* In 2012, for instance, the climate-skeptic economist Bjørn Lomborg was able to parlay this enduring aversion into a cover article in *Foreign Affairs* magazine titled "Environmental Alarmism, Then and Now."

For this reason, the notion that there might be a link between resource costs and the Great Financial Crisis will, I think, still strike most economists as far fetched. In what follows, I shall try to explain how and why a link exists. It runs partly through the direct effects of higher costs, but much more through the indirect channels of market instability, financial speculation, and investment uncertainty. All of these help to explain why we must now think again about the inevitability of a return to sustained growth. After a daydream of thirty years' standing, it's time to consider again the possibility that the 1970s were not an interlude brought on by shocks, bad management, and policy mistakes—but instead, in certain respects, a harbinger of the world conditions that we now face, and from which we will not, on this occasion, so easily escape.

Three

The Great Delusion

Paul A. Volcker became chair of the Board of Governors of the Federal Reserve System in August 1979. Ronald Reagan took office as president of the United States in January 1981. These two men would restore American power, preserve the American lifestyle in broad terms, and set the course of economic expansion in America until the century's end. As someone who became executive director of the Joint Economic Committee in January 1981—charged with causing as much damage and annoyance to both of them as I could—I did not think so at the time. However, like many on the Democratic left, sympathetic to the interests of workers, unions, and the manufacturing industry, a skeptic of monetarists, supply-siders, and the free-market mantras of that period, and as an economist brought up largely ignorant of the physical basis of the production system, I did not understand how the Volcker-Reagan policies would play out.

Stripping away the smoke screens of ideology and public relations,[*] what Volcker did was very simple. He used the strategic price that America continued to control—namely, the world interest rate—as a weapon against the price of the strategic commodity that America no longer controlled, which was oil. Over the 1970s, as oil prices rose, much of the world had gone into debt, mainly to the commercial banking system of the United States. Thus most of the world, especially Latin America, Africa, and parts of Asia, was vulnerable to the interest rate weapon. Two notable exceptions were China and India, which had steered clear of commercial bank debt. But before 1980, neither of these vast countries was an important force in world trade. That would, of course, change in time.

Under the pressure of high interest rates, the real value of the US dollar (weighted by trade) rose by 60 percent. High interest rates plunged the indebted countries of the developing world into a twenty-year depression, removing them from effective competition for the world's resources. Inequality soared.[†] (In sub-Saharan Africa, far from the radar screens of American policy makers or their economists, the human implications would be cataclysmic.) The response was commodity dumping, which made real resources cheap for the rich countries once again.

High interest rates, a strong dollar, and capital inflow lifted constraints on US imports, so that the Reagan tax cuts and military spending programs could restore economic growth in the United States, whatever the price of oil and whatever the trade deficit. But ultimately even the oil cartel could not withstand the strain of the larger global depression, alongside the Iran-Iraq War. Prices fell. And so, by the mid-1980s, this most critical resource was flowing cheaply to the Global North once again. In a few more years, the combined pressure of debt, high interest rates, and low world energy

---

[*] I have discussed the economic ideologies of the Reagan-Volcker period at length in an earlier book, *The Predator State* (2008).

[†] For a discussion of the effect of the debt crisis on global inequality, see my *Inequality and Instability* (2012).

prices would help stress the Soviet Union—an energy supplier—to the breaking point. When the USSR collapsed in 1991, so did its internal demand for steel, nickel, gas, and many other products, including oil, which eventually found their way to world buyers, further depressing prices.

Now new centers arose to meet America's demands for light manufactures. The first would be Mexico, but that country would hold center stage for only a short while. By the time the North American Free Trade Agreement (NAFTA) came into force in early 1994, Mexico's moment of rapid industrial growth, which had started in the 1960s under the maquiladora program, was already far advanced. Almost inevitably, given the scale of the country, its financial independence, the capacity of its government, and its internal priorities, the prime role of supplying light manufactures to American markets fell to China. In addition to the glut of commodities, there would now be a vast supply of consumers' goods, ever improving in quality, at prices that would never rise.* And this, together with the low cost of commodities, cemented the end of inflation.

It was an accomplishment for which central bankers could claim some credit. They had broken the back of price-setting forces both in the wider world and at home, and opened the door to the postcommunist globalization. But to admit to this success, in this way, would have been to confess that after the mid-1980s they were functionless. The central banks had helped to set in motion forces that had eliminated inflation for a generation. By their own lights, if that were so, they had nothing more to do. Far better for them to claim that the success was temporary and provisional, and that to preserve it would require constant vigilance, lest by some mysterious, practically magical process, inflation "expectations" be again reignited. With this, the chorus of economists, newly disposed to psychological interpretations, was inclined to agree. The charade of monetary

---

* Later and less important would be the outsourcing of service activities, including computer programming, back-office functions, and call centers, to English-speaking developing countries, especially India.

policy vigilance continued year after year. In his memoir *The Age of Turbulence*, Alan Greenspan acknowledged that the collapse of inflation was a worldwide phenomenon, owing largely to the end of the USSR and the rise of China. This was a remarkable admission for a central banker, though whether Greenspan realized he was conceding that he, as Fed chair, did not deserve to be credited for the long price stability of his tenure is not quite clear.

Thus the Reagan tax cuts, growing military budget, and the high dollar did restore the national capacity to spend, and investment and consumption in the United States recovered from the harrowing recessions of the early 1980s. The world, long since deprived of access to American gold, went on holding dollars—or, more precisely, Treasury bills and bonds. China eventually became the largest such holder. And this enabled the American trade deficit to go on and on, with each year's deficit simply added to the external debt. Imports helped sustain real American living standards, while putting a ceiling over domestic labor costs. To the fury of American labor, reduced to near impotence, and to the frustration of Democrats and liberals, a grateful American population kept the Republicans in power. For the most part, American lives went on as before. Eventually even productivity growth recovered. Most important for our purposes, the economists' faith in stable long-term growth was restored. The 1970s became just a bad memory, and destined to fade, as bad memories do.

But there was a catch. The American lifestyle would now be fueled not by the growth of wages and personal incomes but in the main by changes in the structure of households and by increasing personal, household, and corporate borrowing. There would be more earners in each household, and more debt. Reagan and Volcker completed with astonishing success the transition from the multilateral, structured, and negotiated international monetary world of Bretton Woods to a free-floating, unstable world that nevertheless remained centered on the dollar and on the American financial markets. United States Treasury bonds became the de facto reserve asset of the whole world. But at the same time, the American family became the motor of worldwide demand growth*—so long as it was willing to add job to job and debt to debt, secured mainly by the equity in the American home. This was the new world order: better living through financialization.

In 1991 an apparent threat to this new order emerged very briefly. President Saddam Hussein of Iraq invaded Kuwait—a country he charged (accurately enough) with stealing oil from under Iraqi soil. No compelling American interest was directly involved, but the episode was an affront to the *appearance* of American power. President George H. W. Bush dispatched this affront with his hundred-hours war, reasserting American military dominance as though Vietnam had never occurred. Thus the elder Bush completed the cycle of illusions that Reagan had begun.

Ultimately William Jefferson Clinton inherited an apparently made-to-order world. It had just one military superpower, the United States, with its financial sector at the top of the global pecking order. This combination was the true basis of the domestic prosperity of the Clinton era. Funds flowed in, stocks boomed, and there was vast investment in new technologies, bringing the entire country to full employment for the first time since the late 1960s. Unemployment fell below 4 percent for three years in a row, while inflation did not budge. Tax revenues surged, and, unexpectedly, the federal budget went into surplus. Alan Greenspan, an old libertarian turned chairman of the Federal Reserve, became a bit of a folk hero, partly because he allowed the boom to continue in the face of those economists who claimed that runaway inflation would result and partly because (under the prevailing economic theory) he reaped praise when the predicted inflation did not occur.

To most ordinary Americans, the effects of the New Economy were highly favorable, even bordering on the miraculous, given the experi-

---

* The Greek economist Yanis Varoufakis has described the United States since 1981 as the "global Minotaur," a reference to the denizen of the labyrinth, into which much disappeared but from which nothing emerged.

ences, challenges, and disputes of the 1970s. Americans had seen unions crushed, factories abandoned, entire industries either moved offshore or replaced by foreign competition. Much of the former industrial heartland remained in deep decline, parts of it a wasteland. Yet (and despite the continuing fixation of some progressive American economists on the apparent stagnation of median real wages) for most Americans, day-to-day living standards did not fall, and if they had fallen for a time in the 1980s, then in the late 1990s, they rose to new highs. Poverty hit historic lows. Food and fuel were ultracheap. So too were light manufactures such as clothing, shoes, and the panoply of solid-state electronics, available in discount outlets everywhere; these came, of course, from Asia. As the technology revolution took hold, communications costs tumbled, thanks to optical fiber. Home ownership, stoked by federally supported credit programs, continued to rise. The stock market boomed. If life seemed good, for most people it *was* good.

And as the millennium ended on this high and happy note, what were the economists thinking?

For the most part, they took the news as it came. Things *seemed* fine. Therefore they *were* fine. The storms of the 1970s had left no permanent trace. What could an economist raised in the tradition of the optimistic 1950s and 1960s say except that good policy and good luck had combined to produce a good result? To some, it even appeared we were in a "New Paradigm"—Alan Greenspan's favored phrase. To put the same thought in old-fashioned terms, productivity growth had recovered (for reasons always slightly beyond understanding), and the United States had seemingly met the conditions for a steady-state growth path. In 2001 two highly respected economists who had served in government in the 1990s, Alan Blinder and Janet Yellen, published a book titled *The Fabulous Decade*.* The dispute between conservatives and liberals was now largely over how to divide the

---

* In 2014, Janet Yellen would become the first woman to chair the Federal Reserve Board.

credit, as between the revolutionary Ronald Reagan and his custodial successor, Bill Clinton. It wasn't much of a dispute, since there seemed to be plenty of credit for both.

With hindsight, the 1980s became years of heroic vision, as Volcker (with Reagan's support) set the monetary ship to rights, restored the credibility of the Federal Reserve, and eliminated inflation. In so doing, it was said, wise policy undid the errors and ambitions of the 1970s, while consigning the political and economic leadership of that era—Nixon, Ford, Carter, and Volcker's predecessors Arthur F. Burns and G. William Miller—to obloquy and oblivion.* The explanation for full employment was not the credit boom or any compelling public policy intervention. It was only that time had passed, restoring equilibrium. And luck, since the "shock," a cartel-induced rise in oil prices, did not recur. Meanwhile, in the prevailing view, it was discipline and vigilance at the Federal Reserve that had kept inflation expectations from reemerging. As a result, long-term interest rates fell. The presumed consequence was steady growth, once again, without inflation. In a 2005 paper celebrating the long tenure of Alan Greenspan at the Federal Reserve, the aforementioned Alan Blinder and Ricardo Reis asked whether Greenspan was the best central banker of all time or just the luckiest. "Both," they answered.

So began the legend of the "Great Moderation." Not for the first time, economists took a run of good news and converted it into a parable with a moral. In the seemingly successful 1960s, it had been the American Keynesians who'd been the revisionists, making the case for the triumph of economic management—their own—subject only to the minor and tolerable trade-off between lower unemployment and higher inflation. In the 1990s, the "New Classicals"—the radical conservatives of that era—seized on the stability of economic growth after 1980 to proclaim the wisdom of a noninterventionist, "responsible" fiscal stance, combined with

---

* Robert Samuelson's 2010 history *The Great Inflation and Its Aftermath* is a useful example of this frame of mind.

a monetary policy focused on price stability alone. In 2003 the Chicago-based Nobel laureate Robert Lucas proclaimed that the "central problem of depression prevention has been solved, for all practical purposes, and has in fact been solved for many decades." The comment eerily resembled Milton Friedman's concession four decades earlier that "we are all Keynesians now."*

The term *Great Moderation* owes much of its popularity to one Ben Bernanke, a professor at Princeton University who was appointed to the Federal Reserve Board by President George W. Bush in 2002. In a talk to the Eastern Economic Association in early 2004, Governor Bernanke outlined the evidence that a Great Moderation had occurred, and posited three possible explanations, which he called "structural change," "improved policy," and "good luck." Bernanke's comments are worth reviewing, as they give a reasonable survey of the mainstream economist's perspective on the history of the period before the world fell apart.

Structural change, as Bernanke defined it, might include "improved management of business inventories, made possible by advances in computation and communication." He also mentioned "the increased depth and sophistication of financial markets, deregulation in many industries, the shift away from manufacturing toward services, and increased openness to trade and international capital flows" as possible "examples of structural change that may have increased macroeconomic flexibility and stability." Bernanke gave no evidence on any of these points and no great weight to any of them. He also passed over "good luck" on the (slightly odd) ground that if luck were the cause, nothing much of policy importance could be said. Bernanke therefore focused on the remaining explanation: better policy. To begin the argument, he invoked one of the favored devices

---

* Although Friedman was cannier, writing to correct the context: "As best I can recall it, the context was: 'In one sense, we are all Keynesians now; in another, nobody is any longer a Keynesian.' The second half is at least as important as the first." Letter to *Time* magazine, February 4, 1966.

of the economists and cited the general agreement of other economists with what he was about to say:

"Economists generally agree *that the 1970s, the period of highest volatility in both output and inflation, was also a period in which monetary policy performed quite poorly.* . . . Few disagree *that monetary policy has played a large part in stabilizing inflation,* and so *the fact that output volatility has declined in parallel with inflation volatility, both in the United States and abroad, suggests that monetary policy may have helped moderate the variability of output as well."* (Emphases added.)

Things are as they are because economists say so.

To rephrase the argument: with a central bank credibly set against inflation, the economy would gravitate toward greater stability and resilience in the face of external shocks. With lower inflation, Bernanke said, "the dynamic behavior of the economy would change—probably in the direction of greater stability and persistence." Further, he argued, the "external shocks" such as oil price increases would themselves be less likely because they were really internal and not external at all. Thus, he wrote, "the extraordinary increases in nominal oil prices in the 1970s were made feasible by earlier expansionary monetary policies rather than by truly exogenous political or economic events."

The remarkable thing about this statement is the mind-set it reveals. It is close to the historical facts, yet without ever discussing them in detail. We cannot learn, for instance, precisely what Bernanke means by "earlier expansionary monetary policies." Is this a reference to the Vietnam War? To Nixon's 1972 reelection campaign? It might be either one. Matters that one might think relevant—such as the changing geophysics of energy (domestic peak oil) or the changing balance of power in the world (the collapse of the USSR, the rise of China)—are not discussed in any way that betrays that they might have been important, either to the favorable past or the worrisome future. The structural changes mentioned—mainly deregulation in various industries and sectors—are noteworthy, as they were the kind of policy change that free-market theory approves of in the first place.

And the discussion is sealed within the boundaries of accepted theory. The outcomes of the model are carefully separated from "exogenous" events. A few convenient policy themes, which fit into a favored narrative (financial innovation, deregulation, and free trade), are mentioned to provide an aura of context. The argument is then wrapped in backward induction, in which the preferred conclusion (that better policy led to improved outcomes) is inferred from the improved outcomes. Alternatives are ignored.

And the upshot? Back to the basic growth theory! With good policy and no shocks, sustained growth is possible once again. All that matters is to get "savings" to the right rate. Nothing else—not resources, not the environment, not the legal system, and not the structures of international finance—enter into the picture in any concrete or material way. There is no reason why sustaining the normal long-term rate of growth should be impossible or even difficult.

In this world, what could produce a crisis? Apart from something unforeseen and unforeseeable—or a gross dereliction of monetary duty by the central bank—it's difficult to imagine how a complete and ongoing breakdown might occur. And central bankers promised that they had learned from their mistakes of the 1970s and would not repeat them.

Under the prevailing theory, apart from shocks, the only way things could go wrong was for the central bank to commit policy errors. And since the central bank did nothing more than control the gross flows of money and credit, policy errors were of just two possible types. Policy could be too easy, or it could be too tight. A loose credit policy and excessive money creation would lead to inflation. Or given too little credit and money creation, there might be *deflation*, a general fall in prices. Within the theory, these were the only dangers against which the central bank needed to be on guard. Further, errors of either type were easily detectable. They would show up in money growth and then in price changes. The fact that prices were nearly stable meant, ipso facto, that the central bank had been doing its job correctly. Far be it from a central banker to master the larger world of industrial profitability, job gains and losses, the buildup of private debts, or the balance of supply and demand in the commodity markets. Let alone the malfeasance of private bankers.

Bernanke's argument—which is a fair statement of his official viewpoint—makes clear why he and other economists were unable, at least in their formal reasoning, to conceive in advance of the events of 2007 to 2009. In the theory to which economists of this type subscribed, such events were shocks, the origins of which were necessarily "beyond the scope of the theory." Unlike in the 1970s, they could not have been the result of defects in policy. Policy had changed. Mistakes were no longer being made. The responsible authorities had learned the lessons of that decade. There could not have been an undiagnosed weakness in the structure of the economic system, for that would imply a problem with the now-governing economic models. A disaster could come only from the outside.

Furthermore, within the scope of economic thinking, no other source of disaster—such as the risk that deregulation and desupervision might unleash a wave of fraud, abuse, and malpractice that could lead to the destruction of the banking system—was even in the realm of conceptual possibility. Since these were matters excluded from the theory, no time or energy could be devoted to thinking about them. Let me say it again. People with this mentality, mind-set, and analytical framework were (and still are) vested with the control of regulation in the financial sector.

And so, when the 2008 crisis hit, the phrase "no one could have known" reverberated through official Washington and bankerly New York. Of course, there is a little difficulty; in fact, what was coming *was known*, well in advance, to some people. As Michael Lewis reported gleefully in *The Big Short*, there were investors who made hundreds of millions of dollars betting on the upcoming disaster. But those people were not economists. For the case of the mainstream economists, it was actually true that "no one could have known." If you were the sort of person who could have known—or, even worse, who did know—then by definition you were not a mainstream economist. Therefore, you were "no one" in the eyes of those who were the guardians of professional identity. Your views, however lucrative, did not count. And secondly, for the economists, it was axiomatic that shocks *cannot* be foreseen. If they could have been, steps would have been taken, under the market system, to prevent them. That this did not happen meant that the dangers were beyond anticipation. One might ask, Why does one need economists, if this is how they think?

To analyze the world in this way requires, in effect, the redefinition of human experience into a special language. That language must have a vocabulary limited to those concepts that can be dealt with inside the model. To accept these restrictions is to be an economist. Any refusal to shed the larger perspective—a stubborn insistence on bringing a broader set of facts or a different range of theory to bear—identifies one as "not an economist." In this way, the economists need only talk to one another. Enclosed carefully in their monastery, they can speak their code, establish their status rankings and hierarchies, and persuade themselves and one another of their intellectual and professional merit.

A community and a line of argument constructed in such a manner are unlikely to be well prepared for an event like the Great Financial Crisis.

Four

Tweedledum and Tweedledee

It would not be fair to say that there were no disagreements within the leadership of the economics profession in the years before the storm broke. On the contrary, there were intense debates. But what were they about? In a remarkable essay, "How Did Economists Get It So Wrong?" in the *New York Times Sunday Magazine* in September 2009, Ben Bernanke's erstwhile Princeton colleague Paul Krugman surveyed how leading economists thought—or failed to think—in the run-up to the crisis.

Krugman's essay is about two groups, which he calls "saltwater" and "freshwater" economists. They tend to call themselves New Classicals and the "New Keynesians," even though one is not classical and the other is not Keynesian. One might speak of a "Chicago school" and an "MIT school," with the latter loosely extended over Harvard, Yale, Princeton, Berkeley, and Stanford. They are the now somewhat distant intellectual heirs of Milton Friedman on one side and of Paul Samuelson on the other, but with a good deal of interbreeding in the years since those two masters passed their prime.

Most of all, they are academic tribes. And while the differences between them were once quite important, in recent times they have become both secondary and obscure. The two groups share a common perspective, a preference for thinking along similar lines and for restricting their intellectual reach to their own community, giving themselves a sphere within which their judgment would not be challenged by outsiders. Their concern, first and foremost, is with establishing personal position in a complex system of rankings. Krugman describes this instinct as a "desire for an all-encompassing, intellectually elegant approach that also gave economists a chance to show off their mathematical prowess." This is exact and damning: it was in part about elegance and in part about showing off. The café society of the academic economist is not about taking on the problems of the larger world.

The failure to foresee, forewarn, or forestall the crisis was shared by both groups. In the years before the economy went bad, the high theorists of economics were not riven by a feud between Pangloss and Cassandra. Within their charmed circle, there was little debate over dangers, risks, challenges, and the appropriate policies associated with such developments in the modern world as globalization, financialization, inequality, or the rise of China. History and law played as small a role as geophysics and political geography, which is to say almost no role at all. It was, rather, a chummy conversation over the proper way to model the behavior of rational agents, interacting in more or less efficient markets. And if you didn't think that question was the central one, well, you weren't really an economist, were you?

Paul Krugman contends that the economists "mistook beauty for truth." The beauty in question was the "vision of capitalism as a perfect or nearly perfect system." To be sure, the accusation that a scientist—let alone an entire science—was seduced by beauty over truth is damaging. The formulation raises a raft of questions about the role of objectivity, the use of evidence, the nature of truth, and the place of economics among the sciences. Do biologists, for example, spend their time pondering the "beauty" of a "vision" of the living world as a "perfect system"? Do geologists worry about whether the beauty of rock layers is or is not perfect? The very mind-set is mystical.

But also, what exactly was beautiful about the "vision" that *capitalism*—normally thought of as a particular phase in the history of economic development, is "perfect or nearly perfect"? Krugman doesn't say *why* economists came to this point of view or why anyone might be disposed to accept it. Instead, he notes that the mathematics used to describe the alleged perfection is "impressive-looking" and "gussied up with fancy equations." In relation to the notion of beauty, this too is a most telling choice of words. "Impressive-looking" and "gussied up" are not phrases often used to describe the *Venus de Milo*. One brings to mind, say, your high school principal; the other, the Place Pigalle.

Economists using mathematical expressions to decorate arguments about the perfection of market systems may believe that their work is beautiful. Outsiders see instantly that it isn't. Quite apart from the messy problems and ugly realities of the economic world (capitalist or otherwise), no one with a sense of aesthetics would take the clumsy algebra of a typical professional economics article as a work of beauty. The main purpose of the math is not to clarify, or to charm, but to intimidate. And the tactic is effective. An idea that would come across as simpleminded in English can be made "impressive looking" with a sufficient string of Greek symbols. A complaint about the argument can be deflected, most easily, on the ground that the complainer must not understand the math.

And what are these mathematical discussions about? In a paper written for a midlevel professional audience, Professor Ricardo J. Caballero of MIT—the chair of the top-ranked department—raises the kind of concern that professional economists find worthy of attention. It has to do reasonably enough with the relationship between a model and the world it is supposed to represent. In raising this concern, Caballero calls attention to the grip that a complex method can have on an academically ambitious mind: "What does concern me about my discipline, however, is that its current core—by which I mainly mean the so-called dynamic stochastic general equilibrium approach—has become so mesmerized with its own internal logic that it has begun to confuse the precision it has achieved about its own world with the precision it has about the real one" (Caballero 2010, 85).

So what, then, is the "dynamic stochastic general equilibrium approach"? It is a model that predicts, let's say, the future rate of growth by assuming that all of the agents in an economy interact, directly or indirectly, subject to a certain amount of random error. *Dynamic* refers to the movement of the variables over time; *stochastic*, to the presence of random error; and *general equilibrium*, to the interaction of agents.

Since this sounds far too complicated for a compact model—and it would be, if taken seriously—DSGE model builders adopt a radical simplification. Instead of agents that are different yet interacting, they assume that all players in the system are essentially the same. That is, they build their models around "representative agents." In the simplest form (and yes, there are more complex versions), all actors (since they all have the same information and the same powers of reasoning) can be treated *as if they were all exactly alike*. That being so, the economy can be modeled as though there were just one person in it, predicting the future with foresight based on an accurate model, as much calculating power as required, and subject only to random (hence unpredictable) shocks and errors.

Since this is a technical issue, it may be best here to cite Caballero in his own words:

Take for example the preferred "microfoundation" of the supply of capital in the workhorse models of the core approach. A key parameter . . . is the intertemporal substitution elasticity of a representative agent, which is to be estimated from micro-data. A whole literature develops around this estimation, which narrows the parameter to certain values, which are then to be used and honored by anyone wanting to say something about "modern" macroeconomics . . . What happened to the role of Chinese bureaucrats,

Gulf autocrats, and the like, in the supply of capital? A typical answer is not to worry about it, because this is all "as if." (Caballero 2010, 89)

Two things are notable in this passage. One is how it describes the "representative agent" approach as one in which all differences between economic players—their wealth, their outlook, the laws and habits by which they are bound—are deemed irrelevant from the start. And the other lies in the repeated use of the passive voice, with its overtones of enforced lines of thinking. When Caballero speaks of the "preferred" approach, one may ask, preferred by whom? For what reasons? And when he says that certain values "are then to be used," who is the implicit commissar giving the instruction? From whom does the "typical answer" come? The hidden hand carries a whip.

Caballero moves on to the question of beauty, in the context of a model of business cycles—so-called real business cycles. He holds that the ebb and flow of the economy is due to waves of technological change, which lower the return on some activities (horses, buggies) while raising them on others (pavements, automobiles). Though Krugman derides this approach as "silly," asking "Was the Great Depression really the Great Vacation?" it is rooted to a degree in the history of technology, which does tend to come in waves. Yet Caballero does not see this. Instead, he writes: "The beauty of the simplest barebones real business cycle model is, in fact, in its simplicity. *It is a coherent description of equilibrium in a frictionless world*" (my emphasis, Caballero 2010, 90).

A person not previously instructed in economics might again ask, "Whatever for?" What's the value of coherent description of a fantasy world? Of a state that does not change? Of a world where interaction is characterized by a complete lack of structure? How can one analyze technical change as though it were "frictionless," when the essence of disruptions caused by technology is that the old collapses quickly while the new takes a long time to build? It's baffling, this business of frictionless models. Why should we find it useful to treat the financial relationships of human beings, organized in complex societies, on planet Earth, "as if" they were the force of gravity on objects in empty space? It's *as if* one were to take the starting point of life science as the study of conditions in the asteroids. Sure, the result might be interesting, in some abstract sense. You may even think the model beautiful. But it is too far from the object of interest—life on Earth—to cast useful light on it. And starting there will not get you where you might like to go, and where you might expect to go, if you instead started with a microscope, a petri dish, and a sample of swamp water.

Flaws and Frictions

The function of the pure, or freshwater, version of the doctrine of efficient markets was to orient the discussions in economics around a particular—*admittedly extreme*—vision of economic life. Even those who objected to this vision had to engage with it. The layered complexity of the vision, the subtlety of the claims, meant that it took mental effort to come to grips with what was being said. To articulate a dissent without becoming a heretic was a delicate task. The profession would reward those who kept to just a few points of departure from the pure model, and punish the rest. In this way, the debate stays within the tribe, and the purists, though sometimes embattled, preserve their importance.

The dissents that are admitted come from those who prefer, so to speak, to add a few pinches of salt to the water. That is the approach to which Caballero turns his attention next. It is an approach that Krugman describes as the "flaws and frictions" method, and both of these saltwater economists advocate moving it "from the periphery to the center" of analytical economics.

Their method consists of taking the sterile starting point of frictionless equilibrium, and introducing a complication—usually just one at any given time. The most famous and primitive of these is simply to assert that "wages are sticky" and so fail to adjust to restore full employment. An older generation of "flaws and frictions" economists (Lawrence Klein and Paul Samuelson) pioneered wage stickiness as their preferred way of reading the message of Keynes on unemployment in the Great Depression. The young Joseph Stiglitz was the most famous modern practitioner of this method of slight deviations, having built his critique of orthodox theory on the concept of "asymmetric information": a perfect world gone sour because some know more than others. Paul Krugman, as a young economist, upended conventional trade theory by introducing the concept of "increasing returns" into the formal models. George Akerlof has in recent years done something similar with "animal spirits." By introducing a flaw or a friction, a mainstream economist can capture some useful feature of the real world and yet graft it onto the purist models in ways that do not compromise his or her professional standing.

In this vein—and faced with the reality of the financial crisis—Caballero introduces several possible notions. There could be "a sudden rise in complexity followed by widespread panic." Or "a negative aggregative shock [which causes] debt to become information-sensitive." Or it may be useful to modify the notion of rational expectations by permitting the possibility of "Knightian" uncertainty: the idea that certain kinds of events are so inherently uncertain as not to be subject to probabilistic assessment. Such events are neither Black Swans nor Fat Tails, but truly unknowable. The sudden recognition that some things (previously thought knowable) cannot be foreseen could cause a realization that prior probability calculations were no good, destroying confidence. This in turn might motivate sharp changes in behavior.

Where do these ideas come from? Not from evidence; there is none. Not from weighing the favored (DSGE) model against alternative approaches to modeling the world. The prevailing view doesn't admit to the existence of such alternatives! Never does it invoke the flow of history, in any detail, to assess whether this or that model can account for a range of facts. The economist's goal is instead to develop the *simplest possible* story from the starting point of particles in frictionless space that might possibly generate a pattern of behavior, similar in certain broad respects to the events we have observed. Once the desired pattern—perhaps it will be called a "bubble"—has been generated, the argument rests. The theory of the case has been presented, until some other economist comes along to show how it might be done in some even simpler way.

The common method of both the freshwater and saltwater economists knits them into a single community as economists, while excluding all others. The differences between the two groups can be quite bitter; they tend to turn on whether a "flaw" or a "friction" is a sufficient cause for breaking with the code of self-adjustment in the economy and nonintervention by the government. Thus, do "sticky wages" or "asymmetric information" or "animal spirits" (or "efficiency wages") justify a program of public spending to create jobs? Freshwater economists say no: all periods of apparent unemployment are due to an incomplete adjustment of markets to a changed equilibrium state, but the adjustment must go forward, at whatever cost, until it has been completed.

Saltwater economists disagree. For the saltwater group, "stimulus" is sometimes an effective remedy to an economic downturn. For some in the saltwater camp (notably Krugman and Stiglitz), the flaws and frictions are large and pervasive enough to justify large and forceful action, since otherwise the market failures will persist for a long time. For others (notably Ben Bernanke), the point of stimulus is temporary and provisional. It is to help along a recovery that will eventually happen in any event.

Despite the modest nature of the differences between freshwater and saltwater, the tensions between the two have reverberated through the policy debates that followed the outbreak of the Great Crisis. Initially, the most obvious fact was that in frictionless equilibrium, even with "stochastic disturbances," crises of the type we were living through could not occur. To get from that starting point to anything remotely approaching the events of the real world would require a massive "external shock"—the functional equivalent of a meteor hitting from outer space—perhaps something involving technology, or a war. That was the logic of the theory. But where was the shock? The freshwater school had no idea and suggested no candidates for this role. So at first it did not occur to the Chicago school even to defend its own ideas, and the apostles of free and efficient markets fell silent for a little while.

Their silence allowed the saltwater school to fill the airwaves and newspapers with flaws and frictions. For Stiglitz, in particular, the essence of the crisis was the failure to recognize that flaws and frictions actually predominate in economic life, and especially that asymmetric information is a dominant feature of markets. This permits insiders to take advantage of outsiders. It makes it possible for contracts to fail. And it opens the door to the possibility of bank runs, panics, and crashes spreading across the globe, demanding the intervention of the public sector to regulate imprudent behavior, offset liquidity preference, and support effective demand. In his book on the crisis, *Freefall*, Stiglitz writes: "Agency issues and externalities mean that there is a role for government. If it does its job well, there will be fewer accidents, and when the accidents occur, they will be less costly. When there are accidents, government will have to help in picking up the pieces" (Stiglitz 2010, 17).

This is the saltwater version of the story: accidents happen. Since accidents happen, the market system needs some help from government agencies. It needs help from government—the patient parent—to clean up the mess after accidents occur. But *fundamentally*, beneath the "flaws" and the "frictions," accidents are accidental. They are to be expected in general, but not necessarily in any particular case. In this way, Stiglitz mans the left flank of reputability, and his critique, while biting in certain respects, leaves the centrality of the freshwater economists intact. If nothing else, Stiglitz and Krugman need their Chicago counterparts as punching bags.

And *all* the economists agree that the normal end state is one of full adjustment to the normal condition of full employment. At that point, the economy returns to its potential and has the capacity to go forward along that path. Thus, in a 2011 speech, the then chairman of the Federal Reserve, Ben Bernanke, could say: "Notwithstanding the severe difficulties we currently face, I do not expect the long-run growth potential of the US economy to be materially affected by the crisis and the recession if —and I stress if—our country takes the necessary steps to secure that outcome" (Bernanke 2012, 7). Chairman Bernanke had every reason to expect that, among economists, this statement would be uncontroversial.

But suppose that the crisis represents a threshold—a passage into a different future—from which the former "long-run growth potential of the US economy" cannot be attained? How can we even assess such a possibility? To do so, we need to explore some ideas dangerous enough to get one excluded from the mainstream. And there are many of these. But perhaps the most useful place to begin is with the best-established, most fully developed rejection of the idea that capitalism is "perfect," "nearly perfect," or "beautiful": the critique of capitalism that originates in the writings of Karl Marx.

The Marxian View

Marxian analysis has many factions and currents. For a generation or more, partly as a relic of the political currents of the 1960s, the dissident tradition represented most commonly in many American economics departments has been a strand developed in the 1970s at the University of Massachusetts Amherst, after the radicals led by Sam Bowles (along with Herbert Gintis and Arthur MacEwan) were denied tenure at Harvard in the early 1970s. It has roots also in the stagnationist analysis of an earlier pair of dissidents, Paul Sweezy and Paul Baran, who, already in the 1950s, were writing skeptically about growth theory. There is, of course, a rich body of similar thought in European, Latin American, and Asian Marxism, and some of that thought was also transplanted, by academic back channels, from time to time to the United States.

While the neoclassical growth theory takes steady-state equilibrium as its base case, the Marx-Baran-Sweezy-Bowles-Gintis position has been that capitalism is unstable and crisis inevitable. This theme roots the risk of crisis in specific properties of capitalism, monopoly capitalism, and finance capitalism. It leaves open, and even encourages, the thought that a different social system might be *less* unstable and less prone to crisis. And that has been the obvious historical weakness of the argument, given that over many decades, the cataclysm that would bring down capitalism did not occur—and that the Soviet Union went down first. Even though there was nothing in the American Marxian view that especially favored the USSR, it was easier to believe in the fall of capitalism when some other system seemed possible. Still, the conviction remained: the capitalist system was so fraught with contradictions that it had to fail at some point.

In a useful paper in 2004 titled "Crunch Time for U.S. Capitalism," the South African economist Patrick Bond summarized the major Marxian crisis-is-inevitable arguments. They were of two major types: one based on cutthroat competition (Brenner, 2003), and another based on the over-accumulation of capital (Meiksins Wood, 2005, and Harvey, 2005, with various qualifying views as presented by Arrighi, 2003). One of these emphasized the inability of capitalist firms to control their own markets; the other focused on the drive for apparently greater efficiency and reduction of labor costs in the production process. Both of these deep causes would generate a falling rate of profit, and so the crisis in question would be a crisis of profitability within the capitalist system. It would thus manifest itself, at some point, in a collapse of investment and production, and of employment.

Class struggle and power relations generally remain at the heart of this analysis; the tension between capital and labor is the motive force of history. The "falling rate of profit," "rising organic composition of capital," and "crisis of realization" have been part of the lexicon of Marxian analysis for much more than a century, and the Bond paper shows that they remain the central ideas. Moreover, investment, production, and employment did decline in the crisis. To describe what happened as a "crisis of realization" would not be unreasonable as a first cut. In this sense, Marxians predicted the crisis in general terms and were not surprised when a crisis happened.

But the issue remains: How *closely* did the Marxian vision of what would happen correspond to what did happen? In other words, does the Marxian lexicon give us what we need, if we want to understand events in fine detail? Or to put it another way, if we'd had the events and not the lexicon, would we have derived the lexicon from the events?

Here the central issue is the role of finance. Was the Great Crisis a *financial* crisis, and—if it was—what is the importance of the financial aspect to our understanding? As we have seen, the economic mainstream has difficulty with this concept because there is no mechanism in mainstream theory for understanding how financial events affect the real economy except momentarily. Apart from loose references to bubbles, mainstream economics is built around the notion of equilibrium in the real economy. Except for transient shocks, in the mainstream view there can be neither crisis nor "financial crisis." Marxians take the opposite view: they expect crisis, and they do not expect the system always to recover. Since banks are leading capitalist institutions, they are not surprised that crisis should surface in finance. The problem for Marxians is that finance explains nothing on its own. In their vision, the role of finance is substantially cosmetic. The true difficulties are deeper, rooted ultimately in class struggle, imbalances of power, the spur to accumulate capital, and the use of technology as a weapon against the working class. For Marxians, these are the fundamental causes of crisis.

Marxians see that the operations of the banks can obscure these underlying conflicts, giving an illusion of prosperity for a time. The accumulation of unsustainable debt in the private sector is the means to this end. For a time, as debt grows, production will continue and employment will be maintained. But the process cannot be maintained: when the illusion shatters and everyone sees that the debt cannot be repaid, crisis must follow. Arguing in this vein in a paper that gives the financial history in detail, Brenner (2009) recapitulates that the crisis "manifests huge, unresolved problems in the real economy that have been literally papered over by debt for decades, as well as a financial crunch of a depth unseen in the postwar epoch." Note the term "papered over," which captures exactly the tenor of the relationship between finance and the underlying "real economy."

The Marxian tradition thus shares with saltwater and freshwater economists a focus on the deep structure of relationships that underlie and transcend finance. For Marxians and anti-Marxians alike, finance is largely a veil over deeper forces. The difference between them lies in their analysis of those forces. The mainstream position supposes harmony and continuity, though perhaps with flaws and frictions, while the Marxian tradition supposes that there will be conflict and crisis. For saltwater, freshwater, and Marxists all, finance is a way of shifting the timing and perhaps the incidence of these deeper matters. None see it as the *central* or *motive* force. Thus it is almost as difficult for the Marxians as it is for the mainstream to think or speak of a "financial" crisis, except as an adjunct to the difficulties of the real economy.

John Bellamy Foster and Robert McChesney (2012) are Marxian early adopters of the there-will-be-no-recovery position. But while their book *The Endless Crisis* follows Paul Baran and Paul Sweezy in recognizing the role of finance capital in the modern system, the crisis that they identify is not, strictly speaking, a financial crisis. In their analysis, finance is part of the burden on the economic system, and the resulting rise in inequality, alongside low growth of wages, is a cause of the unmanageable expansion of household debts. Yet the crisis itself, as identified by Foster and McChesney, is a crisis of monopolism, of overaccumulation of capital, and of the excessive size of the financial in relationship to the "productive" sector of the economy, along with the phenomenon of "superexploitation" associated (they argue) with the move of manufacturing industry to China. What happened within the financial sector, and to the financial sector, and what was done by the financial sector, appear almost incidental and are barely analyzed in their book.

It is possible, of course, that finance *is* a veil over a "real system," which can be understood in deep terms without clear reference to the financial sector. But there is something unhappy about this way of thinking. It leads to an analytical tradition in which the superficial evidence of recent events—that the financial system collapsed—is dismissed as epiphenomenal. Meanwhile, analytical energy is diverted to forces such as "class struggle" and "cutthroat competition" that can barely be observed, and the key roles in the drama are assigned to actors who remained throughout in the shadows.

It is fairly easy, in applying a template of this kind to facts, to get the big picture right but the details wrong. For example, the crisis that Bond anticipated back in 2004 was a crisis of imperial overreach, set off by a collapse of the dollar due to unsustainable US current account deficits and the military stalemate in Iraq, with these events precipitating a loss of confidence in the United States as the anchor of the global power system. A crisis of that type might have happened. But it never did. The actual crisis proceeded differently through a collapse at the core of the private financial sector: beginning in the United States and reverberating to Europe, including to the smaller, peripheral countries of the Eurozone. Nothing happened to the dollar; on the contrary, it went up. The Marxian instinct was right: they understood, as the mainstream did not, that the system was unstable. Something very bad could happen. But the actual river of history flowed in a different channel.

Five

The Backwater Prophets

In his 2009 *New York Times Sunday Magazine* essay on the failures of
the mainstream economists, Paul Krugman devoted just two sentences
to the existence of economists outside the saltwater-freshwater axis. "Of
course," he wrote, "there were exceptions to these trends: a few economists
challenged the assumption of rational behavior, questioned the belief that
financial markets can be trusted and pointed to the long history of financial
crises that had devastating economic consequences. But they were swimming against the tide, unable to make much headway against a pervasive
and, in retrospect, foolish complacency."

It was a refreshing admission, and yet there was something odd about
the role of this short paragraph in the essay. It's a throwaway. Apart from one
other half sentence, and three passing mentions of one person,* it was the

---

* The Yale financial economist Robert Shiller, author of *Irrational Exuberance*, and a 2013
winner of the economists' Nobel Prize.

only discussion, in a 6,500-word essay, of those economists who got it right. They were not named, their work not cited, their story untold. It's not that there hasn't been any recent work into the nature and causes of financial collapse. It's not that no economists foresaw that a financial crisis was coming. Such economists have existed for a long time. But they are neither saltwater nor freshwater—nor Marx-water—but something else: backwater.

Backwater economists are the unpersons of the profession. Long before the crisis, those inclined to study the instabilities and weaknesses of the economy, without necessarily taking to Marxism, were shunted to the sidelines within academic economics. Their articles appeared only in secondary journals, or in newsletters and even (more recently) in blogs with names like *Naked Capitalism* and *Naked Keynesianism*. Many who betrayed skepticism too early in their careers by doing economics in this way were discouraged from academic life. If they remained, they were sent out into the vast diaspora of lesser state universities and liberal arts colleges. There they would struggle with heavy course loads, and, if they did manage to publish, they could safely be ignored.

Let us venture out into these hinterlands and attempt a survey of the main currents that didn't get it wrong. I will offer three groups, without pretending to be comprehensive. The first is pragmatic and statistical, based on the concept of bubbles, with the claim that indicators can identify them and predict the onset of crises most of the time. The other two make more use of a theoretical framework, which is to say that they try to embed the prediction of crisis into a framework of cause and effect.

The Pragmatic Practice of Bubble Detection

One of the least obscure among the backwater traditions seeks to identify financial bubbles—the peculiar indicia of an imminent crash—by statistical means. Dean Baker of the Center for Economic and Policy Research in Washington is a preeminent practitioner of this craft, with a clear claim to having seen the "housing bubble" when academic economists largely could not. As far back as 2002, Baker wrote: "If housing prices fall back in line with the overall price level, as they have always done in the past, it will eliminate more than $2 trillion in paper wealth and considerably worsen the recession. The collapse of the housing bubble will also jeopardize the survival of Fannie Mae and Freddie Mac and numerous other financial institutions." The prediction was spot on,* and it was made five years before the event. So we should ask: What was the method and how does it work?

As discussed in the prologue, a bubble is an image, or metaphor, of an ephemeral departure from the normal underlying state, with the property of gradual expansion (departure from normal) followed by sudden collapse (return to normal). The notion of bubbles cannot be separated from the notion of an underlying normality. A *permanent* departure from a previous trend would, by definition, not be a bubble. The bubble becomes, for this line of thinking, the entirety of the problem. Allowing the bubble is tantamount to enabling the subsequent crash. While a single bubble in isolation is arguably innocuous, a series of bubbles and busts is worse than the postulated alternative of steady growth, even if the trend under the two alternatives happens to be the same. If one accepts the bubble image, correct policy therefore consists of preventing bubbles from developing, so as to preserve the underlying normality of the real economy; the alternative to bubbles is steady growth at the same average rate.

Preventing bubbles requires a method for detecting them as they arise. The method is to spot indicators, usually in the form of a ratio of two measures, that are departing sharply from their historical norms. An example would be the price/earnings ratio in the stock market—say, for technology stocks in the late 1990s. When the p/e on Nasdaq stocks reached unprec-

---

* As were the words of Jane D'Arista, a financial noneconomist with broad practical experience in banking regulation, in work based on the flow of funds (2002): "The bursting of the mortgage bubble could unleash broader financial disruptions with deeper macroeconomic implications than the shakeout following the S&L crisis of the 1980s."

edented highs, it became clear that it was unlikely that the prices would continue to rise. Thus to justify holding the stocks, the earnings on those stocks would have to rise dramatically. Otherwise prices would have to fall, as the stocks could not remain competitive with other financial assets. The argument made at the time, notably by Federal Reserve chair Alan Greenspan, was that a New Paradigm had come into being and that earnings would rise to the degree required.* Of course that didn't happen; instead, the bubble collapsed and prices fell. In the 2000s, an analogous ratio was the price/rental ratio in the housing market, and the logic of the argument is the same: either rents would have to rise, or housing prices would fall. The extent of deviation of this ratio from past norms, coupled to the scale of the housing stock, gave a measure of the scale of the bubble itself—something that Baker eventually calculated at about $8 trillion for housing.

In these two cases, the method worked. But as with any ad hoc method, the possibility exists that it may fail. The method relies on the expectation that past historical values are normal and will prevail in the long run, but what is normal is not necessarily permanent. The "normal" price/earnings or price/rental ratio *might* change. It is not quite enough to assert, in effect, that the claims of history are eternal. Maybe there is a New Paradigm at work, after all? Or perhaps changes in other forces that affect the system, such as tax law or interest rates, are changing the normal relation of one thing to the other? To see that this is not the case, in a particular instance, one needs an argument—a theory—as to *why*, exactly, the particular trend under inspection cannot be sustained.

The next two groups of economists tried, in advance of the crisis, to understand the unsustainability of the system. They did so in distinctive ways, but what distinguishes their approach from the mainstream, the Marxians, and the bubble detectors is a full engagement with the financial

---

* This was also the view of James K. Glassman and Kevin Hassett, authors of a notorious book titled *Dow 36,000*.

aspects of economic life. There is in these views no intrinsically "normal" condition. The mechanics of finance have the property that they are sometimes sustainable for a time, but that—under certain conditions—they reach the limits of sustainability. The sustainable periods coincide with economic growth, not coincidentally but because expanding finance and economic growth are the same thing. The reaching of limits produces crisis, as growth cannot continue once credit expansion is withdrawn. Each group is perhaps best described by linking it to the prominent economist whose ideas either inspired or most closely framed the argument. These are the Anglo-Irish Cambridge economist Wynne Godley and the financial theorist Hyman Minsky.

Godley and the National Income Identities

The work of John Maynard Keynes is linked to the accounting framework that we call the National Income and Product Accounts, developed by Simon Kuznets as Keynesian ideas were circulating in the early 1930s. Total product *is* the flow of expenditures in the economy; an increase in that flow *is* what we call economic growth. The flow of expenditures is broken into major components: consumption, investment, government, and net exports, each of them subject to somewhat separate theories about what exactly determines its growth or decline.

Accounting relationships state facts about the world. More precisely, they define the terms within which we understand the world. In particular, the national income identity states that total expenditure is the sum of its components. This implies, without need for further proof, that the reciprocal relationship between public deficits and private savings is also a fact.* That is, every dollar of public deficits corresponds exactly to a

---

* The income identity is $C + I + G + X - M = Y$. In the standard notation, Y is income, C is consumption, I is investment, G is government spending, X is exports, M is imports, T is

dollar of savings in the private sector, either domestic or foreign. This is not a theory. It is not a conjecture. It is a fact, based on the way we do the bookkeeping. If the government puts a dollar into the private economy, via spending, over and above what it removes from the economy via taxes, then the private economy must have one more dollar on its books than was there before.

To put the point in a slightly different way, the financial balance of the *domestic* private sector—the excess of saving over investment in private domestic firms and households—must equal the sum of the government budget deficit and the net export surplus. Increasing the public budget deficit increases net domestic private savings (for an unchanged trade balance), while (for the same reason) an increased trade surplus also increases net domestic saving. Conversely, increasing net private savings increases the budget deficit. This is because with more saving, there is less consumption, less income, and less economic activity to tax. Hence tax revenues fall and deficits rise.

Wynne Godley and a team at the Levy Economics Institute built a series of strategic analyses of the US economy based on these accounting relationships. Their argument centered on America's international trade position, which they considered to be unsustainable (Godley, 2008) because the trade deficits were too large at full employment. They showed that the public budget surpluses of the late 1990s corresponded to an excess of investment over saving, and this was the reason why full employment was possible. The eventual cost of servicing the debts that financed the investments, they argued, would force private companies and households into financial retrenchment, which would in turn drive down activity, collapse the corresponding asset prices, and cut tax revenues. The result

---

total tax revenue, and S is saving. The second relationship is $(S - I) = (G - T) + (X - M)$, where S is defined as $Y - C - T$. $(G - T)$ is the budget deficit (ignoring transfer payments) and $(X - M)$ is the trade surplus. To know any two of the terms within brackets is, by definition, to know the third.

would drive up the public budget deficits, while reducing imports and therefore the trade deficits. And thus, more or less precisely events came to pass, both in the Nasdaq slump in 2000–01 and in the financial crisis of 2007–09.

Godley's method is similar to Baker's in that an unsustainable condition may exist when an indicator (such as the price/earnings ratio for stocks) deviates far from prior values. The difference is that Godley's approach is embedded explicitly in a framework of accounts; the choice of variables is systematic rather than ad hoc. This focuses attention on major macroeconomic indicators such as the private savings ratio or the current account balance. The question, then, is whether a particular state of the accounts is sustainable, or not, in terms of the political, contractual, or behavioral environment. It is a macroeconomic question—but it also goes no deeper than the accounts that give us our portrait of macroeconomic conditions. There is no underlay of the "real" economy, and so the analysis is spared both the mainstream notion of an underlying real equilibrium and the Marxian notion of an underlying intractable state of conflict.

In the late 1990s, the US government budget went into surplus for three years. Most commentators at the time gave credit to President Clinton's economic policy, including especially the tax increases enacted in 1993 as part of the deficit-reduction plan. But this was doubtful, considering that the budget forecasts did not project that the modest measures then enacted would produce a surplus in the government's accounts.

Godley's approach called attention to the fact that the public surplus was driven by private debts. The surplus was the accounting counterpoint to another unexpected event: namely, the information-technology boom. As companies borrowed to invest in technologies, they created incomes. The taxes paid on those incomes drove up public revenues, creating the budget surplus. The important questions were: How long could such a situation be sustained? And what would happen when it stopped? Official opinion in the last years of the Clinton presidency held that the New Paradigm could continue over an entire decade, with public-sector surpluses until the last

The End of Normal

dollar of national debt had been repaid. Godley's analysis made it clear immediately that this was very unlikely. The increase in tax revenues brought on by the borrowing-and-spending boom in the private sector depleted net financial assets in the private sector. These could be replaced by capital gains—for a time. But at some point, the plausibility of continued capital gains, on top of what had occurred already, wore thin. Dow 36,000 was not going to happen. Companies and households cashed in their chips, the stock market collapsed, and the 2001 recession killed the surplus.

Conversely, in a downturn, large public-sector deficits are inevitable. They are made so by the private sector's return to net saving. As long as the private sector is anxious to build up financial assets and repair its balance sheets, private spending will be low and public deficits will be large. Policy makers can't do anything about this unless they can somehow change private-sector behavior. Otherwise public budget deficits have to be large enough to permit the financial accumulation—or deleveraging—that the private sector is determined to achieve.

If public surpluses are unsustainable because of private debts, public deficits have a different problem. Private markets have no problem with the public debt of large countries, but public policy makers do not tolerate them well. Policy makers generally don't see, don't think much about, and don't understand what is happening on the books of the private sector. They tend to think of public deficits as a policy instrument per se, something under their control, and for which they may be held to account. But if they act on this belief, cutting spending and raising taxes just at the time when the private sector wants more cash in its own pocket, the private sector will respond by cutting back even more. The economy will collapse further. That is the dilemma of austerity policy.

The willingness of foreigners to hold US government bonds as reserve assets creates another counterpart to the US public budget deficit. Foreigners earn dollars by exporting more to the United States than they import from the United States. They convert their dollars into Treasury bills and bonds, because the latter pay interest and the former do not. Their willingness to hold dollar assets, in turn, supports the value of the dollar, which raises imports and reduces exports, and so reduces tax revenue at the US Treasury, compared with what would otherwise be. So long as the world wishes to add to its reserves of Treasury bills and bonds, corresponding US budget deficits are inevitable. Deficits will grow, in either a growing or volatile world economy, as the desired stock of reserves grows. From this it follows—as a simple consequence of Godley's balances—that any desire to eliminate the US budget deficit corresponds to a desire to eliminate the US position as the supplier of financial reserves to the world. It seems, though, that not one political leader or journalist in ten thousand understands this—or will admit to it, if they do.*

Minsky and Nonlinear Financial Dynamics

The framework of financial fragility offered by Hyman Minsky shares one key trait with the national-accounting framework emphasized by Godley. Under both, the intrinsic stability of the system is not prejudged. That question is left open. The system may be stable, or it may be unstable. It tends neither toward an equilibrium nor inexorably toward breakdown. The task of the analyst, making use of the framework, is to assess whether particular conditions are sustainable, for a time, or whether they are leading toward crisis. This shared trait gives the Godley and Minsky analyses their value for our purposes and in our situation.

Minsky's core insight was that *stability breeds instability*. Periods of calm, of progress, of sustained growth render financial market participants ill contented with the normal rate of return. In search of higher returns, they

---

* And what drives the reserve asset decisions of foreign central banks? Why do they buy and hold US Treasury paper? Will anything ever drive them to sell their Treasury bonds for euro assets, or anything else, forcing down the value of the dollar and putting an end to the American position as the "global Minotaur"? If we knew the answer, we could know the expected life span of the dollar-based international monetary system.

seek out greater risk, making bets with greater leverage. Financial positions previously sustainable from historical cash flows—*hedge positions*—are replaced by those that, it is known in advance, will require refinancing at some future point. These are the *speculative bets*. And then there is an imperceptible transition as speculative positions morph into positions that can be refinanced only by new borrowing on an ever-increasing scale. This is the *Ponzi phase*, the end stage, which must collapse once it is recognized to exist.

Minsky thus argued that capitalist financial instability is intrinsic. It arises from within. It does not require external disturbances, or shocks. There is no such thing as an equilibrium growth path, sustained indefinitely. However, a provisional, contingent form of stability is possible. It consists of keeping the system going forward on a steady keel for as long as possible. The public responsibility is to regulate financial behavior, limiting speculation and stretching out the expansionary phase. Abuses and their consequences are inevitable, and the dynamic of a successful policy ensures that it will be challenged by reckless behavior sooner or later. This does not mean that prudence and good management are pointless. Minsky's prescription is first to be vigilant and wary, and then to deal with the abuses and their consequences as they occur, and, finally, to have a government and central bank large enough to stabilize the economy when collapse eventually occurs.

When lined up against the mainstream or the Marxian views, what is radical about Minsky's thought is that it begins and ends within the financial system and never ventures outside of it. There is no separation between the financial sector and the real economy. The level of employment, the rate of inflation, the pace of investment and technological change all operate through credit decisions made mainly by bankers and other financial institutions. Finance is the *only* way to understand the economy. There is no such thing in economic life as a nonfinancial event, and the instabilities of finance are the same instabilities that afflict ordinary businesses and ordinary working people. While openness to instability distinguishes

Minsky from the mainstream, the prism of his financial viewpoint sets him off against the Marxians and also distinguishes his line from Godley's.

Minsky was not a mathematical theorist, but his approach has strong conceptual ties to recent applications of nonlinear dynamical systems to economic problems; for example, in the work of Peter Albin (1998), Barkley Rosser Jr. (with Gallegati and Palestrini, 2011), and Ping Chen (2010). Nonlinear dynamical systems are models built from simple equations—often just one equation. The equations have two properties. First, they incorporate a nonlinear feature such as a kink or a curve or an exponent—something that was missing from the complex, multiequation linear economic models that first became fashionable in the 1960s.* Nonlinearities would have made those systems unsolvable. Second, the output of the equation is fed back into the equation as an input in the next iteration. Thus the equations model the development of a system over time.

A key property of nonlinear systems is the appearance within them of *phase transitions*, which are changes in the qualitative characteristics of the outcome as some controlling parameter varies. These are akin to the change of water from ice to liquid to vapor, depending on temperature. At one setting of the control, the system can deliver a single equilibrium—a frozen state, so to speak, just as in mainstream analysis. But as the parameter varies, behavior will change. The next phase will be one of repeating cycles, where the system jumps from one outcome to another—say, from a high-output to a low-output position. Then it will start jumping between four possible outcomes, and then eight. Finally, there is a transition to a state called "deterministic chaos." In the chaotic state, even though the next outcome is always perfectly determined by the equations, the actual result jumps around unpredictably, within the limits of the system. Knowing where you are—or even all of past history—conveys no information about where you will be a moment hence.

---

* The models of Data Resources, Chase Econometrics, and Wharton Economic Forecasting Associates were prominent examples.

Phase transitions define the boundaries between qualitatively distinct states. The crossing of a boundary marks the passage of the system from one characteristic pattern of behavior to another. The change may be from apparent stability to instability, and from instability to collapse. All of these possibilities are inherent; there is no need to go outside for a "shock." It follows that stable prosperity is never a New Paradigm. It is simply a contingent state that may be maintained or lost, depending on how the system is run.

A virtue of this approach lies in the way the mathematics mimics history, evolution, and even the behavior of mechanical systems. There are rules and often boundaries (tolerances), yet there are not predictable outcomes. Even if the properties of the system are understood perfectly, the precise nature or timing of the next catastrophe cannot be known. You have to live the life to know exactly how it ends. The late Peter S. Albin made this point beautifully back in 1998.

Thinking about the economy in this way may seem unnecessarily abstract. But the Minsky model has clear implications for the role of government. The job of government is to regulate. The point of regulation is to keep a potentially unstable system operating within safe limits so far as these can be known. In particular, the point of financial regulation is to maintain the financial system within a stable and relatively desirable phase—either hedge or speculative—and well away from the phase boundary associated with Ponzi finance and collapse. Easier said than done! As with car engines, airframes, and nuclear reactors, even though you know the boundary is out there, you can't know exactly where it is. Getting closer to it—pressing the envelope—gives you higher performance. Crossing it gives you disaster. The choice of the margin of safety is a judgment call.

In this way, dynamical systems resemble the behavior of engines of all types, which typically have three operational phases. They can be "off," in which case the next period's state is exactly the same as the present. They can be running "normally," in which case the next period's state is connected smoothly to the current state or perhaps to an oscillating alternative. Pushing them to the limits of normal gives peak performance. Pushed past their limits, they can overheat, burn out, or melt down—in which case they must be rebuilt before they can be restarted. Attempting to operate a machine that has flirted too closely with the border of breakdown is dangerous. And a financial system is more like a nuclear reactor than it is like a car, so far as we consider the consequences of getting the control settings wrong.

When the effects of disaster are catastrophic, the policy guideline is clear: Play it safe. Keep away from the boundaries. Stay well within the zone, for as long as you can, in the face of pressures to move to the edge. But this way of thinking played no role in the way that mainstream economists reasoned about the appropriate posture of policy toward financial crisis. For the saltwater and freshwater groups, there is only a safe zone. They have never been in a stopped car, nor have they ever experienced a crash.*

Thus insouciance and fatalism combined to justify inaction. In the 1980s, insouciant economists favored using "market discipline" rather than supervision to oversee the behavior of savings and loans. In the 1990s, they helped dismantle the barriers—notably the Glass-Steagall firewall between commercial and investment banks—that helped to keep the financial system shy of the Ponzi phase. (Whether that barrier was still functioning is a separate question.) They permitted the Commodity Futures Modernization Act of December 2000, which made it impossible to regulate credit-default swaps. They opposed the Tobin tax on financial transactions, the purpose of which was to "throw sand in the gears" of financial markets and slow them down. In perhaps the most grotesque case, in the early 2000s, Alan Greenspan publicly encouraged the mass adoption of speculative (adjustable-rate, payment-optional) mortgages. Here the officials charged with preserving the safety and soundness of the financial sys-

---

* Pushing the metaphor just a bit, the Marxians are more like motorcyclists. They know very well that they are going to end up in a crash at some point—but it doesn't stop them.

tem not only acquiesced in private-sector overconfidence but also pushed the system to the danger zones.

The concept of a "margin of safety" applies in Minsky's analysis to the books of individual firms and banks. It may be applied equally well to the design of regulation and supervision in the face of uncertain economic conditions. But to understand what it means to be reasonably safe, we need also to understand the nature of risk. We need to have a broader picture of the world in which we live.

Part Two

The Four Horsemen of the End of Growth

Six

The Choke-Chain Effect

The economics of growth that came of age after World War II made essentially no reference to resources, to their cost, to diminishing returns, or to resource rents. For Americans, oil, having displaced coal in transportation and home heating, was still mostly from Texas and its surrounding states, and it was cheap. Vast reserves in the Persian Gulf ensured ongoing abundance even as Europe and Japan recovered. Competing demands from elsewhere in the world were modest, since the Soviet Union was self-sufficient in energy and China a minor presence in the world economy.

There was no reason to expect any early change in this state of affairs, and those who suggested otherwise were not well received. Oil shortages

This chapter owes a large debt to Jing Chen, a Chinese-Canadian physicist-turned-economist with a clear vision of the parallels between biological and economic systems. Our joint work may be found in the *Journal of Economic Issues* and the *Cambridge Journal of Economics*. Readers may find this effort to summarize and explain relatively hard going. If so, my apologies.

had been predicted repeatedly, and the predictions had always proved wrong. As the known pools were drained, it would always pay to discover more. And even after the largest and most accessible hydrocarbon reservoirs had all been tapped, we could still expect that technology would improve the efficiency with which existing resources could be extracted, until such time as a new and better form of energy came into being. Oil had, after all, displaced coal (as a transportation fuel) even though vast reserves of coal remained at hand. In a long series of S curves illustrating the diffusion of new techniques and resources, history demonstrated that innovation produces an overlapping sequence of transformations, always in the direction of lower costs and higher living standards. For the postwar generation, the *Limits to Growth* debate was a study in the foolishness of pitting mechanical projections of depletion and shortage against this record.

Behind the scenes, serious people thought about these issues in a darker way. The United States did consume a much larger share of world resources than its population share, and this was a major contributor to high American living standards. The government knew this. It was an injustice to be protected. Much of the work of the clandestine services in the 1950s and 1960s, in Iran, Iraq, the Congo, Central America, Indonesia, and Brazil, among other places, went to ensure that American firms and consumers had ongoing favored access to the oil, copper, uranium, and timber of those places, and even their sugar, bananas, beef, and coffee. Much later, similar concerns surfaced in the circles that decided on military intervention in Afghanistan and Iraq. But this went undiscussed, for the most part, in academic economics.

An economics that took resources for granted, that ignored resource rents and also the workings of finance in the resource markets reflected both the self-confidence of postwar high liberalism and a degree of insecurity with respect to the communist challenge. Marx in his day had quite a lot to say about imperialism, the demand for resources, and for markets.

Such was the basis of his appeal in the Third World. The response of Cold War liberals was to try to distinguish capitalism, based on free and equal trade, from imperialism, which was based on a tricky technical concept called "unequal exchange" (Raffer, 1987). In its political self-image, the United States was not an empire but an empire destroyer. Its contemporary politics were anticolonial; that the reality seemed otherwise to many Vietnamese was inconvenient, but a detail.

Social and economic critics in this period thus tread a delicate path if they wished to remain relevant in the contemporary politics of the United States. The path had to respect the boundaries that separated the liberal from the radical. The liberal position sought to share and extend the benefits of growth to the poor countries; thus the development and aid project, writ large. To suggest that resources were limited and their distribution inherently unjust—that was a task for the unfashionable fringe. To admit that the country was living high on the world's resources was also to raise sticky moral questions about the lifestyle of everyone in America, including one's own.

On these issues, the Keynesian alternative to mainstream economics—in the traditions of Godley and Minsky—had little to say. The post-Keynesians focused on questions that could be raised within economics: accounting, financial instability, organizations. They did not venture much into the relationship between economy and the broader physical world, nor into the geopolitical implications of patterns of resource use. They did not broach seriously the question of resource costs, or enter the emergent field of ecological limits and constraints. In the 1950s and 1960s, that would be left to even more isolated figures: notably Kenneth Boulding at the University of Colorado and especially Nicholas Georgescu-Roegen of Vanderbilt University, whose masterwork *The Entropy Law and the Economic Process* appeared in 1971.

Georgescu-Roegen observed that that economic reasoning, as developed in the dominant traditions, was not in line with the second law of thermodynamics.* This is the great principle that entropy constantly increases, that heat always travels from a hotter to a colder object, that time moves always forward and never back. Entropy is irreversible. Models of equilibrium systems, favored by economists and at the foundation of the growth theories, were by definition stable and even reversible. Any change brought on by a policy (or shock) could be offset by a policy (or shock) in the opposite direction.

Georgescu-Roegen insisted that economic activity is like all forms of activity, whether organic or mechanical. It consists in concentrating useful energy, in deriving satisfaction from it, and in releasing the residues as waste. Efficiency is defined as the ratio between satisfaction and waste. If the resources can be replenished, the process can be repeated. If the resources cannot be replenished, or if the waste fouls the environment, the process must come to an end. A given resource can be used only once; its use is a historical fact; once done, it cannot be undone. To quote P. G. Wodehouse quoting Omar Khayyám: the moving finger writes, and having writ, moves on.

Organisms develop structures—biological, mechanical, and social—to transform resources into forms they can use. These are called *fixed costs*, because the structures required must be built before production occurs. You have to commit in advance to a strategy—to a technology—for extracting and using resources. Costs are then fixed to the extent that this strategy cannot be changed in a short period of time. The use of resources that changes with the level of production is called *variable cost*. Different economic systems have different combinations of fixed cost and variable cost. When there is no production, variable costs are zero, but fixed costs still have to be paid.

Overall, a system will function if the value of total resources extracted

---

* In his great 1989 book *More Heat Than Light*, Philip Mirowski explained how twentieth-century economics derived from nineteenth-century physics, as it was before the second law of thermodynamics had been understood.

exceeds the cost of extracting them, both measured in energy units. This is an energy surplus. To get that surplus, you must have some prior investment otherwise the variable cost just equals the output, and there is no net gain. Larger animals and bigger corporations, which have made such investments, tend to have longer lives and to be the top predators in their respective food chains—they have developed advantages, and they have reserves. For this reason, what economists in the Austrian tradition have called "roundabout" means of production—methods using more capital—have an evolutionary advantage when resources are cheap.

Typically, a more efficient system requires a larger investment in fixed costs: to get better, you need to be bigger. Yet the converse is not necessarily true. Systems with high fixed costs may be efficient or inefficient. That depends on their design and engineering, on how well suited a particular technology is to the environment in which it is installed, and on the stability of that environment over time. In times of plenty and stability, natural selection and economic policies generally aim to increase fixed costs by accumulating capital through investment. Efficiency then has the potential to increase, so long as resources remain cheap. Stability is important because it is possible to justify high fixed costs only if the system is expected to remain profitable, earning a surplus, for a long time. Higher resource costs and instability, therefore, are big threats. They can destroy a surplus and make a big fixed system unsustainable.

To think in concrete terms, consider the difference in agricultural techniques between a poor country and a rich country. In poor countries, farming is often done by human and animal labor. The energy extracted from the land, which originates in sunlight, barely exceeds the energy required to cultivate it. For this reason, poor peasant farmers are thin. Production and consumption are local. Both are vulnerable to drought and flood and thus to famine. Peasant farming is precarious. But on the other hand, farming as a way of life in poor countries is very stable. It carries on for centuries, even millennia, with little change. While natural calamities are disastrous for individuals, they do not threaten the underlying way of life, which will be reproduced as before once the calamity is over. That is because the fixed costs are low. It does not take much to rebuild the system.

In rich countries, farming is embedded in a vast industrial system that provides machinery; chemical fertilizers; markets, including futures markets; and transportation of the eventual produce to distant consumers. This system is much more productive: yields and living standards are much higher. Why? Because the energy of the sun is supplemented by other energy sources, especially oil and gas, which power the machinery and are converted into fertilizers, enriching the soil. Division of labor makes possible the efficient application of the extra energy. Crucially, the energy cost of extracting these resources, during the two centuries of their common use, has been far below their energy value.*

But suppose that energy cost rises? It may rise because the costs of extracting oil from the deep seabed or from tar sands is higher than the cost of extracting it from onshore fields, now depleted. Or it may rise because of market power in the extraction and distribution of energy, creating a situation of artificial scarcity, transferring real wealth from consumers to producers or to middlemen. What happens then? The peasant farmer who does not rely much on outside energy only lightly affected. But the costs of fertilizer, transportation, and farm machinery all rise. The initially high profitability of industrial farms will fall much more sharply than the profitability—initially low—of the subsistence farm.

Efficiency is a matter of design, scale, and control. As noted above, big animals are efficient. They live a long time, range over great territories, and can often consume a wide range of foods. Yet they are not numerous, not flexible, slow to reproduce, and therefore may be vulnerable to extinction if conditions change, cutting the surplus and making the raising of young more difficult. Small animals, on the other hand, are numerous,

---

* The relation between these two quantities is called the energy return on investment (EROI), about which I have learned a great deal from the work of Charles Hall.

short lived, adaptive, reproduce in large numbers, invest little in their off-spring, and are the species' survivors in hard times. The same rule applies to business firms and whole economic systems. Great companies flourish when resources are cheap and conditions are stable for a long time. Small companies come and go. They change with circumstance but not in basic type; when destroyed, they can be replaced. Their proprietors rarely become rich unless the business also grows big. Great corporations, on the other hand, can concentrate great wealth, but they are prone to great busts.

The bigger the firms, the larger the share of fixed costs in total costs. Networks, infrastructure, trained personnel, management, research, and capital equipment are among the fixed costs, as are pensions incurred on past labor. Hourly labor and materials are variable. The greater the fixed costs, the longer a company, project, industry, or technology must last in order to justify the initial investments, and the more the need for control over circumstances, including political stability, resource costs, competition, and the market, stretching far into the future.

For this reason, only in times of optimism, security, and confidence will great projects be undertaken by private firms. Only then are they foreseen to yield great rewards—and only then will financing will be available for them at low rates and for long terms. We can identify the nineteenth-century British Empire, combining predatory access to resources, dominant technology, military power, and enforced peace as a famous instance of an optimistic age. Not by accident, Victorian expansion and foreign investment were financed partly by bonds with no redemption date, called *consols*. They were a financial instrument suited for an empire on which the sun would never set.

A second instance is the United States and its sphere of influence after 1945. Part of the goal of the postwar world order known as the Pax Americana was to liquidate previous empires: notably, the bankrupt British and what remained of the French. Another goal was to contain the rise of new empires, especially the USSR. A third was to thwart the destabilizing efforts of revolutionaries to create truly independent zones. The first two efforts succeeded almost completely, and the third did as well, with the major exceptions of China, Vietnam, and Iran, and the irritating one of Cuba. The result was to stabilize the US financial position, permitting America to run large trade deficits without penalty. This advantage continues, even in the age of crisis. Thus the United States has had no difficulty selling Treasury bonds at terms extending to thirty years—a sign that despite all difficulties, the country as a political entity is expected to endure.

But when resources are scarce and expensive, when uncertainties loom large, then time horizons shorten. Scale is limited, and total surplus or profit is less than would be available to the large enterprise under stable conditions. Since profits are less, distributive conflicts—among labor, management, owners, and the tax authorities—become more intense. Confidence in good outcomes wavers. Under these conditions, fewer large projects will be undertaken, and maybe none at all. There is a reason why under certain conditions one buys backup generators and bottled water. But no one would prefer doing so, and no country that relies on backup generators and bottled water will ever reach the living standards accessible via power lines and fixed pipes.

To illustrate the role of uncertainty, consider the development of hydroelectric dams. In the United States, hydro development advanced rapidly in the 1930s. Why? In part because America was militarily secure. There was no chance that the dams might be destroyed in warfare—as German dams, built in the years before aerial bombing, would later be during World War II. In Latin America, the prevailing peace among Brazil, Paraguay, and Argentina made possible the massive hydro development at Itaipu on the Paraná River. Egypt, on the other hand, ran a big risk with the Aswan High Dam, which subsided only when peace with Israel was reached in 1978. In China, the vulnerability of large hydro projects to attack from either the United States or Russia remained extreme until the late twentieth century. In the interim, China's electrical power development relied heavily on coal. Coal plants are far less efficient than hydro, but if they are destroyed in warfare, there are no disastrous consequences downstream. Only when the threat of attack disappeared in the mid-1970s could China begin to develop its largest hydropower resources, notably the Three Gorges on the Yangtze River.[*]

Government policies influence economic performance by affecting the structure of the economic system. A lower interest rate, by making large initial outlays financially feasible and projected cash flows from the distant future more valuable, tends to encourage investments with high initial fixed costs. Higher tax rates also tend to encourage increased fixed costs. Activities involving variable costs (labor) are generally taxed heavily, whereas those that depend more on onetime investments are taxed more lightly. In fact, machinery investment is generally heavily tax-subsidized. For once a building, a piece of machinery, or a dam is in place, the equipment remains in use, but the economic effort to produce it will not be taxed a second time. Labor, on the other hand, is taxed constantly, and the cumulative tax on employment adds up over time. Conversely, low taxes and high interest rates encourage an emphasis on variable costs. It is not accidental that more-developed countries often have high taxes and low interest rates, whereas in poorer countries, taxes tend to be low and interest rates high.

Technical progress is often achieved by moving to systems with higher fixed cost. Technology enables one to tap into resources that were previously not economical. For example, new horizontal drilling and fracturing technology enables natural gas companies to develop shale gas on a large scale. But at the same time, more advanced technologies are more resource intensive. Hydrofracking requires large amounts of water. The net effect of technology on resources evolves over time. When the rate of consumption of resources becomes higher than the rate of renewal or discovery, resources will become scarce. In a resource-scarce environment, social

---

[*] I'm grateful to Ping Chen for this insight into Chinese energy policy.

systems with higher technology require more resources to support the technology. As a result, net resources available for consumption—water, fuel, biofuel feedstocks with food uses, such as corn—may decline. This will lower living standards, and it will do so more sharply if a country hangs on to the technology that it can now no longer afford.

If a firm or economy cannot generate a surplus, it will first consume any reserves that may be on hand. Next, scarcity can sometimes be relieved by borrowing from outsiders against future production—incurring a debt. In the case of scarcity or diversion, barring a favorable turn of events, contracts will be broken, and resources promised to outsiders will not be delivered. This is a historic cause of wars.

The final remedy for scarcity is to eat the seed corn, curtailing investment. Then present standards will be maintained for a time, but those in the future decline. It will become ever more clear to those living in the present that the future will be dreadful. Public authority must then choose between maintaining investment by force or allowing the present generation to use up the resources required to keep the future generations alive. There is no reason to believe that the democratic decision made by the living in the face of their present needs and desires will be the decision that would maximize the chance of long-term system survival. The unpleasant conclusion is that it is possible for a society to *choose* economic collapse.

What is true of societies is also true of firms. Global empires breed transnational corporations, with big technical projects (pipelines, nuclear power plants, global air networks, communications), long design horizons, and the need for stability and growth. When resources are cheap and markets are growing thanks to falling costs, companies of this type expand. But when resources become scarce, markets contract, and the potential for growth vanishes. Business cycles may then become instruments of policy. Downturns can be inflicted on purpose, when it suits the leaders of enterprises, to squeeze out competition, control costs, and open market space for new investment.

Normally, the same markets that are shaped and disciplined by business-cycle policies are protected against outsiders by tariffs and by patents and often by the imposition of standards and other nontariff barriers. That was not the case in the United States for the Asian competition of the 1980s. The strategic role of the rising countries of Asia, their technical excellence, and the powerful lobbying presence they developed made it impossible to block their rise in American markets. What started as a resource-cost disadvantage for American firms turned into a permanent trade deficit.*

In response to their declining industrial position for thirty years, the most advanced countries (and especially the United States) have been undergoing financialization. The large banks have grown to over half of all banking; and banking at its peak earned 10 percent of all wages and 40 percent of all profits. This is not a surprise. Large banks are some of the highest-fixed-cost social structures. They are very efficient at making money—for themselves.

Compared with real products, financial products are highly uniform and of great volume. Yet the cost of producing them is almost entirely paid up front. It pays to invest heavily for products with large volumes. For example, index arbitrage takes advantage of price differentials between spot and futures markets; it is essentially risk free and can be very profitable. But opportunities for arbitrage disappear seconds after they arise; index arbitrage requires quick calculation and execution. Since the quickest arbitrageurs take almost all the profits, there is a strong need to develop the best customized computer systems, which are extremely expensive, and to bid heavily for the top talent to run them. The prize for coming in first is a winner-take-all position; one thinks of Morgan Stanley or Goldman Sachs.

---

* The voluntary export restraints in autos of the Reagan period were designed to slow the penetration of Japanese cars, but in ways that permitted higher margins per unit and ultimately market dominance in the higher-quality segments.

High-fixed-cost systems have multiple vulnerabilities. At the enterprise level, these include more efficient rivals within the same market space—in the case of US manufacturing, the emergence of German, Japanese, Korean, and later Chinese competition, all challenging the market share required to keep unit costs low. Resource costs may rise for technical reasons, squeezing the surplus. There may be wars and revolutions, which can create political conditions that drive up the cost of resources even more, as in 1973 and 1979. It is normal, when uncertainty rises and profits fall, to bet on a return to ordinary business conditions. It is also normal enough to be wrong about that bet.

Futures markets bring expected future conditions into play in the present. There are two main possibilities: future resources can be expected to be either abundant or scarce. When net abundance prevails, the price will tend to fall toward the variable cost of the most efficient suppliers, and more expensive producers will struggle. Net abundance is unstable for this reason. That is why cartels emerge: they put a floor under the price, preserve some margin to cover fixed costs, and enable the higher-cost operators to continue to work. But cartels are also unstable. There is a tendency to overproduce, which undermines the cartel. In Texas, under the Railroad Commission, as with the world oil cartel under OPEC, the danger was always that more supply would enter the system, forcing down prices and destroying the solidarity of the cartel.*

When a resource is scarce, the price dynamic is the opposite. Prices will now rise, and they will rise past the cost of production of even the most expensive producer. How high can they go? The limit on prices will be not what it costs to meet demand at the margin. It will be the highest

---

* The National Industrial Recovery Act of the early New Deal was designed to support cartels so as to maintain prices and curtail overproduction—the opposite of antitrust enforcement. The Agricultural Adjustment Administration served a similar goal. Both have been maligned by modern economists, who maintain that the problem of excess supply can be dealt with by increasing total demand. But it is not self-evident that this is always true, nor that total demand is necessarily easy to increase.

price that consumers can bear, the highest they can pay without curtailing their demand. Futures markets will push the price quickly toward that limit. Traders do this by taking a long position in a commodity or an index fund and then rolling it forward as the delivery date approaches. It then pays for producers and speculators to hold the resource—to refrain from pumping, to slow down tankers, to fill storage tanks—to take advantage of the still-higher prices that will come quite soon. This is a condition that regulation used to try to thwart by limiting speculative positions in the futures markets. Without effective limits, futures markets facilitate this game.

In a world where resources have become scarce, and also financialized, the end result is not an indefinite series of price increases. Instead, it is a cycling of both key resource prices and economic activity. Prices rise, under the pressure of speculation, until there is a collapse of consumer demand. Then they fall again until consumers recover. But once consumers do recover, prices start rising again. Soon enough the fact of cycling creates anxiety, since everyone knows that the current price, whatever it is, will not endure. Anxiety diminishes the incentive to make long-term investments. New refineries (for instance) are not built, because while prices may be higher in the short run, there is no assurance that they will remain high enough, long enough, to justify the investment. The result is that net scarcity, once established, tends to persist unless some radically new technology comes along.

What is the effect of chronic net scarcity on profits? First, increasing resource costs will be deducted from the profitability of high-fixed-cost systems. Such costs are a direct drain on the surplus of the system. When the price of oil goes up, every oil user suffers a cost and profits squeeze. The producers get a corresponding gain, but there are fewer producers than users, and many of them are overseas. There is no automatic recycling of the displaced profits from the producers to the users—and if there is, it happens usually on commercial terms that cannot be sustained. So the choice is between a slump now and a debt crisis later.

Second, doubts associated with expected cycling of resource prices dampen investment spending. This too hits the profits of energy users, whose goods now have a smaller market. So even if the direct cost of energy in the economy is a low share of total activity, an increase in energy prices may have a big effect on the total pool of available profits. That is why the oil shocks of the 1970s led to recessions. It was not their direct impact on the disposable income of consumers that mattered so much, but that they hit at current business profits and also introduced doubts about the prospect for future business profits. On both counts, investment declined, and so did employment and total output.

This tightening we may call the choke-chain effect. It comes into play when there is (a) a net scarcity of a critical resource, in the sense that total demand exceeds total supply at the habitual price, and (b) when the supply of the commodity can be manipulated by hoarding and speculation. Like a choke chain on a dog's neck, the effect does not necessarily prevent economic expansion. But once the use of energy resources *accelerates*, prices rise rapidly and then profitability falls quickly. This curtails investment, sows doubt about the sustainability of the expansion, and may also provoke a (perverse) tightening of the other domestic levers of policy. Only a slump can then relax the grip of the chain.

The cycling of energy costs seems so obviously a huge part of US economic history after 1970 that it is difficult to imagine a narrative that does not emphasize it. The same is true for continental Europe, as it is for the United Kingdom in the presence (now waning) of North Sea oil. One may note also the fortuitous role of oil in Norway, gas in Holland, and nuclear power investments in France, giving those countries a buffer against rising oil prices not available elsewhere in the short run. That postunification German energy strategy has relied on the supply of Russian gas also scarcely needs stating. And Chinese external economic strategy clearly aims at stabilizing the supply and cost of energy and other resources over as long as can be reliably managed. So even though the choke-chain effect is not a staple of growth economics—quite the reverse—its presence is no secret to policy makers anywhere.*

What about hydrofracking? The phenomenon of fracturing shale for oil and natural gas has suggested to many that resources will soon again become cheap, restoring net abundance, business profitability, and the prospects for sustained growth. There is a boom in the business, and the United States is (as of present writing) on track to surpass Russia as the world's largest energy producer. Moreover, natural gas prices in America are less than a third of what they are in Europe. Has the choke chain been lifted, and not a minute too soon, by a miraculous technological advance?

At this stage, it is too early to tell. Clearly, there is an enormous amount of shale gas to be had. Enthusiasts abound, but so do skeptics, and the business person making investment decisions has no firm basis for judging either side. The key issue appears to be the rate at which new wells are depleted, and specifically the age at which they lose pressure. Depletion rates are coming into focus, but the technology is too new to know how long the wells will last. Only time will tell. However, the fact that, in many eyes, American prospects are distinguished from those of Europe by the presence of shale gas in Texas and North Dakota, is a sign that—implicitly at least—the role of resource costs in economic growth has finally become very clear.

Climate change has no *current* bearing on the argument. The disaster of global warming may be mitigated by aggressive action to reduce carbon emissions. Whether that happens—or not—does not affect the econom-

---

* Nothing in this argument has to do with the threat of a peak in *global* oil production, except that rumors of such a peak may influence speculation, hoarding, and current energy costs. Whether peak oil is already here, as some maintain, or whether it is ten or thirty years out is relevant to growth today only insofar as the peak will affect prices and import costs now. Similarly, the rumor of a peak may prompt speculative behavior that drives up prices whether an actual peak is imminent or not. We may therefore safely leave the mysteries of global petroleum geology to those who hold those secrets.

ics of a cost squeeze in the short run, unless the prospect of aggressive mitigation begins to change current business expectations and planning. And that would require the costs of climate change to be incorporated, through public policy, into current business decisions affecting energy use. The problem is obvious: the big costs of climate change proper lie in the future. And even though major reductions in carbon emissions are necessary for the sake of the survival of organized life in its present form on the planet, achieving them will also be costly, and a large share of current energy-using business activity would become unprofitable and be curtailed.

It may be petty to discuss mere economics in the face of existential ecological threats, but the fact is, business decisions are made in the here and now. In a broad sense, a low cost of resources has to underpin the profitability of all business activity. The rising cost of resources in the 2000s necessarily meant a squeeze on resource users. The rise peaked on a wave of hoarding and price speculation when oil touched $148 per barrel in the summer of 2008. It then subsided with the slump—an excellent example of the choke-chain effect. At present writing, oil prices near $100 per barrel have become customary, and we appear to be living in a world where the long-range prospect still includes a choke-chain acceleration of resource prices when the growth of demand threatens to accelerate again.

So far as I'm aware, no study of the *financial* crisis has yet suggested that resource costs lie at the heart—or near the heart—of it.[*] But it remains equally true that resource costs have moved from the shadows, and are now understood by all informed, practical people to play a central role in economic performance—even though formal economics continues to neglect them. They are the simplest, clearest way to understand the crisis

---

[*] At a meeting in 2009 to advise on the direction of the Financial Crisis Inquiry Commission, I suggested that the oil price spike should be examined. The view of the other participants was that it was not sufficiently central, and I did not try to press the point.

of the 1970s, and why inflation emerged then but disappeared in the 1980s and 1990s. They can also help explain why the energy-using world fell into troubles again after 2000, just as resource costs roughly doubled in relation to the prices of goods and services produced in the resource-using lands. And why, meanwhile, the energy-producing world, in the Middle East and in Latin America, experienced no financial crisis at all. No one suggests that resource costs alone are the full story of the Great Crisis— only that they are one underlying part of it. For now, that is enough.

Seven

The Futility of Force

If the resource costs facing the industrial world have been first a propellant to and then a restraint on growth, then it is necessary to examine the role of military power as the guarantor of acceptably low resource costs. Since the start of the industrial revolution, the world has been dominated by those who had access to resources on preferential terms: the British and French empires, Russia, the United States. Those countries and empires lacking cheap resources, including the Ottomans and the Chinese, found themselves weak, thwarted, and in decline. The Germans and the Japanese, attempting to create such empires and gain such access, were turned back in major wars. In the Pax Americana that followed, resources remained cheap through 1970, in part because of their internal presence on American soil, and in part because the American military guaranteed the stability of the great prizes in the Persian Gulf and elsewhere. The presumptive effectiveness of US power was tested in Vietnam, reaffirmed in the first Gulf War, and unchallenged in the post–Cold War era until the aftermath of September 11, 2001.

If one rereads the pyramid of books that appeared on the reach and role of the United States in the early years of the "global war on terror," one finds that whether they favored or were opposed to "empire," they rarely raised the issue of capability.* The superiority of American power, measured by advantages in ships, planes, bases, and spending, was self-evident. That the power would be used effectively for the most part was assumed. Events would soon demonstrate that the assumption was without merit. But they also showed something else, quite different and unexpected: in the face of a world economic crisis, military power, however great, has in general become a sideshow. It is not merely that the United States can no longer dominate the world in military terms. Rather, the nature of military power has become such that no dominant power can any longer exist.

In 2004 the Harvard historian Niall Ferguson published *Colossus*, a case for empire in principle and for empire run by Americans in particular. *Colossus* took an unsentimental view of the history of American interventions abroad and yet still made an argument for their necessity. Ferguson did not try to prettify the record, from the Philippines to Vietnam. He did not try to argue, as others have done, that the US mission in the world was nonimperial, that the American mission was qualitatively different from the earlier European world realms. Instead, his thesis was a practical one, in two parts: that the job of managing the world commons must be done by someone, and that however ugly the American imperial tally sheet may be, it looks good in comparison to all the others.

For Ferguson there is a general case in favor of empires and a specific argument for American empire. The general case, Ferguson states, "is always the case for order. Liberty is, of course, a loftier goal. But only those who have never known disorder fail to grasp that it is the necessary precondition for liberty. In that sense, the case for American empire is

---

* Michael Mann, *Incoherent Empire* (London: Verso, 2003) is a significant exception.

simultaneously the case against international anarchy, or, to be precise, of a proliferation of regional vacuums of power" (Ferguson 2004, 28).

We shall leave aside some of the assumptions left implicit in this statement. Is the alternative to empire really "international anarchy"? Is self-determination a modern hoax? National independence a romantic illusion? If there is no imperial power, and specifically no American imperial power, does that mean that "regional vacuums" necessarily emerge? If they do, what does it mean, and is it so bad? Does the wider world, in general, see American motives through the same warm and fuzzy lens that Americans use to judge themselves? Ferguson's sweeping style is not intended to make it easy to discuss these questions, but that's not important for present purposes. In the wake of 9/11, the issue was tested on narrower grounds.

The case for the actual use of military power to impose order on an otherwise anarchic world, then, is the case that order *can be imposed*. That order can be imposed *and maintained*. That this can be done *by force*. Was this ever true? If it was ever true, is it true now?

As to the first question, there is little doubt. For a long time, empire was an effective instrument of world order. That time began in the early nineteenth century, when the great advantages of the machine age combined with an improving art of public administration to give imperial powers the combination of defensible motivation and overwhelming advantage of force.

These two developments revived what had been, up to that point, a fading political form. European global empire (as distinct from the vast but still limited imperial realms of China, India, Egypt, Greece, Rome, Mexico, and Peru) began with global navigation, which led to contact with native populations in the Americas and the Pacific. Being global at a time of slow and uncertain communications, it was necessarily loose. The fruit of oceanic navigation and continental discovery, global empires in their first phase were built on depopulation by disease, on slavery, and on plunder—first of existing artifacts, later of mineral resources, later still of land and labor. Public administration for other purposes was, largely, limited to keeping rudimentary order and the saving of souls.

In this first global era—let's say from the sixteenth to the eighteenth centuries—control by the central power depended on the loyalty of small local elites transplanted from the home country. This was limited by distance, by the cost of maintaining armies across a vast ocean, by the passing of generations since settlement, and, on the colonial side, by an extreme but not unreasonable aversion to paying taxes. It is no mystery why the first British Empire—in what is now the United States—fell apart in the late eighteenth century. Nor is there much doubt as to why in the early nineteenth century, the Spanish and Portuguese dominions in South America slipped away.

The second wave of empire was different. By the midnineteenth century, it was possible to promise to bring both industrial investment and modern government to the conquered lands. Winston Churchill, no less, put it this way, describing his expedition to the Mamund Valley of Afghanistan in *My Early Life*: "Into this happy world the nineteenth century brought two new facts, the breech-loading rifle and British government. The first was an enormous luxury and blessing; the second, an unmitigated nuisance" (Churchill 1930, 135).

The model, in a way, was Napoleon, whose armies marched against feudalism in central Europe (up to a point) under the banner of revolution and law. But Napoleon tread on contestable ground, on territories part of, or close to, other European empires, and (in Spain and Portugal) on the headquarters of European empires past. (A century later, Hitler would face the same problem.) India, Afghanistan, and Africa were something else, as was Siberia to the tsar or the Wild West to the United States.

The imperial powers of the nineteenth century scrambled for territory that for the most part they did not have to win by force of arms from a comparably powerful party. For the Europeans, this was preeminently in India, Southeast Asia, and the East Indies (where trading dominions gave way to outright administration) and in Africa. For the United States and Russia, the expansions were, at first, in the vast adjoining lands. Why did these ventures arise, and why did they succeed, even after the earlier ones had come to an end?

The answers lie in the railroad, the telegraph, the machine gun, the steamship, and in the political reforms in Europe that offered some justification beyond plunder—at least to the imperialists—for the advance of Western civilization. Against opposition that ranged from neolithic to feudal, in many cases overawed or bought off, the power of Western industry was beyond challenge. Against previous government, in some cases the new empires brought advantages to some local elites—though this was not the case for Belgium in the Congo, or the effect of white settlement in the Dakotas on the Sioux. When there was resistance, nineteenth-century mores and racial attitudes condoned a response of absolute violence. From the standpoint of Punjabis or Algerians or Vietnamese or Native Americans, the new empire was a permanent condition; resistance was quixotic. And so the pragmatic came over to the imperial side, and the empires flourished.

Until the twentieth century. The First World War was a contest between empires, a clash of industrial systems, draining to all of them whether defeated or victorious. The Second World War was fought in large part to prevent Germany and Japan from creating new empires on the models of Britain, France, America, and Russia from just a couple of generations before—empires based on territorial expansion, the subjugation and sometimes the extermination of native peoples, and the use of colonial territories as a base for resources and a sink for industrial goods. The outcome of that war discredited empire generally. It set the stage for national independence of almost all colonies in Africa and Asia; an independence to be guaranteed by the United Nations. Independence did not come easily everywhere, as the French still had to be beaten in Vietnam and fought to an ugly standstill in Algeria, while the British fought in Malaya and Kenya, though not in India, which held financial high cards and used

117

them. But independence came. Apart from the curious case of the Soviet Union, the anti-imperialist power that was the only new empire to emerge from World War II, only Portugal held out for another thirty years. The Portuguese empire was, however, a remnant from the first global era: neither a major source of wealth nor a sink for industry at that time. And Portugal had been neutral in the world wars. While poor, it wasn't bankrupt when they ended.

As the second wave of European global empires faded, Ferguson saw the rise of a new one *on the same model,* only thinly disguised behind the United Nations and the rhetoric of national self-determination. This was the empire of America. Like its immediate predecessors, the American empire is rooted in industrial and military power alongside efficient public administration, the latter arising from a professional military with exceptionally dominant technologies and (as these things go) a decent professional and self-disciplined approach to the tasks of conquest.

Ferguson thus places the postwar reconstruction of Germany and Japan in the category of American *imperial* success stories, motivated partly by the classic imperial concern with fortifying the far frontiers of empire against its rivals—in this case, the Soviet Union. He sees the end of World War II as a passage *between* empires, and not, as most would have had it, as a challenge to the concept of empire in itself. The cynical corollary is that the national independence and the international structures of world governance established after 1945 were a sham.

Yet it was not in the defeated Axis countries that the might of the American military and the power of the American political and administrative example would be tested. That happened first in Korea, where US forces narrowly escaped defeat at the hands of the North Koreans and then of the Chinese. And then it happened again a decade later in Vietnam.

Ferguson's analysis of Vietnam is interesting for the frank brutality of his views. He argues that the United States was winning the war at the end, that it could have won had it pursued the endgame with still greater force and determination, and that military victory would have preserved an independent, friendly, and anticommunist South Vietnam. It is possible, too, that he is right, a least so far as the conventional conflict with the North Vietnamese army is concerned. As he notes, American technologies improved and adapted to Vietnamese conditions, battle tactics grew more effective as the war came to a close, and that in 1972 the North Vietnamese invasion was stopped by US air power. Maybe, in military terms, the NVA could have been fought to a standstill.

Vietnam was a difficult place to fight. The opposition had safe havens in Cambodia and Laos that were hard to reach and supply routes that were difficult to obstruct. But Vietnam also had many of the attributes of earlier, more successful colonial wars. There was a massive imbalance of means, a largely rural battlefield, and the potential for the unlimited application of force. Ferguson thus holds that the United States lost the Vietnam War for political reasons—because American political leaders either lost or never had the stomach to fight it out to the end. And that raises the question, why did the political reasons prevail? If greater force could have won that war, why wasn't it used? Is there anything to be learned from the fact—if it is a fact—that the political questions proved decisive?

Brutal though it was, there were political restraints on the war in Vietnam, and they existed for good and sufficient reasons. The experience at the Yalu River in 1950 had not been forgotten—that moment when an overstretched American advance to the Chinese frontier was beaten back by a far less well-equipped army fighting near its home ground. American presidents knew that a fight with China on its own frontier was a bad risk. And there was another factor, never far from their minds: the atomic bomb. Of course, no American president would risk coming under atomic attack. But equally, no American president wanted to face a situation where a US atomic bomb might need to be used: for example, to rescue a garrison beleaguered as the French were at Dien Bien Phu, Vietnam, in 1954.* For

---

* Use of the bomb had been suggested to President Harry Truman in Korea. Top policymakers do not forget these things.

these reasons, American leaders were not about to press matters to the point of fighting the Chinese People's Liberation Army. There would be no invasion of North Vietnam, no bombing of the Red River dikes, or attacks on shipping in the harbor at Haiphong.

Television was another new factor. Unlike in every war up through the 1950s, unlimited violence in the south of Vietnam could not be concealed in full from the public at home. And once exposed, again contrary to the mores of an earlier time, it was certain to provoke wide objection. Thus the way the war was prosecuted began to have a direct bearing on how long it could be prosecuted. A war that was waged with too much open savagery could not be sustained. No previous imperial power had faced this problem, except possibly France in Algeria just a few years before.

The political climate had also changed in Vietnam itself, as it had in every previous colony. Fifty years earlier, a Vietnamese might reasonably believe that the French intended never to leave. Empires were the way of the world. An office under the French was secure; indeed, there was no other way to advance. Even Ho Chi Minh, the nationalist revolutionary who became the first president of the Democratic Republic of Vietnam, began as a student in Paris. By the 1960s, this world had disappeared. The Americans in Vietnam were, and always would be, a temporary presence. Our purpose, we said, was to "train Vietnamese to do the job." Since everyone knew this, everyone in Vietnam had to know there would come a day when we would not be there to protect our local friends. This fact had to deplete South Vietnamese enthusiasm for a fight to the finish.

And so, in April 1975, the day of the helicopters came, when Saigon finally fell to Hanoi's army, two years after the US troops had gone home. After the loss of Vietnam, the American military did take stock of its limitations. Under President Jimmy Carter, there were no wars at all. Ronald Reagan, despite his cowboy persona and his early increases in the military budget, was also reluctant to make direct use of military force. In the Reagan years—apart from the brief debacle in Beirut, Lebanon—the US limited itself to proxy wars (as in Angola and Nicaragua), and to cakewalks, as in Grenada. Even in Grenada, as John Tirman relates in his book on the arms trade, *Spoils of War*, the resistance of the armed forces on that tiny island caused a certain amount of casualties and consternation (Tirman 1997, 95–96). In 1989 George H. W. Bush conducted an invasion of Panama. It was an ugly business that killed hundreds, but the quick and dirty violence was shielded, largely, from the American public.

Not until 1991 did the United States again attempt an actual war, the one-hundred-hours operation to clear the Iraqi army from the Kuwait desert, to chase them out of Kuwait City, and to immobilize them in Iraq proper. Being distant, and against a foe of some apparent strength, Operation Desert Storm required a costly and dramatic buildup. But the fight itself was easy: open-country warfare with overpowering air superiority and limited objectives against an obsolete, overextended, and demoralized opposing force, much of which had deserted before the battles began.[*]

The first Gulf War "kicked the Vietnam syndrome," or so it was widely said. But it proved nothing about the reach of military power in general terms. It obscured, rather than transmitted, the lessons that the USSR had been learning the hard way, in the decade before, in Afghanistan. Nor would the US military be seriously tested at the end of the decade when it confronted the forces of Slobodan Milosevic in Kosovo, notwithstanding that the air campaign unexpectedly took seventy days, did not destroy the Serb forces, and illustrated for close observers some of the ways that crude countermeasures can frustrate aerial bombardment. Those seeking affirmation of their view that with the end of the Soviet Union the United States had become an unchallengeable superpower—a hyperpower—would have to wait.

Then came the attacks of September 11, 2001, the "Pearl Harbor of the twenty-first century," as the neoconservative group called the Project for

---

[*] About a third of Saddam Hussein's army in 1991 was Kurdish, a population with no interest in fighting for him, given his long history of oppression and even genocide against the Kurds.

a New American Century had foretold and as President George W. Bush noted in his diary that night. September 11 opened the door to a vast military buildup, going far beyond the scale of the actual war that followed, to disrupt Al Qaeda and chase the Taliban from power in Afghanistan. As the US military (and its allies) rolled toward Kabul in late 2001, there were essentially no political limits to what the Pentagon could spend. And no effective constraints on its planning.

But Afghanistan, too, was too small a war—or so it seemed for the first several years—to impinge heavily on the American view of war itself. According to the Congressional Budget Office in 2007, military operations in 2001 and 2002 increased by only $14 billion and $18 billion, respectively, above baseline. The direct economic effects were, therefore, trivial. What mattered much more were the unlimited scope the Pentagon now had to prepare for future wars, and the boost to confidence that came from an easy win. Afghanistan, in other words, was (in the early days) a cakewalk that fostered an illusion.

In early 2003 came the invasion of Iraq. Here it was at last: a war of conquest and occupation, of a large country, against a large army. Here was the test of the hyperpower hypothesis—of the idea that the United States could rule the world through "shock and awe." The test was announced with a wave of war fever, perhaps not seen since Pearl Harbor. Those who expressed skepticism were either shunned or ignored.

We know now the outcome of that test. It may be useful to list some of the reasons why it turned out as it did. It may be useful to explore why, a decade later, after an estimated $800 billion in direct costs (and much more in indirect costs and costs still to be paid), the United States would withdraw from Iraq after having achieved only its most immediate objective: namely, the downfall of Saddam Hussein. Iraq plainly did not reverse the pattern, evident since at least the French departure from Algiers, that empires cannot be maintained.

Why is this so? Why have wars of conquest and occupation become so hard?

The first reason is surely urbanization. The preindustrial countryside of Africa or India offered (and in many places, such as Libya, still does) vast fields of fire. From a dominant hill or from the air, you could slaughter at will. A village in the way could be burned or razed. Moreover, troops could move, camp, and protect their positions with pickets and sentries. Cities, on the other hand, are confections of concrete and steel and a warren of tunnels and basements. Short of atomic weapons, they are impossible to destroy completely. The streets restrict the motion of vehicles, making them easy targets. All of the advantages of open-field warfare disappear.

Second, there is the evolution of weapons. In the imperial heyday, it was said, nothing could withstand, or counter, the firepower of the industrial army. As the poet Hilaire Belloc put it in the late-nineteenth-century: "Whatever happens, we have got / The Maxim Gun, and they have not."

Those days, however, disappeared very long ago. In the modern world, shaped charges (which direct the power of high explosive through a wall or the side of a tank) are prodigiously powerful, cheap, and easily concealed. As terror weapons, they are also useless to the occupying power, while invaluable to the resistance. For more general explosives, the car makes a powerful means of delivery: the "poor man's air force." Failing the car, the human suicide bomb is versatile and effective. We have learned that there are many ways to induce people to blow themselves up, whether they volunteer for the duty or not.

Third, there is the presence of the media, of modern communications, which now go far beyond the role already played by television cameras in the Vietnam War. Today practically every scene can be recorded and broadcast. The norms of human conduct are never fully respected in war, as in Iraq the US assault on Fallujah or incidents such as the Haditha massacre demonstrate. Nevertheless, the presence of digital cameras, cell phones, Facebook, and now Twitter ensures that atrocities will be followed closely the world over. And that means that the scale of *permissible* violence is lower than it was in past times. The subjugation of an occupied people through the systematic application of terror alone is largely ruled out. The same goes, for the most part, for the use of torture in prisons, as the Abu Ghraib debacle seems to have impressed even on military authority in the United States.

Fourth, in the modern world, the occupier's individual tour of duty is relatively short. Soldiers and their officers rarely stay on station more than a single year; and if they return later, it will generally be to a different assignment. They come and they go home by jet. This too is in contrast to the imperial armies of a century back, to which many men committed practically their entire working lives. The result can only be diminished personal relationships, mutual trust, and, therefore, reliable intelligence between the occupation force and the local population. Further, the civilian administration of occupation is no longer an established profession. It became in Iraq a field for amateurs, often with careers or political ambitions back in the United States. It is not possible to forge an effective ruling elite from untrained and incompetent short-termers.

Fifth, the modern occupation is always limited in time. Nobody any longer conquers territory for the sake of annexing it. Israel on the West Bank and the Golan Heights is practically the only exception in the world today and has earned pariah status in much of the world for violating that norm. The occupied population knows for certain that there will come a day, someday, when the occupiers leave and the collaborators can be dealt with. For this reason, the permanent local proxy official has disappeared. Those who work for the occupiers are either careful to maintain back channels to the other side or hope anyway to move their families to safety in Tucson before it's too late.

Sixth, soldiers in the occupying army are much more expensive and much more precious than ever before. They are no longer the expendable sons of the farm, of a class not far removed from serfdom, scarcely educated and easily replaced. There is the problem, in an all-volunteer force, that they must be recruited. There is the problem that, with sophisticated equipment to manage and maintain, they must be well trained. And there is the problem, in a mass media democracy, that their deaths and injuries are events of political consequence. None of this was true even a half century ago, when cannon fodder was still the principal use to be made of the enlisted man.

These reasons amount to permanent changes in the calculus of warfare. Together they alter the ratio of costs and benefits of waging wars of occupation and control. And they help explain why the Iraq War did not end with the conquest of Baghdad, why an ultimate stalemate took another five or six years and was achieved, in the end, largely through politics rather than force. If the lessons hold, and there is no good reason to suspect they will not, a similar war involving the outright conquest of a large state is unlikely to be attempted again—perhaps not by any power and almost surely not by the United States. Meanwhile, the war in Afghanistan—more rural, on the whole, and in a lower key—continues, but perhaps not for much longer. At current writing, US policy is clearly searching for the exits.

The long aftermath of September 11 thus tested the uses of military power in the modern world. After the quick conquests of Kabul and Baghdad, enthusiasm ran high. But in the way of war, it soon gave way, month by month, to frustration, sorrow, and the counting of costs. In the early going, we were told that the war on terror might never end. A decade later, the American taste for distant conflict had waned. Libya was handled, for the most part, from the air. The war in Pakistan is a matter mostly of drones in remote spots. In Syria, the threat of military reprisals for a chemical weapons attack on civilians was withdrawn, with diplomatic help from the Russians, partly because it was clear that there would be no favorable military result. North Korean threats are being met, to date, by sensible caution and reliance on the Chinese. At present writing, there is even the prospect of a negotiated settlement with the Islamic Republic of Iran.

Is war over? Unfortunately not. But the wars of the present and likely future will be fought in territory that has never been industrialized and will never become so, in places rarely seen by the world press, and with little direct involvement of advanced-country military forces. The Age of War as We Knew It does appear to be ending. With the death in early October

2013 of North Vietnamese general Vo Nguyen Giap, at the reported age of 102, the world may have lost the last of the great military leaders in such wars. Giap had fought the Japanese and defeated the French, Americans, and Chinese in a sequence of wars estimated to have claimed between two and three million victims. Outside Africa, there seems almost no prospect of a future war on that scale. And the reason is clear enough: under modern conditions there is no profit in the game.

Some people believed that the Iraq War was intended to give the domestic economy a boost, so let us turn quickly to that argument. As the war got under way, total military operations ramped up by a factor of four—to $80 billion in 2003, $88 billion in 2004, and an average of $90 billion in both 2005 and 2006. The increase in military spending in 2003 amounted to about two-thirds of 1 percent of the US annual gross domestic product at that time. In the second quarter of 2003, as troops poured into Iraq, national defense spending added 1.45 percent to the rate of growth of the GDP.

This amount was higher than the contribution of military spending to growth in any single quarter since at least 1971. But outside that second quarter of 2003, the Iraq War's directly measured effect on American GDP was barely perceptible. Over the full year of 2003, the direct effect of increased military spending on GDP was just 0.36 percent; it was 0.26 percent in 2004, and less than a tenth of 1 percent in 2005 and 2006. The theory of the multiplier suggests that one might increase these effects by 50 percent or even 100 percent, to take account of downstream repercussions on private spending. But even if one allows for a generous multiplier, overall the impact remains small and ends soon.[*]

The reason the effect of the Iraq War on economic growth tailed off so

---

[*] Total costs add up over the years. Linda Bilmes and Joseph Stiglitz (2008) emphasize long-term costs, including for veterans' care, which are accrued over many years, and macroeconomic costs, including an estimated effect on the price of oil. See Peter Orszag (2007) on certain points of dispute in the calculations.

quickly, in spite of the war going on and on, is that to have a continuing positive effect on economic growth, *the increase* in spending has to be repeated year after year. Adding *one* increment to total spending (about $90 billion per year, in this case) raises GDP *once*, even if total spending at the new levels continues in the years that follow. Maintaining spending at any given level, once achieved, adds nothing more to the *growth rate*. Thus although the total cost of the Iraq War far exceeded the woefully underestimated prewar forecasts, it was nevertheless still very small in relation to the scale of the US economy, and its direct effects on economic growth also ended quickly. This was true once again, even though the war continued for eight years. From the standpoint of American economic performance, at least as measured by the national income accounts, the consequences of public spending on the Iraq War were small from the start. They were practically irrelevant after 2004.

In the mid-2000s, disenchantment with the Iraq experience lent weight to another line of economic argument: that the United States was endangering its world position by "imperial overreach." The ostensible threat was to the international role of the dollar. The worry was that key countries elsewhere in the world, seeking an "asymmetric" response to shock and awe, would show their resistance to American military power—and their disagreement with our Iraq policy in particular—by ceasing to hold US Treasury bonds as a financial reserve, preferring instead the debt issues of Europe, Japan, Russia, or even China. In that event, the value of the dollar would fall, inflation in the United States would rise, and living standards would fall. This would be the way—some feared and others hoped—the world would punish the United States for the arrogance and the crimes of the George W. Bush administration.

Nothing of the kind occurred. The exposure of American strategic frustration in Iraq and Afghanistan had no detectable financial consequences. The vast sums wasted on the war and the occupation seem not to have mattered to the interest rates paid on US government debts. That oil concessions in Iraq and gas pipelines in Afghanistan never materialized seems not to have mattered either. The neo-imperial exercise came and went, and it is hard to find a clear-cut trace of the financial costs. There were costs, of course: in social investments not made, in public capital not maintained or repaired, and in lives damaged or ended. But these are costs absorbed by individuals and by their communities. They are visible enough—but only if one knows how to look.

When the financial crisis hit, it came from another direction: from within the US economy and its private sector, not directly from the violent misdeeds of the government. An ironic result was that in the crisis, the US government bond was just as much a safe haven as it ever had been in the past. The entire war on terror, intended by its authors to be a permanent feature of economic and social life—and seen by its detractors as a threat to the American place in the world—seemed to have faded away, leaving its traces only on the psychology of its perpetrators and its victims. In that sense, it was a sideshow. What it proved, though, it proved beyond question: that the dangers we face, and in particular the barriers to economic growth, have no remedy by military means.

Eight

The Digital Storm

What is the bearing of technical change on the prospects for growth? To most people, the answer must seem self-evident. Technical improvements are part of growth. If they accelerate, growth increases, and if they decline, growth slows. Since we are in the midst of a vast transformation—the digital revolution—then technology* must stand as our best hope for rescue from economic stagnation. I shall argue that this hope is misplaced, even though I accept the common view that the rate of technical change is very great. On the contrary, the vast transformation now under way is

---

* In common use, the word *technology* now refers mainly to computers, telecommunications, the new media, and the new social networks. This is evidence of the plasticity of the word, and *plasticity* is a polite word for "formless." In a broader sense, technology has been around since the Neolithic; as it relates to machinery and industry, the word dates from 1859. The term *high technology*—what we now think of when "technology" is mentioned—came into use a century later, according to a new-media source, the Online Etymology Dictionary at www.etymonline.com/index.php?term=technology.

being managed in a way that will act as a third great barrier to a renewal of growth or return to high employment.

Economists love to debate the effects of technology on inequality, on employment, on growth. And they frequently assert that one country has "more advanced" technology than another. Yet if you ask what technology *is*, and how they measured it, they cannot tell you. Technical change has no stable definition and no unit of measure. Sometimes the economists count patents, as though the patent were a unit of technological change. If you ask for evidence of this, there is none. Patents record inventions. The rate at which they are issued measures the activity of the patent office.

Notwithstanding, the framework of growth theory maintains that—*in some sense*—technology is an element of the growth process. Its effect is to raise the real standard of living by delivering more and superior products for a lower real cost and price. It follows that if in some sense technical change were to slow or stop, growth would also slow. Intuitively, without new technologies, growth would be limited to the gains that may be had from adding more machines *of the same type*. A technically stagnant society would soon hit the barriers and bounds of rising resource costs and diminishing returns to scale. And apart from that, it would be a bore.

Solow's growth model opted to treat technology as a leftover: as that part of growth that could not be accounted for by increasing labor hours or a larger capital stock. This approach evaded all problems of measuring technology, on the assumption that labor, capital, and output *could* be measured. It turned out that what labor and capital couldn't account for was enormous. In the 1950s and 1960s, the "Solow residual" was estimated to amount to some 70 percent of economic growth. Because measured growth was much more rapid than the increase of population or the value of the capital stock, the force of technology—whatever it was—did most of the work in explaining growth in that model.

Can growth of this type continue? Only if technology (whatever it *is*) continues to advance. And given the speed (whatever *that* means) with which digital devices have been transforming life in recent decades, growth must be accelerating on that account alone. So it's perhaps astonishing that some economists now entertain the opposite view and argue that we have already entered an era of technical stagnation. But that is the view of one of the most authoritative students of growth theory and growth accounting: the economist Robert J. Gordon of Northwestern University.

In a 2012 working paper titled "Is US Economic Growth Over?" Gordon compares innovations of the digital age with those of the industrial age that came before it. He notes that the industrial age gave us glass windows, flush toilets, airplanes, highways, piped water, central heating, and air conditioners. The gains from industrial technologies took advantage of efficiencies that were available in that age of discovery, given advances in materials, engineering, hygiene, and energy use. But they were onetime changes. There will be no replacement for glass window coverings that will improve on glass as much as glass improved on cloth or waxed paper. There will be no new power plant for the airplane that will improve it as much as the turbofan jet improved on the propellor. From this foundation of engineering efficiencies, Gordon argues that we are now experiencing an exhaustion of possibilities that will prove tantamount to the end of growth.

The notion of waves of technological change, of industrial revolutions, forms part of the structure of Gordon's argument. His message is that the latest wave, the digital wave, does not improve life, or economic welfare, by very much. Smartphones are just reduced versions of the . . . phone, fax, mails, computer, calendar, calculator, compass, newspaper, television, movie theater, and deck of playing cards. They provide nothing new, nothing of great importance, and what they replace was available before. And therefore they cannot add very much to economic growth, measured in "real" terms. That, so far as I understand it, is the nub of Gordon's case.

But what does "real" mean in this context? How can we judge by how much the "real living standard" has improved by taking all of these functions and making them available in a single pocket-sized packet? If Gordon has a specific metric of human satisfaction in mind, it appears to be the reduction of physical effort required for survival, health, and comfort. On those criteria, smartphones do poorly. They contribute next to nothing to survival or health, and not much to comfort.

Yet to compare the smartphone to the glass window is not a comparison based on the continuing experience of any actual person. In the digital age, there are few who ever directly experienced the transition to glass windows. So there is almost no one around who can report whether his or her personal welfare was improved more by one technology or the other, and even if there were, we need not use that person's testimony as dispositive evidence for everyone else.

Economic output consists entirely of goods and services for which people are willing to pay. Beyond the measuring rod of money, efforts to compare effects on well-being are just guesswork, inherently subjective, as generations of welfare economists have pointed out. And so, even though the answer may *seem* obvious, it is not. We cannot compare improvements in an age of scarcity with those in an age of affluence, and we cannot know whether Facebook and Twitter contribute more, or less, to human welfare than (say) did the railroad or the electric water pump.* We are therefore obliged to consider the impact of the new technologies on their own terms.

---

* Solow's approach to measuring the contribution of technology to growth ran into another difficulty already back in the 1950s, when some economists realized that the capital stock was also unmeasurable. If there could be no clear measure of how much capital there was, there could also be no clear distinction between what was "capital" and what was "technology." Beyond that, as perhaps should have been obvious all along, technology is embodied in equipment (Salter 1964, 14–15). One cannot add together machines of different types and vintages in any rigorously meaningful way, because as designs change, the thing you are measuring changes. Technology and capital are inseparable in principle, and *neither* has any standard physical unit of measure. The effect of this is to obviate growth accounting; if the elements of growth cannot be counted, then measuring their contributions to growth is not a meaningful procedure.

Growth accounting focused our thinking about technology on output per person, which it took as a measure of benefit *to the consumer*. Yet in the sweep of the history of economic thought, this is a recent view. The classical tradition that prevailed before World War I had an entirely different view of what technology is and does. It did not see technology as even remotely intended to raise living standards. The effect on psychology was therefore irrelevant. Rather, the classical economics held that new technologies were created mainly for control and for cheapening the production process, and especially for cheapening labor. Technology was a tool in the arsenal of capitalist competition, the purpose of which was to increase the efficiency of labor, or what Karl Marx called the "extraction of surplus value." Technologies made possible—as Marx pointed out—the lengthening of factory hours, the use of women and children in manufacturing, and the speeding up of production lines. John Stuart Mill concurred, famously conveying his doubt that any machine had ever lightened the workload of any human being.

The classical point of view would have placed the digital technologies in a different light. What do they really do? A modern vision of the classical economist might point (for instance) to their role in facilitating distributed production and outsourcing, in bringing cheap labor into direct competition with that of the developed world. Indian call centers would not be possible without satellites and fiber-optic transmission lines and electronic switching. Nor would today's transnational production networks for fashions and electronics. In the nineteenth century, the steam-powered drivetrain brought English ten-year-olds under the discipline of the machine. In today's world, the fifteen-year-old Chinese villager gets the same doubtful benefit from instant contact with San Jose, California, or New York.

The big function of the new technologies is to save labor costs. They do this by replacing expensive labor with cheap labor at a remote location. Or they do it—it amounts to the same thing—by replacing on-site labor with a machine. Thus checkout clerks are replaced by card readers; bank tellers, by ATMs; bookshops, video stores; and music distributors disappear as communication, information, and entertainment move to handheld devices, and as retail shops give up their ghosts to e-commerce.* Whether a general rise in living standards happens as these developments unfold may be debated either way. But, beyond doubt, incomes concentrate in the hands of the high-tech tycoons; those who are displaced suffer a loss of income, while those who manage to hold on to jobs in the affected sectors may well be less skilled, less credentialed, and less well paid than their predecessors were.

In his 1942 book *Capitalism, Socialism and Democracy*, Joseph Schumpeter called attention to the role of technology as a tool of competition between enterprises in the struggle for market share. The point of technology, Schumpeter, believed, was *just as much* to destroy as to create. Only by destroying the old markets could one release purchasing power to support the profitability of new ones. For Schumpeter, therefore, slumps were a necessary part of this process. Old structures, companies, markets, and jobs *have* to be destroyed when and as new ones emerge. There is no guarantee that the new processes will reemploy those displaced from the old ones. As a rule, they will not. There is also no guarantee that the rise of purchasing power and living standards in the wake of a technical revolution will come at any definite remove of time from the destructive phase.

Schumpeter coined the phrase "gales of creative destruction" to describe how technical change overturns the structures of economic life, reducing great factories and whole production systems to waste and rubble and the masses to unemployment. But he was aware that at the same time, these same changes *did* have the potential to raise living standards for the population at large. Schumpeter did see in technology what Marx (and other classical economists) had missed: namely, that cap-

---

* An economist working for Federal Express tells me that the small size of smartphones has a measurable effect on the Asian-US airfreight business, since many more units can be packed onto a single plane, and so the demand for pilots and crews has fallen.

italism could thrive on working-class markets if it managed to produce goods that the working class could somehow manage to buy. And perhaps because he had moved from Austria to America in 1932, Schumpeter had seen something that the relatively cloistered Briton John Maynard Keynes either did not see or chose not to emphasize: there was a large element, even in the Great Depression, of technological transformation of this type.

The effect of tractors on farming is an example. These mechanical devices, first diffusing broadly in the 1920s, displaced draft animals and the humans previously devoted to their use and care. Horses and mules on American farms declined from some twenty-five million in 1920 to around eight million in 1950. (This was not, in general, good for the horses.) Some seventy million acres of American forage land could now be turned to crops or cattle, about the same as the entire acreage devoted in 1950 to wheat (USDA 1950, 16). Together with chemical fertilizers, pesticides, and hybridization, these changes raised the output of American farmers. But they also displaced farm labor to the cities and towns, where that labor did not have the purchasing power to absorb the new output. The agricultural depression was one of overproduction and of the collapse of prices and profits.

Underlying this change was the rise of oil as a transportation fuel. Though the famous field at Spindletop blew in 1901, making it the first gusher of the Texas oil boom, peak production there was achieved only in 1927, and the East Texas Oil Field was discovered in 1930. These and related finds established Texas as the leading oil producer in the United States and, at the time, in the world. Liquid motor fuel made possible the mechanization of farming. Hydrocarbon-based fertilizers replaced animal waste and replenished the depleted soils cheaply. Trucks extended the reach of farm-to-market commerce. Asphalt, a by-product of oil refining, would become available to pave the roads.

As Schumpeter saw, in this situation creation came first, and destruction followed. The use of trucks in America was spurred by the army in

World War I, a development that prompted Thorstein Veblen to remark that "invention is the mother of necessity." After the war, the now-mature invention was turned to civilian use. Fertilizer used the same chemicals that made the explosives in artillery shells and (later) aerial bombs— something of which we were recently reminded by the fate of West, Texas, where a retail fertilizer facility happened to have 270 (unreported) tons of ammonium nitrate on hand. In April 2013 the town lost 140 houses and other buildings, give or take, when a fire set the chemicals off. Fifteen people died and more than 160 were injured.

The spread of tractors, trucks, and industrial chemicals to the farms in the 1920s was financed by bank loans. And so when the financial system collapsed in the early 1930s, the farm sector especially was exposed. Farming, a leading purchaser of new technology at the dawn of the age of oil, and a source of superabundance, was for that reason the first great victim of the Depression. This was why the Agricultural Adjustment Administration became the first great priority of Roosevelt's Hundred Days.

The oil revolution was an energy revolution, affecting transport, propulsion, heating, cooling, and power. Since energy underpins all activity, the rise of oil eventually opened pathways for growth that had not been there before, from cities in the hot and humid South, to suburbia, to aircraft. But it did not eliminate the previously dominant fossil fuel: namely, coal. Nor did it preclude the development of alternatives, including nuclear power and natural gas. Coal continued to be mined and burned in vast tonnages—but it was now diverted from ships and trains and home furnaces, largely for the narrower purpose of powering electric generators. The concentration of coal on electricity meant that electricity-consuming sectors could also expand more rapidly than they could have done before. To begin to realize these changes, however, took two decades—from the early 1930s to the early 1950s—and the financial and political transformation that was accelerated by another world war.

Ultimately the consumer culture configured itself around a new economy based on automobiles, garages, and repair shops, suburbs and shopping malls—and cheap electric power. The farm boys and girls (and their children) became mechanics, or went to factories, or into construction, or into the shops—or to college. Highways and airports came to dominate the American transportation system. Passenger railroads nearly disappeared (though freight rail, powered by diesel, flourished). City centers withered. The postwar generation grew up under this pattern of American development—a set of fixed costs—which with the rising relative price of oil is now in decay.

Fast-forward to the 1990s, and to the information revolution. Just as all activity uses energy, all economic activity processes information. And so, like the internal combustion engine boom, the information-technology boom affected most of what human beings do. But the information revolution was, if anything, even more comprehensive than the oil revolution had been before it. There were (and are) very few ways in which information is processed that cannot be transformed from analog to digital. Thus the *form* of almost all activity—especially in the service sectors—was *transformed* by this shift and by the rapid increase in the speed and capacity of information processing.

In Schumpeter's creative phase, for those who grasped the potential, there was unlimited money to be made. The young technologists of the late 1990s became the Henry Fords and Alfred P. Sloans of their age. So they borrowed and invested, and for a brief period their activities boosted total demand and delivered a few years of full employment prosperity to the entire country. This was the moment that corresponded in many ways to the stock-fueled boom of the late 1920s. But, of course, they *overinvested*—as their predecessors had also done. There was superabundance, as there had been on the farm and in the early automotive years. And they overleveraged in order to overinvest. When the reality of overinvestment set in, prices fell, the boom collapsed, and the moment of generalized prosperity came to an end. But, just as in the late 1920s, the technology did not disappear. It continued to evolve and to spread. As it did—Schumpeter once again—the destructive phase came to the fore.

Already in the early days, the computer developed the capacity to displace the arts of typewriting, bookkeeping, filing, and draftsmanship. When linked to routers and fiber-optic cable, it could go on to displace the mail, the telephone, the phonograph and CD player, the camera and film, board games and sports, the movie theater and the VCR and the DVD player, not to mention the clock and the watch. It long ago displaced the physical bookstore and is now displacing the physical book, the newspaper, the magazine, and the academic journal, not to mention the physical library as a repository for these things. Televisions have survived only by having been transformed into computers with large screens. Analog signals have left the airwaves. In rich countries, cathode-ray tubes are now scarce as typewriters. There is no equivalent here of the persistence of coal in the oil age.

While the patterns of creative destruction generated by oil and information resemble each other, there are important differences. Most notably, automobiles wear out on their own. The heat of the engines, the friction of the road, rust, and collisions limit the effective life of any car or truck. And this is true even before the notorious effects of planned obsolescence. The effect is to create an ongoing demand for new cars, and also a vast industry devoted to maintenance, inspection, and repair. Roads, too, need to be rebuilt and expanded, and houses built with garages for all the cars. In the transformation to a car-and-oil culture, there was work for many who were not engaged in the building of brand-new cars. The technology destroyed jobs, but it also gave rise to many new jobs as it developed and matured.

With computers and the internet, this scope for secondary employment is far less. Hardware wears out slowly because it has few moving parts and because it is operated, for the most part, in stable, clean, temperature-controlled offices and homes. The infrastructure—optic cables and routers, say—once built, lasts a long time. There is no equivalent of the effect of a heavy truck on tarmac. And when the hardware does wear out, it is replaced. Because of the cheapness of components, repair is rarely preferable to replacement, and so the computer-repair sector remains small and is shrinking as the equipment becomes ever more uniformly solid-state. The replacement industries are remote, as are many of the software jobs. Software lasts indefinitely unless compromised by viral attacks; it may be updated or replaced automatically with no on-site labor required.

Thus if the new industries wish to grow, they must constantly produce new designs and new products. Software must be upgraded. Hardware must be upgraded to run the upgraded software. Faster speeds, more storage, and bigger caches—these are quality improvements, but in many applications, they are eaten up by more demanding programs. (As they used to say in the trade: what Grove giveth, Gates taketh away.)[*] Most of all, the big thing is new applications: new ways to make the computer (or the tablet or the smartphone) the platform of choice for tasks previously done elsewhere and otherwise. Thus new ways for the information-processing device to perform tasks that used to be carried out by someone else for money; new ways to kill off activity elsewhere; new ways to devalue somebody else's skill. New ways to waste time and new ways to show the world that one has time to waste.

The ratio of jobs killed to jobs created in this process is high. The service and office workers, checkout clerks, account managers, and salespeople whose jobs can be consolidated and rendered redundant by the digital revolution are the modern version of the horses driven off their Depression-era farms. And the process does not stop: the costs saved by moving to digital platforms continually claim new victims as prices fall and technical barriers to introducing the new methods in one venue after another are overcome. Moreover, many of those displaced are not only unemployed but also obsolete. They had fairly narrow skill sets to begin with; now they are useless.

---

[*] The references are to Andrew Grove, former CEO of Intel Corporation, and to Bill Gates of Microsoft.

This is the two-edged sword of creative destruction. At one level, living standards do rise, as the cost of creating, processing, sharing, and communicating drops toward the time value of the human labor involved. Music, film, reading, writing, talking, and flirting—around the world, instantly— have been rendered universally available and practically free of marginal cost. Gordon argues that this is not very important, compared with being relieved from the daily drudgery of carrying water from a well. But the sex drive is strong! There is no standard measure that can weigh it against the need for clean water. All the economist knows—all the economist can know—is that people take the opportunity to send messages freely. Since the service is not priced, the valuation to place upon it (the consumers' surplus involved, to use the textbook jargon) is not known and not easily discovered. An unpriced service simply drops out of the GDP.

For the large numbers of people once sustained by the now-displaced activities, on the other hand, actual living standards decline. Having lost their jobs, they lose their incomes. This is the effect that the classical economists emphasized. That they can communicate for nothing or check the news or download songs and movies or watch sports or listen to the radio from around the world is offset, for them, by the reality that they cannot maintain payments on the houses in which their computers and internet connections reside.

A part of the cash flow that previously supported those people—the managers and the checkout clerks, the secretaries and the TV repairmen, the booksellers and the reporters and the photo-lab technicians—now flows instead to a minute number of people at the top of the digital food chain. This was a dominant source of rising inequality in the late 1990s, when fully half the rise in income inequality measured across counties in the United States could be accounted for by rising incomes on Wall Street, in three counties of Silicon Valley, and in Seattle.* It continued to be a

---

* I have documented this point in *Inequality and Instability*, based on calculations by Travis Hale.

large part of the continuing high inequality in the decade that followed, although the locus of most rapidly rising incomes shifted, first to the military-heavy counties around Washington, DC, and then to the most flagrant centers of real estate speculation in the months before the collapse.

The rest of the cash flow that technology eliminates finds no immediate outlet. Businesses that had previously met a larger payroll now meet a smaller one. Their cost saving, like all saving, implies lost employment, diminished incomes, and the waste of displaced human talent. This affects all those directly displaced and also those who previously worked to provide goods and services to those now unemployed. In effect, the "saving" disappears. There is no paid activity to replace the activity lost. The plain result of the new technology is unemployment.

In this sense, the digital products all around us have cost us millions of jobs. How many? It is practically impossible to say, and the reason for that is, you can't distinguish a job lost to technology from a job lost to a business slump. The two are, actually, the same thing. In the nature of business cycles, jobs are lost in slumps. That is when businesses must either downsize or fail. So we attribute the job losses to the slump. But if that were all there was to it, the jobs would reappear with economic recovery. But they have not. As economic recovery begins, businesses find that in the next round of investments, the next redesign of their operations, their needs can be met with fewer workers.

These issues have, I think, been confused more than clarified by the recent contributions of some economists and students of business management. In a book titled *Race Against the Machine* (2011), Erik Brynjolfsson and Andrew McAfee of MIT rely on an alleged acceleration of technological change—something that for the reasons already given is no easier to demonstrate than Gordon's slowdown. But neither acceleration nor slowdown in the pace of change is necessary for labor-saving. All that is required is that the decision to hire a new worker, or to replace a departing one, be weighed against the economic attractiveness of a piece of equipment. Machines—like the horses of yore, incidentally—do not require health insurance or social security contributions or even wages. As those costs rise they would become more attractive, even if there were no further change in the reach or cut in the cost of the technologies at issue.

A scholarly debate has also broken out over whether it is possible to measure the effect of technological change on jobs over the years since 1979. In a useful paper in late 2013, Lawrence Mishel, Heidi Shierholz, and John Schmitt of the Economic Policy Institute survey the claims and the evidence, concluding that one cannot find an important effect of technology on middle-income jobs and therefore on polarization of employment. They show, correctly, that the important job losses and structural changes occur after the Nasdaq peak in 2000—when high-wage occupations especially suffered—and especially after the crisis of 2008—when jobs of all types were lost. Hence the argument that technologies were destroying jobs in the period beforehand carries little weight.

But the inference drawn by Mishel and company that the losses incurred since 2000 are a reversible consequence of slow growth, and then of the great slump, seems to me unwarranted. The slump created new facts for private business. In its wake, employment decisions will be different than they would have been otherwise. And the labor-saving potential of new technologies will be exploited more aggressively than it would have been had no slump occurred.

If this is correct, the result will be a permanent move toward lower rates of employment in the private, for-profit sector. If incomes formerly provided in that sector are not replaced, then a larger part of the total flow of demand formerly provided there will disappear. People formerly employed, who might otherwise find something remunerative and useful to do with their time, will find that there is no way to sell their services. GDP will follow employment down, not so much from a shortfall of total demand, but from a failure to find specific ways to place purchasing power in the— diffuse, decentralized—hands of those who would best use it to give their fellow-citizens work.

This is not to disparage the digital age. People choose digital products, more or less freely, over the technologies they used previously. The new technologies do save resources. They do help business cut costs, and businesses have to control costs or they do not survive. And it would all be worth it if we could only find some other way to maintain, up to a point, the incomes and consumption possibilities of those who have been affected: keeping them in their homes, their kids in college, and their medical bills paid as required. Few would return to a world of push-button telephones and stamped letters; such a world remains available, after all, but who inhabits it? If we miss our defunct bookstores and regret our failing newspapers, it's because of the comforts and pleasures of browsing—leisure activities, really—not so much because they afforded superior access to information.

What happened to jobs when the petroleum revolution—otherwise known as the Depression—dumped America's horse tenders and ploughmen and carriage makers and all the rest onto the labor market? At first it was a disaster: millions hit the rails, or set out in trucks, and landed in camps and Hoovervilles. But then came the New Deal, which employed those millions on public projects, rebuilt the country in the years from 1933 to 1936, and brought the unemployment rate down from 25 percent to below 10 percent—if one counts, as one should, those working on public projects as employed.* Then after the retrenchment and recession of 1937–38 came the Second New Deal and then the mobilization for war.

The war eliminated unemployment altogether. The jobs it created, by and large, did nothing on the productive side: the soldier and the weapon builder do not add to consumption or living standards. In the war, new business investment and much production other than for war materiel stopped, so as to conserve strategic resources. The war also did not leave

---

* In an important essay, "Time for a New New Deal," Marshall Auerback (2008) has pointed out that historians of the New Deal have generally failed to count as employed those working for New Deal agencies—a fact that causes them to exaggerate greatly the extent of unemployment from 1933 to 1936. See further discussion in chapter 11.

in place a large new body of capital equipment for the next generation to use.* Tanks and artillery and warships have no civilian uses, and most of the aircraft were scrapped. But after the war, the population had, built up and in reserve, a postwar purchasing power, in the form of government bonds, to work down over the following fifteen or twenty years. This provided the financial basis for a new economy and enabled a (more or less) smooth transition. By the 1960s, the destructive phase of the oil revolution was practically complete. The countryside had emptied out, the railroads had shrunk, the collieries were no longer making deliveries to home furnaces. The horses were long dead.

And so came the years of economic growth, during which employment could be maintained and expanded largely by ramping up the production and consumption of the new, oil-based generation of services and goods, to which were added the benefits of cheap electricity fired by all that displaced coal. The effect of the car and the truck and the aircraft, of the suburb and the appliance, was to make possible a growth in total employment, absolutely and in relation to the labor force, far greater than the collapse of the ancient ecology of horse and plow and the semimodern technology of the railroad and streetcar had reduced it.

Two more forces bore on the development of a high-employment economy. The first was the initial, early postwar withdrawal of women from the labor force—an ambiguous benefit for those affected. But more family formation meant fewer jobs needed to be created. And at the same time, the family became, for the first time on a mass scale, the wellspring of effective demand. Activities previously performed on an unpaid basis—including the erstwhile labor of the horse, the wife, and the children—became part of the cash economy. As all manner of machines replaced family labor, GDP grew by a process of substitution. Eventually the house itself became a bulwark of purchasing power, detaching the ability to spend, to a degree,

---

* Existing capital was both heavily used and not maintained, so it wore out more rapidly than in peacetime.

from the ability to earn. All of this led toward the financial debacle of the 2000s—but it was good while it lasted.

With the digital technologies, these effects are going into reverse. First, the price of the equipment required to make the new digital products— measured per unit of output—falls rapidly over time, reducing the value of business investment in the GDP. Second, the products themselves replace marketable output. Communications, information, education, entertainment, and (perhaps especially) retail sales, all previously paid for on a per-unit basis, start arriving for free. They are still part of life—of activity—even to a greater extent than ever before. But they drop out from the economy. The activities in question no longer provide income, and so they no longer provide jobs, and so they no longer form part of what we measure when we speak of economic growth. In this sense, the new technologies save both labor *and capital*, which accounts for the fact that the ratio of employment to GDP has not fallen as the technologies diffuse. The main effect is on the measured growth of GDP itself, not on the relationship of GDP growth to employment growth.

Meanwhile, the forces that drove household and family formation in the 1950s and 1960s have been moving in reverse for a long time. In the 1950s and 1960s, having children was cheap. This is no longer true. It has long since dawned on the new generations that the fixed expense is now vast, and that life can be much more comfortable without offspring. Accordingly, fertility rates fall, and women stay in the workforce. In the competition for jobs, they do not yield as a matter of habit and deference to men. So an increased desire for work meets a decreasing offer of employment.

In the 1950s and 1960s, the national financial miracle of the 1940s helped to bring a new technical world—a world that was ready to be born— into being. Over three generations since the war, the middle class has moved from being cash wealthy, to being house wealthy but indebted, and now, in the wake of the crisis, to massively illiquid and insolvent. Working off debts will be the way forward for a long time. There is no simple way, such as was provided in the 1940s by the war, to reverse this situation within a few years.* The great well from which we drew high-employment prosperity in all of living memory has gone dry, and the alternatives—exports, business investment, and government spending—are all too shallow to make up the deficiency.

The normal response of economists to creative destruction has been to wave it away: something will turn up. Theorists of the "real business cycle" assume a cycle: if there is a downturn, an upturn will follow. Keynesians in their modern vein place all of the burden on the shortfall of demand: more spending can always bring the creation of more jobs. And so the economists divide between the fatalists who urge patient acceptance of the prevailing conditions, and those who in slumps urge a "stimulus" and assume that the jobs will follow the money.

There are, in short, reasons to doubt both arguments. Contrary to the real-business-cycle theorists, technology does not move in smooth, repeating waves. The scope of a technology and its effects on the workforce depend on its characteristics. The new digital technologies do not exist merely to provide "real" benefits to the living standards of the population. They are brought into existence mainly to cut costs and to capture market share from older technical forms. Contrary to the Keynesians, one cannot retrieve the jobs merely by spending more money on the existing systems. Given more money, consumers will—in their present strapped condition—mainly continue to pay down debt, as they have been doing since the crisis. Given more money, businesses will mainly invest in new technologies that save yet more labor. Given more money, but not better borrowers or business prospects, banks do nothing at all.

Seen in retrospect, the twentieth was the American Century, for technical and physical reasons. The rise of a cheap fuel; the rise of a mechanical,

---

* The only imaginable parallel, in terms of scale, would be a mass mobilization to transform the economy away from fossil fuels and greenhouse gas emissions and toward some (so far vaguely defined) alternatives. But no one has yet developed the concrete program that would be necessary.

industrial, and electrical civilization to complement it; the creation of a solid financial basis for taking advantage of the opportunities that were there—all played a part. The great contingent events, such as the effect of World War II on the balance sheets of American households into the 1950s, should not be taken for granted. They happened once. There is no compelling reason to expect them to happen again.

Nine

The Fallout of Financial Fraud

Financial fraud plays a large role in journalists' accounts of the Great Crisis, such as McLean and Nocera or Taibbi. It is the focus of work by legal scholars such as Engel and McCoy. It underlies investigative reports, such as those by the Financial Crisis Inquiry Commission and the Senate Permanent Investigations Subcommittee, as well as the memoirs of Neil Barofsky, Sheila Bair, and other senior regulators. It was depicted with scathing force in the 2010 film *Inside Job*. In the popular mind, fraud is much closer to the heart of the crisis than is energy, war, or technological change.

The mere lexicon of the industry is enough to alert one to the central role of fraud in this business. "Liar's loans." "Ninja loans": meaning no income, job, or assets. "Neutron loans": loans that were set to explode, destroying the people but not the buildings. "Toxic waste": the first-loss-bearing "equity tranche" of collateralized debt obligations. This is the language of an industry that is not entirely honest; one thinks of a restaurant where the waitstaff refer to the food as "scum," "sewage," or "sludge."

To put the matter another way, consider the millions of documents labeled "mortgages" that were issued in the 2000s, in the form of 3/27 and 2/28 loans with teaser rates, option adjustable rate mortgages (ARMs), low-doc and no-doc (liar's) loans, and loans with exaggerated appraisals. Were they mortgages in any normal sense of the word? If a mortgage loan is understood to be a long-term loan that is self-amortizing and backed by real property, they were not. What were they then? *Counterfeits* is an entirely plausible term.

Counterfeiting is a very well-understood, ancient trade. To make it work, the counterfeit instrument must be presented to the wider marketplace, with its origins obscured and its bona fides vouched for. This is called *laundering*. It was the function of the ratings agencies to launder the subprime mortgages, turning them into securities of which a high proportion were rated AAA, as sound as the debt of the government of the United States but considerably more profitable to hold. For the ratings agencies, this business rose to be a very large share of their total revenue, so they became (naturally) eager accomplices and saw no need to inquire into the quality of the underlying loans.

Now, when a laundered counterfeit has been produced, it must be sold. This is an operation known as *fencing*—the actual transfer of contraband to a final buyer who may or may not be aware of the origins of the merchandise. Fencing was the task of the commercial and investment banks, of Bear Stearns, Lehman Brothers, Morgan Stanley, Goldman Sachs, Citigroup, Bank of America, Wells Fargo, and JPMorgan Chase, which found buyers for a large share of the goods. The buyers, finally, are called *marks*. And who were they? Very often, foreign investors who were not in positions to examine the goods closely, and took on faith the representations of the banking firms and the ratings agencies. In *The Big Short*, Michael Lewis recounts a conversation between two bankers, one of whom asks the other who, exactly, is buying their merchandise. The answer comes back, "Düsseldorf."

Useful particulars are found in the work of two law professors, Kathleen Engel and Patricia McCoy, *The Subprime Virus*, a study to which they were drawn, in part, by direct observation of the neighborhoods in Cleveland, where the two coauthors happened to live. Here is their description of how the front end of the subprime lending industry worked:

> *Brokers and lenders perfected marketing strategies to find naïve home-owners and dupe them into subprime loans. Some hire "cold callers" who would contact homeowners to see if they were interested in a new mortgage . . . Brokers and lenders . . . scoured files at city offices to find homes with outstanding housing code violations, betting that the home-owners needed cash to make repairs. They read local obituaries to iden-tify older women who had recently lost their husbands, surmising that widows were financially gullible. They also identified potential borrowers from consumer sales transactions. For example, in Virginia, Bennie Rob-erts, who could neither read nor write, bought a side of beef and over 100 pounds of other meat from a roadside stand on credit from the notorious subprime lender Associates First Capital. In talking with Mr. Roberts to arrange the consumer loan, the loan officer from Associates learned that Mr. Roberts had no mortgage on his home. He soon convinced his new client to take out a loan using the equity in his home. Associates refinanced that mortgage ten times in four years. The principal after the refinancings was $45,000, of which $19,000 was paid to Associates in fees. (Engel and McCoy 2011, 21–22)*

Engel and McCoy present another example:

> *In Cleveland, Ruby Rogers had a mortgage-free home she had inherited from her uncle. Citywide Builders, a contractor, helped her obtain a loan through Ameriquest Mortgage to update the home. Over six months, the contractor arranged repeated refinancings of Ms. Rogers' loan until the principal hit $23,000. Of this amount. Ms. Rogers saw only $4,500. Meanwhile, Citywide Builders walked off the job after doing $3,200 worth*

of work on the house. Ms. Rogers was left with a leaking roof, peeling tiles, warped wall paneling, and a hole in the wall. After Citywide Builders went bankrupt, Ameriquest sued Ms. Rogers for foreclosure. (Engel and McCoy 2011, 22)

In a book titled *All the Devils Are Here*, Bethany McLean of *Fortune* and Joe Nocera of the *New York Times* pick up the story of ACC Capital Holding, founded by Roland Arnall in 1998, which was the holding company for Ameriquest and which ultimately "made over $80 billion in loans in 2004, its peak year." McLean and Nocera write:

Arnall followed his old playbook: he made high-priced loans to people who would eventually have trouble paying them back, and he sold the loans to Wall Street . . . Executives were extremely well paid . . . perks were fabulous . . . "the amount of money the company had to throw around was staggering," says a former corporate employee . . . (McLean and Nocera 2010, 129)

and then:

In January 2003 . . . the company hired a mortgage veteran named Ed Parker to investigate fraud in the branches. At first, Parker says, he was hopeful he would be given the authority to do the job right. In his first investigation, he helped shut down a branch in Michigan after looking at twenty-five hundred loan files and discovering that the loan officers were all using the same few appraisers to inflate the value of properties. The fraud wasn't subtle: there would even be notes in the files spelling out the value the appraisers had been told to hit. (McLean and Nocera 2010, 133–34)

Nocera and McLean conclude the Ameriquest story with the confession of a loan officer from the Sacramento, California, office, who wrote:

The Fallout of Financial Fraud

[M]y managers and handlers taught me the ins and outs of mortgage fraud, drugs, sex, and money, money and more money. My friend and manager handed out crystal methamphetamine to loan officers in a bid to keep them up and at work longer hours . . . A typical welcome aboard gift was a pair of scissors, tape and white out. (McLean and Nocera 2010, 136)

Roland Arnall, meanwhile, died in 2008 in his post as United States ambassador to the Netherlands, to which he had been named by President George W. Bush. His confirmation in 2006 had been supported by Senator Barack Obama on the strength of a testimonial letter from Deval Patrick, governor of Massachusetts, who had sat on Ameriquest's board (McLean and Nocera 2010, 210).

How extensive was fraud, abuse, missing documentation, and other forms of misrepresentation in the US subprime mortgage industry in the mid-2000s? In November 2007 Fitch Ratings issued a report on the matter entitled *The Impact of Poor Underwriting Practices and Fraud in Subprime RMBS Performance*. This study was based on a review of a small sample of mortgages made to borrowers with apparently high-quality characteristics (such as high FICO scores), following a much larger survey that suggested that fraud played an important part in subprime mortgage defaults: "Base-Point Analytics LLC, a recognized fraud analytics and consulting firm, analyzed over 3 million loans originated between 1997 and 2006 (the majority being 2005–2006 vintage), including 16,000 examples of non-performing loans that had evidence of fraudulent misrepresentation in the original applications. Their research found that as much as 70% of early payment default loans contained fraud misrepresentations on the application." And there is this:

To gain a better understanding of the situation, Fitch selected a sample of 45 subprime loans, targeting high CLTV, stated documentation loans, including many with early missed payments. In particular, we selected loans that were primarily purchase transactions having a higher range of FICO scores (650 to 770), because high FICO scores and purchase transactions are historically attributes which generally reduce the risk of default. Fitch's analysts conducted an independent analysis of these files with the benefit of the full origination and servicing files. The result of the analysis was disconcerting at best, as there was the appearance of fraud or misrepresentation in almost every file. (Fitch Fraud Report 2007, emphasis added)

Let us therefore stipulate that the Great Financial Crisis was rooted in a vast scheme of financial fraud, beginning with the issuance of millions of mortgage loans to borrowers whose capacity to repay depended entirely on a continuing rise in the resale price of their homes. These borrowers had incomes that were low or unstable, credit histories that were bad or nonexistent, and they lived in homes that were deliberately overappraised so as to justify a bigger loan than the current market value of the property would otherwise support. The loans to them were then sold to large commercial and investment banks, bundled, and the payment streams organized, through a process called *overcollateralization*, in order to support a high credit rating on the derivative securities. For large buyers of these securities (especially the banks themselves), the risk of default was then further obscured by the purchase of credit-default swaps on the entire mess. The regulators, from Alan Greenspan at the Federal Reserve, to the Department of Justice, which might have intervened, chose not to. In fact, they removed barriers and protections and enforcement that had previously been in place. Finally, the securities were offered for sale, and because they carried both a high rating and a decent coupon, they found ready buyers throughout the world.

Yet a peculiar feature of crisis discussions *by economists* is that the topic of fraud rarely comes up. The word *fraud* appears only once in Raghuram Rajan's *Fault Lines*. Paul Krugman's 2012 book *End This Depression Now!* makes almost no mention of financial fraud, apart from this reference to conditions in the S&L industry in the 1980s: "Oh, and loose regulation also created a permissive environment for outright theft, in which loans were made to friends and relatives, who disappeared with the money." On the run-up to the current crisis, this is as close as Krugman comes:

> *We now know that the sale of "asset-backed securities"—basically, the ability of banks to sell bunches of mortgages and other loans to poorly informed investors . . . encouraged reckless lending. Collateralized loan obligations—created by slicing, dicing and pureeing bad debt—initially received AAA ratings, again sucking in gullible investors, but as soon as things went bad, these assets came to be known, routinely, as "toxic waste."* And credit default swaps helped banks pretend that their investments were safe."* (Krugman 2012, 55)

The language appears strong: "reckless lending," "bad debt," "gullible investors." It is actually so weak, in relation to the accounts of close observers, as to border on misrepresentation.

In his 2010 book *Freefall*, Joseph Stiglitz devotes more space to the banks and makes a number of apparent references to financial fraud. There is a chapter titled "The Mortgage Scam" and another titled "The Great American Robbery." But these chapters contain practically no analysis of fraud as such. Stiglitz uses words like *mischief* to describe the behavior of the bankers, and he chastises them for greed and for "preying" on the weak and poor. Here is Stiglitz's five-point summary of financial failings:

> *First, incentives matter, but there is a systematic mismatch between social and private returns. . . . Second, certain institutions became too big to fail—and very expensive to save. . . . Third, the big banks moved away*

---

* As a detail, this usage isn't exact. "Toxic waste" usually referred to the first-loss-bearing, or "equity tranche," of collateralized debt obligations—the part that would fail as defaults started to mount.

from plain-vanilla banking to securitization. Securitization has some virtues, but it has to be carefully managed . . . Fourth, commercial banks sought to imitate the high-risk, high-return of high finance. . . . Fifth, too many bankers forgot that they should be responsible citizens. They shouldn't prey on the poorest and most vulnerable. Americans trusted that these pillars of the community had a moral conscience. (Stiglitz 2010, 114–15)

Forgetting that one should be a "responsible citizen" with a "moral conscience" sounds pretty bad. But notice that the word *crime* does not appear in this passage.

In the American political spectrum, Rajan is a conservative, while Krugman and Stiglitz are liberals. Yet reticence on this matter extends well to their left. In their 2012 book *The Endless Crisis*, the editors of the socialist magazine *Monthly Review*, John Bellamy Foster and Robert W. McChesney, present a Marxist analysis of the crisis, building on the work of Paul Sweezy and Paul Baran in the previous generation. Like those now-neglected forebears, they see a future of stagnation rather than boundless growth; they cannot be accused of gilding lilies. Yet they too make no reference to the role of financial fraud.

It is easy to understand why those in the industry, or connected to it through directorships, consultancies, or friendships and acquaintanceships prefer not to dwell on the criminal foundations of the financial crisis. It is easy to understand why economists who served in government during the era of deregulation and desupervision prefer to frame the issue in less strident terms. They were complicit, or bystanders, or *at best* unsuccessful internal opponents of the actions that set the frauds in motion. The question for us, here, is not one of personal responsibility. Is acknowledging the prevalence of fraud at the heart of the financial crisis indispensable to an explanation for the crisis? Does it make a difference to the capacity of the system to recover? Is dealing with the fraud an essential step on any path to financial stability and progress? On this question, we can distinguish three positions among the economists who downplay the issue.

Market fundamentalists have to hold that fraud was small enough not to matter. Given the record, they cannot deny the presence of fraud and crime in the financial system. But their position requires them to minimize it, to believe that markets are generally effective transmitters of information, difficult to fool, and thus reasonably accurate at pricing assets and evaluating risk. The problem for them is that the weight of evidence, in this case, runs the other way. What we find is that, in the run-up to this crisis, financial fraud was pervasive. In the mortgage and related derivatives markets, it was part, at some level, of nearly every transaction. And the markets tended to reward, not punish, the commission of fraud, by attracting funds to those companies that most successfully misrepresented the quality of their business. In this way, a Gresham's dynamic[*] took over, and the honest players were driven from the business. Market fundamentalists, therefore, have a great deal at stake in minimizing the role of fraud in the crisis: because to recognize the reality is to destroy their worldview.

Fiscal Keynesians—notably, in the present debate, Paul Krugman, who finds himself allied with traditional Keynesians such as Robert Skidelsky (*Keynes: The Return of the Master*) and Paul Davidson (*The Keynes Solution*)—are not market fundamentalists. They have nothing at risk in acknowledging the presence of fraud and in calling for the aggressive prosecution of offenders. But their position is that fiscal (and, in Krugman's case, monetary) expansion is sufficient to end the depression that the crisis has spawned. Krugman quotes Keynes from 1930 on this point, and summarizes: "[T]he point is that the problem isn't with the economic engine, which is as powerful as ever. Instead, we're talking about what is basically a technical problem, a problem of organization and coordination—a 'colossal

---

[*] Gresham's Law held that bad money drives good money from circulation. The Law, which dates from 1858, took its name from a sixteenth-century British financier, Sir Thomas Gresham.

muddle,' as Keynes put it. Solve this technical problem, and the economy will roar back to life" (Krugman 2012, 22). The threat posed by a verdict of systemic, pervasive fraud in the financial system is to this optimistic assessment. Perhaps the issue isn't "magneto trouble" after all. And perhaps a jump start is not the only thing that the economy needs.

For *Minskyans*, fraud is unsurprising. As we've seen, Minsky himself characterized the phase of financial activity just before a meltdown as the "Ponzi phase"—while noting that the term did not *necessarily* imply outright criminality. Rather, the Ponzi phase of financial expansion was the natural outcome of a cumulative accretion of speculative bets, passing beyond the point where they might reasonably be expected to be refinanced, and to the point where they can be sustained only by borrowing to cover the interest on the loans. This situation can continue only so long as it is unrecognized; for once lenders recognize that borrowers are in this position, they face losses mounting at compound interest and have no choice but to cut off the loans, precipitating a crash. After a crash, regulators become vigilant again, and the system picks up once more—slowly perhaps, but building ultimately toward a new expansion phase of the credit cycle.

In Minsky's analysis, therefore, actual fraud is neither here nor there. The system has an unstable dynamic that proceeds whether the incidence of actual criminality in the financial system is greater or less. The Minsky model expects and assimilates wrongdoing but has no great need to take account of the specific facts of wrongdoing in any particular case. And the same holds, broadly, for the Marxians: they expect crisis, stagnation, and even the collapse of capitalism, but they have no need for an analysis of fraud in order to generate these processes in their models. Thus the tribal taboo extends broadly across economics—right, center, and left—and accounts for the strange lightness on the scene of an extraordinarily damaging factual record.

One reason for the taboo appears to lie in an aversion of conservatives, liberals, and radicals alike to the economics of organizations. Organizational economics, or *institutional* economics, is about the conditions under which the organization can function—and the conditions under which it fails. The institutionalist insight is that failure does not come only from external competition. It can come from within. Mainstream economics in the age of the "efficient markets hypothesis" does not consider this possibility, and neither do its liberal-mainstream or Marxian critics. By treating the firm as a single rational actor with a purpose, such as profits or growth, they have achieved a notable simplification on which much of their analytical worldview depends. The thought that the firm might fall apart from inside is ruled out of account, or at best relegated to footnotes, from the start.

Yet the possibility of organizational failure exists. It is a very large, very obvious problem.* To be successful and enduring, an organization must be both purposeful and disciplined. It must be operated as a going concern. This requires socialization of the principal players: they must learn their roles and their tasks, and they must be dedicated to them. They must operate within a reasonable margin of safety, but not so far within it that nothing constructive or adventurous ever happens. The difference between an advanced and a backward society consists largely of the ability of the former and the inability of the latter to develop the necessary degrees of specialization, professionalization, cooperation—and restraint.

To have organizations that endure, they and their competitors must be policed. The key to the effective functioning of an economy dominated by big organizations is to create systems of law, regulation, supervision, and ethics that produce behavior under which organizations serve public purpose, while at the same time meeting the legitimate—which is to say limited—objectives of their private participants and stakeholders. Beyond this, legitimate concerns must also be protected from predatory organizations—pseudocompetitors—that appear to have the same skills

---

* Readers probably do not need to be told of the weight of influence of this writer's father, John Kenneth Galbraith, on these paragraphs. The allergic reaction of conservatives, the liberal mainstream, and the Marxians alike to his 1967 book *The New Industrial State* remains one of their most telling failures.

and abilities but, in fact, do not. Such firms can quickly come to dominate markets, using their apparent financial success to attract capital, boost market valuation, and expand through mergers and acquisitions.

As the criminologist William K. Black has noted, it is logically impossible for the events leading to the great crisis *not* to have been based on fraud. The underlying activity was, after all, loans for *housing*. But by the mid-1990s, housing in the United States was a mature industry, having been backed and supported by government policy since the New Deal. Home ownership rates were already very high. There was no chance of rapid growth in the sector based on the standards for credit and underwriting previously considered acceptable. The only way for the sector to grow *rapidly* was to relax those standards. That necessarily meant seeking out borrowers who did not qualify previously, even while financial innovation made available the funds with which to make the loans. The market for good loans was saturated. But the market for bad loans (the market for loans that will not be repaid) is effectively infinite—by definition, it is limited only by financial imagination, and by the restrictions, or lack of them, imposed by law and supervision.

Black's 2005 study of the savings and loan crisis of the 1980s and his concept of *control fraud*—fraud committed on organizations by those who control them—is a key reference in building the problem of crime into the study of organizations.* The theory of control fraud holds that organizations are most vulnerable to being taken down *from the top*, through devices that transfer funds to the persons who are in control. This can be done in many ways, from the simple device of overpaying top executives to more occult mechanisms that can handle larger sums. Left unchecked, control fraud grows to the point where the self-dealing exceeds

---

* An effort to bring this to the attention of mainstream economists exists, in the work of George Akerlof and Paul Romer (1993), titled "Looting: The Economic Underworld of Bankruptcy for Profit," itself informed by Black's experience as an investigator and whistle-blower in the savings and loan affair.

the amount that the corporation can extract from its environment. At this point, the organization is no longer a going concern; it exists thanks only to false accounting and is doomed to collapse when this is exposed. This is a critical conclusion of Black's analysis: *control frauds always fail in the end.*

Abuse shows up early in executive pay, but—if it takes the usual form of stock options—CEO pay may come mainly at the expense of shareholders and investors. Diluting shares or otherwise stealing from investors does not by itself deprive the firm of resources in the short run. Instead, executive rake-offs foster corporate failure by separating the top executives from the operating management and giving the top echelon no reason to care about the firm's long-term prospects. They have their gain in the here and now, whether the firm succeeds in the long run or not. Indeed, they expect to be gone, personally, before the firm they have destroyed fails.

Looting is another word for the systematic defrauding of the organization itself—as distinct from scams perpetrated on workers, customers, investors, or other outsiders. One can think of looting as a fourth phase in the Minsky process—just beyond Ponzi, so to speak. Recall that to Minsky, the Ponzi phase can arise without criminal intent. One is "in Ponzi" when loans cannot be serviced except by taking out other loans. It is a situation that then presses the debtor into misrepresenting his position, not necessarily for further gain, but merely in order to stay afloat a bit longer. In the opening moments of the Ponzi phase, people initiate their criminal careers. They do so because they see no alternative, short of admitting defeat and going down with the ship.

Looting becomes the rational course of behavior once it's clear that nothing will turn up. By this time, criminal misrepresentation has already occurred. Legal exposure is already there; on that front, the executive has nothing more to lose. Moreover, the firm is destined to fail, and the only issue is, who will get the leavings? The law prescribes an order of priority for bankrupts: senior and junior creditors, secured and unsecured. But the creditors can get only what the insiders have not made off with. So why not loot? There is always the chance that one may get away unscathed, and even if one doesn't, there's a pretty good party to be had in the meantime.

In financial firms, the temptation to loot must be ever present. The firm itself consists of nothing more than the manipulation of money and the exploitation of trust. Financial fraud consists of knowingly making contracts that cannot be honored, and representing them either as the legitimate securities of a going concern or as speculations based on reasonable risks undertaken honestly. There are no cars to crash, reactors to melt, drugs with which to kill people, and therefore the internal reach of professionals (engineers, chemists, doctors) with independent ethical systems is limited. It's all about money. Controls and checks and balances are essential. Weakening or corrupting controls, both internally and by external regulation and supervision, leads toward disaster.

Here again there is the Gresham dynamic: selling good securities is excellent training for selling bad ones. And there are those who so excel at selling bad securities that they specialize in that. Looting has its impresarios who can take a firm that has not yet doomed itself to failure and drive it over the edge. These leaders develop an entire repertory of skills to enhance and prolong their success, including loyal and well-rewarded staff, and good relationships with accounting firms, ratings agencies, and any government officials they may need to intimidate or suborn.

Can anything be done to stop it? The role of regulation and supervision in finance is to reinforce the always perilous position of those professionals who *appear* to have enough ethical sense and fear of punishment to conduct themselves decently in the face of temptation. One condition for this is that temptation not be too great. Another is that detection and punishment be sufficiently common to be taken seriously, although not so common as to discourage ethical people from entering the field.

Fraud will happen in any system. Exposure of fraud will happen if the government puts effort into detection and sometimes even if it does not. But detection can be costly. Exposure carries risks. Unpunished fraud is one type of threat; a climate rife with false accusations is another. Too much zeal, and you may undermine confidence in a mostly sound system, undercutting economic activity and deterring legitimate business risk. The goal of the authorities is (or should be) to maintain a class of bankers who are (for the most part) neither petty chiselers inured to punishments nor robber barons who believe themselves beyond the reach of law. There is a line to be drawn. What is the right level of rigor? What is the standard of tolerance? When should one close a bank and indict the bankers? Is it sometimes better to turn a blind eye, to enjoy the added activity and to hope that the problem of fraud not yet detected is not too bad?

These issues surface repeatedly in the emerging history of the crisis. The memoirs of Sheila Bair and Neil Barofsky show that there was full recognition within government of pervasive financial fraud and an intense struggle over what to do about it. The struggle was won by the do-nothing faction, headed by the Treasury Department, the Federal Reserve, the Securities and Exchange Commission, and the Department of Justice, and lost by the leadership of the Federal Deposit Insurance Corporation and the office of the Special Inspector General for the Troubled Asset Relief Program.

The authorities have taken a clear stand: in their view, as expressed by the actions of the Department of Justice, apart from the singular case of Bernard Madoff, there was no criminal activity in the run-up to the Great Crisis. It is worth remembering that the resolution of the savings and loan scandal saw more than a thousand industry insiders indicted, prosecuted, convicted, and imprisoned. So far in the workout of the Great Crisis, the comparable number of senior bankers most responsible indicted is: zero.

Given the facts of the case, this raises yet another question of responsibility. To what extent did the *government* deliberately foster the frauds that destroyed the financial system? And if it did so, why did it do so at this particular time? Did economic conditions make tolerance for fraud a more attractive strategy in the 2000s than it was, say, in the late 1980s when the savings and loans were cleaned up? Is the government *itself* subject to a

Minsky-Black dynamic, under which successful regulation leads to deregulation, and deregulation leads to disaster?

My argument* is that fraud took over the financial system because it was expedient to allow it. And it became expedient because of the relatively new stresses on the system—on a system that had, up until the 1970s, provided the foundations for sustained and stable economic growth.

When resources to fuel economic growth are abundant, fraudulent activities are not generally tolerated. There are opportunities for "honest profit" and those pursuing such profits work to control the system, which means that they favor enforcement of laws against cheats and chiselers. However, when resources become scarce or expensive, opportunities for large profit for honest business are few. If the *expected* rate of profit—the rate that financial markets insist on as a condition for providing loans—nevertheless remains high, then fraud becomes a main channel to profitability, and fraudulent activities become part of standard practice. Fraud is a response, in short, to the failure of lenders to adjust to a decline in real possibilities. This was the pattern in the information-technology boom, where ultimately the scarce resource was the "viable business plan."

After the technology crash in 2000, there was a steady increase in real resource costs, combined with a depressed view toward new investment possibilities. It became difficult to generate economic growth. It was in the economic systems with the highest fixed costs and the greatest resource dependence that profitability was hit most hard. That would be the United States and also in the southern periphery of Europe. In contrast (as noted earlier), in resource-producing countries and in countries with controlled financial systems, there was at this time no squeeze on economic growth and no financial crisis.

In between the stress and the collapse, there are two more phases that are normal for private companies and public governments. The first

---

* Again, let me acknowledge the contribution of Jing Chen to my thinking on this issue, as expressed especially in our joint note in the *Cambridge Journal of Economics* (2012).

is to obtain new resources under false premises: by borrowing or raising equity on the foundation of unrealistically optimistic forecasts and business plans, in the hope that "something will turn up." Distress borrowing generally takes advantage of differential knowledge: the borrower knows that the situation is dire, but the lender may not know quite how dire it is. Less culpably, it takes advantage of different attitudes toward risk. The borrower has nothing to lose, while the lender can afford to take a gamble. However it's done, it's a desperation bet.

The next phase is for those who control the organization, recognizing that it cannot be saved, to loot it for whatever it may be worth. In this, they may simply sell the capital equipment, pocketing the proceeds. Or they may engage in larger, more sophisticated, and more all-encompassing forms of fraud, using the channels of access that the organization has to funds for as long and as much as those channels will permit, while the reputation of the firm or country remains intact. At this point, of course, collapse is inevitable.

In short, the United States, and the world over which it effectively ruled, enjoyed a quarter century of postwar expansion because of stable governing institutions, cheap resources, the military security provided by nuclear stalemate in the Cold War, and high confidence in future prospects, bolstered—in a minor way, but nevertheless—by the academic construct of the theory of economic growth. Against the Marxians, this view accepts that the system during this period was largely stable and highly successful. Against the market fundamentalists, we see it as having been time limited and historically contingent. While the good times lasted, honest business could make decent profits, and there was, from every political economy standpoint, a powerful politics behind strong regulation and strict standards. Fraud was present in the era of the great corporation in the 1950s and 1960s, but it could not become dominant because the larger polity saw no interest in tolerating it.

Beginning in the 1970s, the conditions for sustained profitability eroded. Rising import and resource costs were emerging difficulties, even as the success of the previous years had made sustained and even increasing profitability a mental habit and a benchmark for business success. There was an inherent conflict between what was objectively possible and what was conventionally expected. Something would have to give. It would not be the expectation.

In the 1980s, resource costs were again beaten down and confidence was restored, but this time at a fearful price in the rest of the world. The global rise in inequality seen during that decade is proof that growth could no longer be shared. And the enduring governance innovation of the 1980s was deregulation: a device openly intended to reduce "burdens on business" and raise its capacity to earn profits at the expense of workers, customers, taxpayers, and honest competition. In the financial sector, specifically in the savings and loan industry, it became clear quite quickly what this meant in practice. The withdrawal of supervision opened the door to industry-wrecking financial frauds, which were ultimately recognized and beaten back, but only at great cost.

Then in the 1990s, the US economy was buoyed, for a few years, by the creative phase of a vast technological wave: the digital revolution. Here genuine innovation, boundless enthusiasm, and sharp practices commingled, so that it's possible to interpret this period as either a bona fide boom or as a fraud-ridden financial bubble—the view, for example, of Robert Brenner (2003). In fact it was both. In any event, there was a powerful element of technological transformation behind it, and the principal destructive phase of the wave (as I've argued) *follows* the creative phase. Meanwhile, the financial weapon wore out, and the United States found itself no longer able, after 2000, to stabilize its external financial position with high interest rates.

So we moved to the 2000s, with rising resource costs once again, the depressing aftermath of the information-technology bust, and (as the decade progressed) the realization that military superiority no longer brought enduring economic benefits. And yet the expectation of steady growth and high profitability still remained, powerfully embedded in the national psyche. No president could afford simply to walk away from that responsibility—and especially not one with as little political legitimacy as George W. Bush. In this environment, financial fraud was not merely an incidental feature. It was the solution to a political problem.

Whether President Bush and his associates understood this is a question for historians to investigate, if they can. The Bush family was no stranger to the financial sector. In 1981 Vice President George H. W. Bush led a commission that helped set the stage for deregulation of the savings and loan industry, and it was Neil Bush, brother of George W., who had served as a director of Silverado Savings and Loan—a notoriously fraud-ridden firm. Be all that as it may, in the fall of 2001, the Bush Department of Justice reassigned five hundred FBI agents from financial fraud to counterterrorism—an understandable move. What was less understandable, however, is that they were never replaced. In 2003 Mr. James T. Gilleran, the head of the Office of Thrift Supervision, held a famous press conference at which he took a chain saw to a stack of federal underwriting standards—an unmistakable signal to even the most slow-witted lender. There was a pattern of promotions inside the regulatory apparatus that placed some of the least effective regulators of the savings and loan era back in charge of large sectors of the financial industry, especially on the West Coast. Complacent leadership occupied other top offices, including at the Office of the Comptroller of the Currency and at the Federal Reserve. The climate of aggressive and sharp practices was established from the top, and the reward was sustained spending and economic growth right through and past the election of 2004 and on into President Bush's second term.

Thus the financial frauds that helped to propel the entire US economy in the middle 2000s were the culminating phase of efforts that had become necessary as far back as 1970 to preserve the pace of economic growth under increasingly difficult conditions. Those efforts had been successful, for quite different reasons, in the 1980s under Reagan and in the 1990s under Clinton—each one, in his own way, slipping the constraints of sound financial practice but mostly getting away with it. George W. Bush's problem was that he was out of good options and had to fall back on a set of rogue institutions, from the mortgage originators to the commercial and investment banks—exploiting the world's belief that the American household sector was a sound borrower, when, in fact, the recipients of new lending at the margins were not sound at all. Exactly as in Russia in the late phase of the Soviet Union and thereafter, the response of those in charge of the strategic enterprises (in our case, banks) to the opportunity they had was to loot them for all they were worth. And so the economy stumbled forward until it could no longer do so, and then all hell broke loose.

The implication is that the collapse is definitive. That it was not followed by a normal business cycle upturn on the model of postwar normality should not come as a surprise. We are at the end of the postwar period, and those models no longer apply. Moreover, it cannot be cured by the application of Keynesian stimulus, along the lines urged by many of my fellow-Keynesian friends. The institutional, infrastructure, resource basis, and psychological foundation for a Keynesian revival no longer exist. The car does not have magneto trouble. Due in part to regulatory neglect—the failure to put water in the radiator and oil in the crankcase—it has suffered a transmission failure. A meltdown.

More gas in the engine will not make it go.

Part Three

No Return to Normal

Ten

Broken Baselines and Failed Forecasts

The Great Financial Crisis broke into public view in August 2007, when the interbank lending markets froze suddenly. It built through that fall and winter to the failure and fire sale of Bear Stearns in March 2008. By then, the US economy was slowing down, and Congress enacted the first "stimulus" package at the request of President George W. Bush. But this was all prologue. Through the spring, summer, and early fall, the official line continued to be that problems were manageable, that the slowdown would be modest, that growth would soon resume. The presidential campaign played itself out that year on topics of greater interest to the voting public: a prolonged debate among the Democrats over the details of health care reform and between the eventual nominees over the war in Iraq. True panic would await the bankruptcy of Lehman Brothers, the sale of Merrill Lynch, the failure of AIG, and the seizure of Fannie Mae and Freddie Mac in September 2008.

Then panic came. Money market mutual funds fled from the investment banks and their debts, which unfortunately, the funds had held. Their depositors then began to flee, seeking safety in insured deposits in the banks. The funds had to be rescued by a guarantee from the president, who duly committed the Treasury's Exchange Stabilization Fund to their support. As depositors then fled the smaller banks to the larger ones, deposit insurance limits had to be raised. Globally, access to dollars dried up, threatening banks, especially in Europe, that needed dollars to service debts they had incurred at low rates of interest in New York. This threatened the collapse, ironically, of foreign currencies against the dollar. Meanwhile, Treasury secretary Henry Paulson and his team struggled to come up with a program that could keep the big banks from sinking under the vast weight of corrupt and illiquid mortgage-backed securities, made against overpriced and overappraised properties, that they held.

Once the immediate panic was quelled, the public's reaction to these events was conditioned by three closely related forces. First, new loans were no longer available—on any terms, let alone the preposterously easy ones of the precrisis years. Second, home values declined, and so even if lenders had wanted to resume lending, the collateral to support new loans had disappeared. And third, there was fear. The consequences were very sharp declines in household spending (and so also in business investment), production, and employment, and a sharp increase in private savings. Households, mired in debt, began the long, slow process of digging themselves out.

In the face of such events, one might think that economists responsible for official forecasting would be moved to review their models. Yet there is no sign that any such review took place. Indeed, there were practically no modelers working on the effects of financial crisis, and so the foundations for such a review had not been laid. Though many observers saw that the disaster was of a type and severity not captured by the available models, they could not change the structure of the models on the fly. So the models absorbed the shock and went on to predict—as they always had done in the past—a return to the precrisis path of equilibrium growth.

Consider the baseline economic forecast of the Congressional Budget Office, the officially nonpartisan agency that lawmakers rely on to evaluate the economy and their budget plans. In its early January forecast in 2009, CBO measured and projected the departure of actual from "normal" economic performance—the "GDP gap." The forecast had two astonishing features. First, the CBO did not expect the recession to be any worse than that of 1981–82, our deepest postwar recession to date. Second, CBO expected a strong turnaround beginning late in 2009, with the economy returning fully to the precrisis growth track by around 2015, *even if Congress took no action at all.*

Why did Congress's budget experts reach this conclusion? On the depth and duration of the slump, CBO's model was based on the postwar experience, which is also the run of continuous statistical history available to those who build computer models. But a computer model based on experience cannot predict outcomes more serious than anything seen already. CBO (and every other modeler using this approach) was stuck in the gilded cage of statistical history. Two quarters of GDP loss at annual rates of 8.9 percent and 5.3 percent were beyond the pale of that history. A long, slow recovery thereafter—a failure to recover in any full sense of that word—was even more so.

Further, and partly for the same reason that past recessions had been followed by quick expansions, there was baked into the CBO model a "natural rate of unemployment" of 4.8 percent. This meant that the model moved the forecast economy back toward that value over a planning horizon of five or six years, no matter what. And the presence of this feature meant that the model would become *more optimistic* when the news got worse. That is, if the news brought word of a 10 percent unemployment rate instead of 8 percent, the model would project a more rapid rebound, so as to bring the economy back to the natural rate. A 12 percent unemployment rate would bring a prediction of even faster recovery. In other words, *whatever* the current conditions, the natural rate of unemployment would reassert itself over the forecast horizon. The worse the slump, the faster the rebound.

Then there was another problem, which has to do with the way that economists inside the government interact with those outside. When the government has a scientific question—say, on the relation of tobacco to cancer or the danger of chlorofluorocarbons to the ozone layer—there is a protocol for getting an answer, which typically consists of setting up a commission of experts who, within a relatively narrow range, are able to deliver a view. That view may be controversial, but there is at least a fairly clear notion of what the scientific consensus view is, as distinct from (say) the business view. For example, the Intergovernmental Panel on Climate Change does not feel obliged to include among its experts the designated representative of the coal companies.

With economic forecasting, there is no such independent perspective. A large share of working economic forecasters are employed by industry— especially by banks. And those in academic life who forecast often make some outside living by consulting with private business. The CBO and the Office of Management and Budget, which do the economic forecasting for the government, are not independent centers but derivative from the dominant business/academic view. Typically, the business forecasters aggregate their views into an average or community viewpoint, and this is published as the "blue-chip" consensus. And here is the result: a vigorous dissent— say, by Nouriel Roubini—in early 2009, making the case that conditions were far worse than they seemed, and that the long-term recovery forecast was wholly unrealistic, would have been immediately classified as an eccentric or unusual point of view. As such, it would be either dropped from the consensus (as an "outlier") or simply averaged in. Either way, it would carry little weight.

And meanwhile, the financial economists—those employed directly by banks being perhaps anxious to avoid having their institutions seized— became a chorus of optimists. In April 2009, for example, in New York City at the annual Levy Institute conference on economics and finance, James W. Paulsen of Wells Capital Management projected a "V-shaped" economic recovery and scrawled "Wow!!" over a slide depicting the scale of the stimulus to that point.* CEA chair Christina Romer polled a bipartisan group of academic and business economists, including those of this type, and senior White House economic adviser Lawrence Summers told *Meet the Press* that the final package reflected a "balance" of their views. This procedure guaranteed a result near the middle of the professional mind-set.

The method is useful if the errors are unsystematic. But they are not. Even apart from institutional bias, economists are by nature cautious, and in *any* extreme situation, the midpoint of professional opinion is bound to be wrong. Professional caution even dampened the ardor of those who may have been ideologically disposed to favor strong action. In November 2008, 348 *left-leaning* economists signed a letter to President-Elect Obama, demanding a stimulus of just $350 billion.† Within a few weeks, a much larger package was on the table, but the hesitancy of the left's position helped to tie the hands of those within the incoming administration who might have pushed for more.

The CBO and the OMB took the measure of these views as though they were an unbiased sample, which they were not, and as though the situation were within the normal postwar range, which it was not. It's hard to imagine a set of forecasting principles and consultation practices less well suited to recognizing a systemic breakdown. Short of a decision to override the forecasting exercise—a decision that could have come only from the incoming president, for which he was not qualified, and that would have been open to criticism as "political" interference in a technical process—there was no way for an unvarnished analysis of the grim situation to make it to the center of policy making.

---

* Paulsen did warn of problems, of which "player panic" was the most important. He would be proved right about the trajectory of the stock market but not about the recovery of the economy. See "Economic and Financial Market Outlook," 18th Annual Hyman P. Minsky Conference, April 16–17, 2009, http://tinyurl.com/8bhr5ar.

† I am grateful to Michael Grunwald for reminding me of this incident. I too signed the letter, but by then my position favoring a much larger program was well-known.

The principles underpinning the models as they were built reinforced the notion that recovery would be automatic and inevitable. A key such principle is that of a "potential rate of total output," or *potential GDP*. This is usually calculated by extending the trend of past growth of total production (gross domestic product) into the future. It is therefore assumed that the capacity to produce continues to grow, even if actual growth and production fall short for a time. The presumption is that the economy can, if properly managed (or not managed, according to ideas about policy), always return to the rate of production predicted by the long-run trend of past output growth.

The concept of a natural rate of unemployment, also known as the "nonaccelerating inflation rate of unemployment" (NAIRU), provides a notional mechanism for the return to potential. The NAIRU idea is that the unemployment rate is determined in a market for labor, governed by the forces of supply and demand, which impinge on the level of wages— the price of labor. If there is unemployment, then market pressures will drive down real wages (wages measured in terms of their purchasing power). This will improve the attractiveness of workers to employers and gradually bring the unemployment rate back to its normal or natural level. The return of employment to normal then implies a return of production to its potential.*

The NAIRU had been a staple of textbook economics for decades, with the mainstream view holding that any effort to push unemployment below 6 percent or 7 percent would generate runaway inflation. Over the 1980s, these estimates came under challenge, and in the 1990s, as unemployment fell without rising inflation, the custodians of natural-rate estimates

---

* If the unemployment rate does not return to its natural rate, the concept implies that something must have interfered. The most likely candidate, in that event, is "wage rigidity." Something must have obstructed the labor market's ability to adjust. This argument, with its implication that labor markets must be deregulated and fair labor standards relaxed or abolished, has been a point of doctrine and propaganda, especially in Europe, for many years.

progressively lowered their numbers. For those who had argued against the high NAIRU, the relatively low NAIRU estimates, on the order of 5 percent, of the postcrisis forecasts produced a bitterly ironic outcome. Previously a high NAIRU had been an excuse for policy complacency in the face of high unemployment. Now the low NAIRU became a reason for considering the high actual unemployment rate to be anomalous—and thus for expecting a rapid "natural" rebound of economic growth—and once again for doing little.

The Christina Romer–Jared Bernstein forecast of early 2009 illustrates this property. Romer and Bernstein, senior economists with the incoming Obama team (and in Bernstein's case, the progressive economists' lone representative on the team), predicted that with no stimulus package, unemployment would peak at about 9 percent in early 2010. *With* stimulus, they held that the peak would be around 8 percent in early 2009, a misforecast for which they were criticized somewhat unfairly.[*] The more important point is that *with or without* stimulus, Romer-Bernstein projected that unemployment would return to near 5 percent by 2014. And they projected that a return to unemployment below 6 percent, expected in 2012, would be delayed only by six months if there were no stimulus. Romer and Bernstein were trapped not so much by the unexpected depth of the slump as by the entirely formulaic expectation, dictated by the NAIRU, of what would happen afterward.

Among other consequences, the official theory of events was forced to concede that the benefits of any fiscal expansion, or stimulus program, would be felt only in the very short term. From the standpoint of the new administration, as expressed by its own economists (perhaps unwittingly, but still), the entire American Recovery and Reinvestment

---

[*] At the time the forecast was made, data on the extent of the collapse were not in yet, and Romer and Bernstein were anyway constrained to use the baseline prepared by the team in place at OMB, which belonged to the previous administration. http://tinyurl.com/82c46mb.

Act (ARRA)—the signature response to the crisis—was merely a stop-gap. It was conceived and designed, at least in macroeconomic terms, as nothing more than a bit of a boost on the way to an otherwise inevitable outcome. In practical terms, it was much better than this, but that fact was downplayed—even concealed—rather than being trumpeted as it might have been.

The grip of higher purpose and long-run equilibrium on the half-hidden mechanics of the forecasting process is actually even stronger than this. Looking out over ten years or so, official economic forecasts tend to show minor *losses* from stimulus programs. This is thanks to what they project to be the financial consequences—higher interest rates—of increasing the government's debt. This effect is supposed to "crowd out" private capital formation that would otherwise have occurred. Once the shortfall in total production is made up, the extra interest burden associated with recovering the lost ground more quickly than otherwise is projected to weigh as a burden on private economic activity going forward. With less private investment, there will be (it is projected) a smaller capital stock and slightly less output, and eventually the gains associated with stimulus will be outweighed by these offsetting losses.

And so the Obama team found itself working from predictions that foresaw a top jobless rate of around 9 percent with no stimulus, and a fast recovery beginning in the summer of 2009 with or without stimulus. Those forecasts helped to place an effective ceiling on what could be proposed or enacted, as a practical matter, in the form of new public spending. When CEA chair Romer proposed an expansion program well above $1 trillion, Lawrence Summers advised her that the number was "extraplanetary." Summers did not necessarily disagree with Romer's estimates; in retrospect, he has said he did not. Rather, his *political* judgment was that to propose such a large plan would undermine the credibility of the analyst, given the weight of the forecasts with both the president and Congress. So $800 billion over two years became the number around which expectations coalesced.

Given the pressure for quick results, the American Recovery and Reinvestment Act tilted toward "shovel-ready" projects such as refurbishing schools and fixing roads, and away from projects requiring planning, design, and long-term project execution, like urban mass transit or high-speed rail. Nevertheless, a large number of such long-term investments, including in energy and the environment, were tucked inconspicuously into the bill, as Michael Grunwald tells in his 2012 book *The New New Deal*, on the expansion program. There was an effort to emphasize programs with high estimated multipliers—"more bang for the buck"—though this was also compromised by accepting tax cuts for political reasons, for about a third of the dollar value. Tax cuts have low multipliers, and especially so when the household sector feels strong pressure to pay down its debts rather than embark on new spending. The bill also provided considerable funds to state and local governments to hold off the sacking of teachers, policemen, firemen, and other local public servants. Such expenditures are stabilizing, but they add nothing to the economy that wasn't already there.

The push for speed also influenced the recovery program in another way. Drafting new legislative authority takes time. In an emergency, it was sensible for Chairman David Obey of the House Appropriations Committee to mine the legislative docket for ideas already commanding broad support (especially among Democrats). In this way, he produced a bill that was a triumph of fast drafting, practical politics, and progressive principle. But the scale of action possible by such means was unrelated to the scale of the disaster. And in addition to that, there was, to begin with, the desire for political consensus. The president chose to start his administration with a bill that might win bipartisan support and pass in Congress by wide margins. He was, of course, spurned by the Republicans; in spite of making tax cuts a major feature of the bill, no House Republican voted for it.

The only way to have avoided being trapped by this logic would have been to throw out the forecasters and their forecasts. The president might have declared the situation to be so serious, and so uncertain, as to require measures that were open ended and were driven by the demand for them—

measures that would not be subject to appropriations limits and that would therefore break, as necessary, all budgetary rules and all the constraints. A program enacted under that stipulation could then have been scaled back, once in place, should it prove to provide more support than the economy required.* In early 2009, that would have been a remote risk.

Of course, forecasting failures became apparent quite quickly when the economy did not remain on the growth track anticipated in early 2009. The following year, too, was a disappointment, as were 2011 and 2012; from the trough of the slump, economic growth never exceeded 2.5 percent. The ratio of employment to population never improved, and unemployment declined largely because increasing numbers of people ceased looking for work. Residential investment in 2012 was half its 2005 levels; total investment remained more than 10 percent below its previous peak.

And what happened when the economy did not cooperate with the forecasts? Did this bring on a review of the models? Again, one might hope so. Again, one would be disappointed. The simple response of the forecasters to the failures was to run the models again, with a new starting point. Thus the five-year window for the start of a full recovery kept receding into the future, year by year, like a desert mirage. In 2009 full recovery was expected by 2014; in 2010 the date became 2015, and so forth.† Each year, the forecasters told us, the world would be "back to

---

* At least three precedents for action of this type come to mind. They are the early New Deal, the mobilization for war in 1940–41, and the Reagan tax cuts of 1981. In the case of the tax cuts, an exaggeratedly negative assessment of the economic conditions of 1980 justified a gargantuan reduction of both personal and corporate taxes. When the economy recovered under the impetus of demand stimulus, the tax reductions were then pared back, with large tax-increase bills in 1982 and 1984.

† The Economic Policy Institute economists Andrew Fieldhouse and Josh Bivens have done excellent work illustrating this point. See Andrew Fieldhouse and Josh Bivens, "Policymakers shouldn't assume that a full recovery is four years away (and always will be)," Economic Policy Institute Economic Snapshot, February 21, 2013, http://tinyurl.com/me6g3wf.

normal"—with full employment, recovered output, and high investment—five years hence.

It's plainly unsatisfactory to forecast in this way. But what's the alternative? To develop a different point of view, one needs a model capable of generating a picture of the future that does *not* necessarily yield a mirror of the past. To do that, one needs a structured grip on the underlying mechanics. One needs a vision of how the economy works, and one needs the courage to assert that vision—ironically—in spite of the fact that it *cannot* be derived from the past statistical record. This is the hard part. But only in this way can one see that the baseline is baseless, that equilibrium is vacuous, that the past growth path is not the single best forecast. There is no known way to build such a model for use by functionaries, and hence no easy escape from the mental traps of statistical prediction.

In an emergency, therefore, forecasts are not only useless but are also counterproductive. Franklin Roosevelt was blessed by history, in that he came to power in an age bereft of national income accounts and economic forecasting models. He was working in the dark, with nothing to guide him but a sense of urgency, the advice of trusted observers, and the observed results of action. So he tried everything, the plausible and the implausible alike, and both received and accepted full credit for the results. If Roosevelt had enjoyed the dubious benefit of today's economic experts, Keynesians and anti-Keynesians alike, he would have never gotten the New Deal off the drawing board.

It is no surprise, then, that in 2008 and early 2009 the policy responses to the crisis were in roughly inverse scale to the influence of forecasting on the decision makers. In the financial sphere, and especially at the beginning, the panic was pervasive and the policy reaction boundless. Forecasts did not matter. The Federal Reserve dropped interest rates to zero, provided unlimited liquidity to banks, and essentially granted the world financial sector unlimited access to cash. Only the element presented to Congress, the monstrous cash-for-trash operation called the Troubled Asset Relief Program (TARP), was limited in scale, to an arbitrary number ($700 billion) chosen for political reasons: because it was "more than five hundred billion and less than a trillion," as one senior Senate staffer put it to me. But TARP was window dressing. Initially, it was designed to have been a scheme of reverse auctions, intended to "discover prices" for the bad assets and so simulate the behavior of the financial markets that suddenly no longer existed. As the notorious three-page proposal made its way through Congress, it became clear that the idea would not work. The auctions could not be up and running in the few days' time available and could not be protected from manipulation even if they had been.[*]

Quite quickly, schemes based on mimicking or supporting markets were replaced by improvised quasi nationalization. Deposit insurance was increased from $100,000 to $250,000 on all accounts and extended to cover business payroll accounts that often exceed that limit for brief periods. The Treasury deployed TARP funds to take an equity position in the major banks, providing them with capital that they needed for regulatory reasons. Further funds flowed to Goldman Sachs, Morgan Stanley, and foreign counterparts such as Deutsche Bank from a decision to pay off the insurance giant AIG's credit-default swaps at face value. Meanwhile, the Federal Reserve took over the commercial paper market, ensuring a flow of funds to major companies that had been relying on money market mutual funds. The Fed also made dollars available on a large scale, at near-zero cost, and created its own (nonauction) support for toxic assets (via the Term Asset-Backed Securities Lending Facility, or TALF; the Public-Private Investment Fund, or PPIP; and other facilities), while Treasury addressed foreclosures with a program called the Home Affordable Modification Program (HAMP), to "foam the runway" for the banking system[†] by stringing out the

---

[*] Mortgage-backed securities are a caricature of asymmetric information. The sellers will always know far more than prospective buyers about the quality of the underlying revenue streams, and this advantage is amenable to endlessly creative abuse.

[†] The phrase was used by Secretary Geithner in the presence of the special inspector general for the TARP program, Neil Barofsky.

process of foreclosure on millions of defaulted or troubled home loans. The Federal Reserve also swapped currencies, to the tune of $600 billion, with foreign central banks so that their national banks wouldn't have to sell off non-US assets in order to meet their dollar liabilities.* Such actions would have driven up the dollar against the Swiss franc, euro, pound, and yen.

The next piece of the policy was to restore confidence, at least in the future of the big banks. To this end, in early 2009 Treasury secretary Timothy Geithner launched a program of "stress tests," the stated purpose of which was to establish the extent to which banks required more capital—a larger cushion of equity—to protect themselves against even worse economic and financial conditions. Whether they gauged this accurately is doubtful, since they did not require banks to mark their failing mortgage portfolios to market prices, and since—contrary to all normal practice—the results of the tests were negotiated with the banks themselves before being released. But the fakery of the stress tests served a larger purpose: it demonstrated to the world that the United States government was not going to assume control over the banks or otherwise let them fail. Bank shares rallied spectacularly.

The great financial rescue of 2008 permitted the banks to continue operations, soon enough free of constraint on activities and on compensation. None of the big banks was seized, no bankers jailed. With bank earnings in full recovery by mid-2009, but nothing else, there was a savage political reaction. The Federal Reserve's programs were, moreover, as opaque as they were Pharaonic, and ultimately an audit ordered by Congress along with disclosures incident to a suit by the Bloomberg financial media company revealed embarrassing abuses, including the participation of at least two top bankers' wives in the TALF program. And so voters punished the bailouts in the 2010 congressional midterms, while a terrified Congress

---

* UBS Financial Services, for example, was said to have dollar liabilities exceeding the Swiss GDP; if it had been forced to liquidate Swiss franc assets to meet its dollar claims, the result would have been an epic crash of the Swiss franc.

enacted, as part of the Dodd-Frank Wall Street Reform and Consumer Protection Act, numerous limits on any future bailout policy.

Nevertheless, the banking system survived. The big banks especially were saved. Their market share increased. Their profits soared, and their stock prices recovered. They could meet their need for revenue by lending abroad, by speculating in assets, and simply by pocketing the interest on their free reserves. Limits on their freedom to maneuver remained minor, as even the weak restrictions imposed in the Dodd-Frank Act came into effect only very slowly. As time went on, the Federal Reserve pursued its programs of "quantitative easing," which were ongoing purchases of assets from the banking system, including large volumes of mortgage-backed securities. While this program was touted as support for the economy, its obvious first-order effect was to help the banks clean up their books and to bury potentially damaging home loans deep in the vaults of the Fed itself, where they might—or might not—eventually be paid.

As for the supposed *economic* policy goal of all this largesse, the president stated it many times. The purpose of saving the banks was to "get credit flowing again." Secretary Geithner stated his view that, as an affirmative policy, the government sought a world financial sector dominated by American big banks, and an American economy in which private banks played a leading role. But it is one thing to have the banks and something else entirely for them to make loans. And loans to support commercial and industrial lending, much less new residential construction, were not on the agenda. New loans to businesses or households? To whom would they have made loans? For what? Against what collateral, with a third or so of American mortgages already underwater? Against what expectation of future profits? Five years later, the banks still had not returned to this business.

In banking policy, as expressed by the president, the dominant metaphor was of plumbing. There was a blockage to be cleared. Take a plunger to the toxic assets, it was said, and credit conditions will return to normal. Credit will flow again. But the very metaphor was misleading. Credit is not a flow. It is not something that can be forced downstream by clearing a pipe. Credit is a contract. It requires a borrower as well as a lender, a customer as well as a bank. And the borrower must meet two conditions. One is creditworthiness, meaning a secure income and, usually, a house with equity in it. Asset prices therefore matter. With the chronic oversupply of houses, prices fell, collateral disappeared, and even if borrowers were willing, they couldn't qualify for loans. The other requirement is a willingness to borrow, motivated by the "animal spirits" of business enthusiasm. In a slump, such optimism is scarce. Even if people have collateral, they want the security of cash. And it is precisely because they want cash that they will not deplete their reserves by plunking down a payment on a new car.

With few borrowers knocking on the door, for banks the safe alternative was to sit quietly and rebuild capital over time by borrowing cheaply from the central bank and lending back to the government at a longer term and a higher rate. For this, there are two tools: the cost of funds from the Federal Reserve, and the interest rate on longer-term bonds, paid by the Treasury. So long as the two agencies are able to maintain the spread—the positive yield curve—between these two numbers, profitable banking is easy. This is what the large money-center banks did in the 1980s after the Latin American debt crisis; it is what the supervisors instructed regional and smaller banks to do in this crisis (by tightening up on underwriting guidance); and it is the preferred solution for all, among bankers and those who supervise them, who like a quiet life. But it does not lead to new loans.

After a certain amount of time, most detached observers would conclude that the purpose of unlimited (and forecast-free) intervention in banking was to save the banks and the bankers. A beneficial effect on the rest of the economy was not impossible and not to be despised. But it was not the objective of policy in the financial sphere.

Overall, the American Recovery and Reinvestment Act poured about 2 percent of GDP into new spending and tax cuts per year, for two years, into a GDP gap estimated to average 6 percent for three years. In other words, as a matter of arithmetic, it might have worked to restore full production at the levels that prevailed before the crisis, if the fiscal multipliers had been close to 2. But under the conditions, and the mix of spending types and tax reductions in the bill, they were not close to that value.

Given the political and economic constraints on the "stimulus package," there remains a puzzle: Why, in the wake of financial calamity, did the US economy fall as little as it actually did? Employment and market incomes fell by some 10 percent. Yet the fall in real GDP—in total output—from 2007 to 2009 was just 3.5 percent; while personal consumption expenditures dropped only 2.5 percent. How come so little? Some are tempted to credit the unlimited actions of the central bank, but as we have seen, without loans there is no monetary stimulus, however low the interest rate.

The answer is that total federal government spending (purchases of goods and services) rose by more than 6 percentage points in the same period; health security payments rose 25 percent; Medicare, nearly 15 percent; Social Security, by over 16 percent; and other income security programs (notably, unemployment insurance), by over 45 percent. Meanwhile, total tax receipts fell over 8 percent. In sum, and notwithstanding the small scale of the ARRA, the federal budget deficit rose to above 10 percent of GDP.

Some of these changes were enacted after the stimulus package, in further measures including extended unemployment insurance, a federal add-on to state plans, and (later on) a 2 percentage-point reduction in payroll tax collections. But most of these changes were *automatic*, which is to say, they too were forecast free. They reflected increased demands on federal programs that already existed, and that had existed for decades, as well as the lucky special circumstance that very high oil prices in 2008 helped produce a substantial cost-of-living adjustment in Social Security in 2009. And they reflected the effect of declining private incomes on tax revenues. Overall, some 10 percent of private incomes were lost in the crisis, but about three-quarters of these losses were made good, in the aggregate, by the stabilizing force of a changed federal fiscal posture—and the resulting large deficits in the public accounts.

What saved the United States from a new Great Depression in 2009 was not the underlying resilience of the private economy or the recovery of the banking sector. And it was not the stimulus program, though that clearly did help. It was mainly the legacy of big government that had been created to deal with the Great Depression and to complete the work of the New Deal. Big government programs—Social Security, Medicare, Medicaid, unemployment insurance, disability insurance, food stamps, and the progressive structure of the income tax—worked to transfer the loss of private income from households, which could not handle it, to the government, which could.

In short, the very scale of government created over the previous century meant that the public sector could step up to meet the needs of the population when the private sector no longer did so. And in the spirit of the age, according to which no achievement goes unpunished, this success—modest, qualified, and relative to expectations, though it was—led to a rapid change in the public debate.

Eleven

The Crackpot Counterrevolution

Walking in New York City in the late winter of 2009, my cell phone rang with an unknown number. It proved to be Amity Shlaes, a financial commentator resident at that venerable bastion of the Establishment, the Council on Foreign Relations, who was organizing a daylong seminar two weeks hence on the New Deal. Would I participate? I agreed, wondering briefly about the topic and the last-minute character of the call. Only later did I realize that I must have been asked in order to lend a trace of balance to the council—on this occasion, in order to protect its reputation.

The analytical star of the council's foray into economic history was one Lee Ohanian, professor at the University of California at Los Angeles, who with coauthor Harold Cole had developed a fresh analysis of the economic impact of Roosevelt's first two terms.* Their method consisted of displacing

---

* "The Great Depression in the United States from a Neoclassical Perspective," in *Federal Reserve Bank of Minneapolis Quarterly Review* (1999).

the postwar neoclassical theory and measurement of economic growth—
especially the concept of potential GDP—back onto the 1920s and 1930s.
In that model, as we've seen, a growth path depends on population, technology, and saving. Thus one can draw a trend line through the economic
growth path of the 1920s and project it forward to 1940, to see what "theory"
would have expected GDP to be by that time had no Depression occurred.
There is a large gap, of course, because the Depression *did* occur. Cole and
Ohanian then identify a series of shocks that they argue can explain much
of the 1930–32 meltdown, including shocks to technology; changes in taxes
and spending, tariffs and trade, and monetary policy; and the collapse of the
banking system. Finally, they ask, in effect, why, eight years later, had the
gap not been erased by the natural recuperative powers of the private economy? Under the model, there "should" have been a rapid and full recovery,
defined as a return to the previous trend. But there was not.

Given the logic of this view, one is driven to a firm—if a bit startling—
inference. Contrary to all previous thought, the New Deal did *not* promote
economic recovery. Instead, it got in the way.

Now, in actual history, by 1936, the United States economy had returned to its previous peak level of real economic activity, and to many,
this might plausibly be counted as the moment of "full recovery." But by
backcasting economic growth theory (which, at that point, was still twenty
years shy of being invented), Cole and Ohanian insist on a higher standard.
To them, full recovery requires a return *to the previous trend*—meaning, to
a situation as if the Roaring Twenties had never come to an end. They then
judge the shortfall from that trend. Naturally, a large shortfall persists, and
that raises what Cole and Ohanian call a "puzzle." Reflection on the puzzle
brings them to their final analytical coup, which consists of identifying
what was new and unprecedented about the years after 1933. Under the
cautious subheading "A Possible Solution," Cole and Ohanian write:

> To account for the weak recovery, these clues suggest that we look for
> shocks with specific characteristics, for example, a large shock which

hits just some sectors of the economy, in particular, manufacturing, and which causes wages to rise and employment and investment to fall in those sectors. We conjecture that government policies toward monopoly and the distribution of income are a good candidate for this type of shock . . . In particular the NIRA [National Industrial Recovery Act] of 1933 allowed much of the US economy to cartelize . . . In return for government-sanctioned collusion, firms gave incumbent workers large pay increases.

In other words, the culprit must have been . . . the New Deal! Without that, the expansion from 1933 to 1936, even though it was already the fastest ever recorded in peacetime,* then or since—would have been even faster. With no New Deal, the economy would, as a whole, by 1936 have returned to where it would have been had the 1920s never ended. In 1999 Cole and Ohanian promised further work to substantiate (or possibly, refute) this conjecture. We need not follow them into the details of this work, except to note that in 2009, in an Op-Ed essay in the *Wall Street Journal*, they affirm their finding. Specifically, they assert that by 1935, when the NIRA was struck down, manufacturing wages were 25 percent above the level that would have prevailed otherwise, and after that, wages were kept high through labor law reform, the spread of trade unions, and collective bargaining. Thus it was higher wages—and not Roosevelt's infamous drive to balance the budget—that account for the recession of 1937–38 as well as the shortfall of growth after 1933.

The brilliance of the Cole-Ohanian argument lies in its faithfulness to the dominant vision of the growth process within modern economics. Cole and Ohanian are quite careful to stay within the boundaries of accepted historical fact. They acknowledge, for instance, what was for contemporaries the "standard definition of the Great Depression, which is the 1929–1933 decline." This is to recognize that at the time, the

---

* Real GDP growth rates were later calculated to have been 10.7 percent in 1934, 8.9 percent in 1935, and 12.9 percent in 1936. See *Historical Statistics*, 3-25, table Ca9-19.

New Deal (and not the war) ended the Depression. There followed, of course, the decisive evidence: Roosevelt's reelection in 1936, in which he swept all the states save for Maine and Vermont. But having adopted the rigorously neoclassical perspective, Cole and Ohanian are obliged to discover that all of this is wrong. The Depression did not end in 1933. Instead, as they put it, "real output remained between 25 percent and 30 percent *below trend* through the late 1930s." Thus the Great Depression continued, against the accepted tendency of all economies to revert to trend. A culprit is required, and what better one than the reckless, illicit, and even unconstitutional interventions of Franklin Roosevelt's New Deal?

To be fair, eminent liberals have on occasion paved the way for this view of the New Deal as an obstruction, by accepting the (much more common) historical view that the New Deal, while helpful, failed to end the Great Depression in a different sense, by failing to restore high employment. Paul Krugman is not innocent of this; in *End This Depression Now!* he writes: "It has always been clear why World War II lifted the US economy out of the Great Depression" (Krugman 2012, 148). In this writing, the New Deal becomes a fairly modest and not very effective economic recovery program within the Great Depression, and the second dip of 1937, as a distinct event, recedes from view. And so the war alone emerges as the Depression-ending phenomenon, a deus ex machina of national emergency rather than an achievement of peacetime policy.

Among the facts often cited to support this view is the claim that unemployment never fell below 10 percent in the 1930s. But this is not true. What we know of the scale of unemployment in the 1930s was reconstructed largely after the fact, in the early 1960s, at which time (and again, to be fair, following the official practice of the 1930s) federal emergency workers were counted as unemployed. Since then, however, the practice has shifted, the emergency workers have been counted as having jobs, and presently accepted statistics show unemployment having declined from 22.9 percent of the civilian labor force in 1932 to just 9.2 percent in

1937.* There were, at the peak, more than 3.7 million emergency workers, or about 7 percent of the 1936 workforce. A 2008 paper by Marshall Auerback usefully summarized what all these people actually did:

> *[Roosevelt's] government hired about 60 per cent of the unemployed in public works and conservation projects that planted a billion trees, saved the whooping crane, modernized rural America, and built such diverse projects as the Cathedral of Learning in Pittsburgh, the Montana state capitol, much of the Chicago lakefront, New York's Lincoln Tunnel and Triborough Bridge complex, the Tennessee Valley Authority and the aircraft carriers* Enterprise *and* Yorktown. *It also built or renovated 2,500 hospitals, 45,000 schools, 13,000 parks and playgrounds, 7,800 bridges, 700,000 miles of roads, and a thousand airfields. And it employed 50,000 teachers, rebuilt the country's entire rural school system, and hired 3,000 writers, musicians, sculptors, and painters, including Willem de Kooning and Jackson Pollock.*

Auerback notes that international comparisons that treat these workers as unemployed unconsciously bias the comparison to other Depression-era countries:

> *Even pro-Roosevelt historians such as William Leuchtenburg and Doris Kearns Goodwin have meekly accepted that the millions of people in the New Deal workfare programs were unemployed, while comparable millions of Germans and Japanese, and eventually French and British, who were dragooned into the armed forces and defense production industries in the mid- and late-1930s, were considered to be employed. This made the Roosevelt administration's economic performance appear uncompetitive, but it is fairer to argue that the people employed in government public works and conservation programs were just as authentically (and much more*

---

* *Historical Statistics*, table Ba470–477, pp. 2–83, and notes on the following page.

*usefully) employed [than] draftees in what became garrison states, while Roosevelt was rebuilding America at a historic bargain cost.**

Modest and ineffective, the New Deal was not.

Why bring all this up here? The importance of the Cole-Ohanian argument extends far beyond its role as a device to reinterpret the New Deal. It serves as a template for a series of economic arguments applied to the present, which I venture to term the crackpot counterrevolution.

Two more examples will suffice to show how the method works and to what ends. One involves estimates of the relationship between the size of government and the rate of economic growth. The other assesses the effect of "activism" in the wake of the Great Crisis.

What is the relationship between government and growth? In a traditional view, long held by economic historians, "the poor get rich and the rich slow down."[†] There is a growth advantage to starting out, if not abjectly poor, then at least somewhat behind. Convergence is the way of the world in the long run—not for every country, but for most, in phases, as time goes on. And as countries become rich, what do they do? They add government services, social insurance programs, and public procurement of goods and services. Rich countries make use of their wealth by building substantial collective institutions. This is not new. It has been true, in general terms, for as long as there have existed nation-states.

Given this fact, what statistical relationship might one expect between government spending and economic growth? Quite reasonably, there should be a negative relationship. It should be true, as a general rule, that countries with bigger governments, being richer, have slower growth. So far

---

* Auerback's article was posted on the website of the Colorado Bar Association in December 2008, and may be found at http://tinyurl.com/nwruh56. In March 2009 Conrad Black published a shorter but otherwise highly similar essay titled "FDR and the Revisionists" on National Review Online.

† The economic historian Walt Rostow so titled one of his books.

there is no basis for disagreement, and (say) the 1998 paper on this topic by Richard Vedder and Lowell Gallaway titled "Government Size and Economic Growth" for the Congressional Joint Economic Committee on this issue is unexceptionable.

But Vedder and Gallaway don't stop with historical description. Like Ohanian and Cole, they extend and invert the argument, changing the lines of causality and upending the historical sequence. Now the size of government, instead of being a resultant, becomes a policy lever, and the relationship between government and growth, instead of being a statistical artifact of the relationship between wealth and growth, becomes a trade-off that can be exploited by policy choice. Want a higher rate of growth? Cut government spending! A simple conclusion for the simple of mind.

To press their point, Vedder and Gallaway describe an "Armey curve"—deftly named for Dick Armey, a former Republican majority leader in the House of Representatives*—according to which the growth rate for the United States would be optimized with a size of federal government at just over 17.5 percent. This was a level last seen in 1965. They conclude that transfer payments—Social Security and Medicare, notably—started impeding growth when they reached 7.3 percent of GDP back in 1974. Yet they find no adverse relationship between growth and defense spending. And they find that other spending, on education, agriculture, transportation, and so forth, *increases* the rate of economic growth.

There is nothing surprising in any of these statistics. They are not absurd. On the contrary, military procurement and highways are direct components of final economic output. Adding a dollar to those accounts adds a dollar, by accounting definition, to real GDP. Transfer payments—Social Security and Medicare—do *not* add directly to GDP. Rather, they move income around within the system, giving some people more to spend, while

---

* And one of perhaps only two in modern times known to hold the PhD in economics; the other being former congressman (later senator) Phil Gramm. Both are Republicans of Texas, my home state, which is well known for electing intellectuals to high office.

others have less. By accounting definition, this should have only (at most) a small effect on growth either way. And as the elderly population grows, the share of services (which the elderly tend to consume) in total output also grows. But producing services, as opposed to physical goods, requires less advance investment—and for that reason alone, the *rate of growth* associated with any given *level of well-being* is likely to decline.

It's therefore quite valid to state that if we were to return to the population structure, social conditions, income level, and resource costs of 1965, we might return to the higher growth rate of that year. It was a year of maximal increase in government spending due to the newly enacted programs of the Great Society and the Vietnam War, both of them direct contributors to output and to economic growth at the time. On the other hand, would this be a good thing? Would Americans be better off? Of course not.

Thus the method of crackpot reasoning. It is to take an attractive objective (higher growth) and a likely correct statistical association (with the size of government) and to combine them to produce a policy recommendation that anyone could see is nonsense—were it not dressed in statistics. The recommendation, in this case, is to return to a share of federal government spending in GDP not greater than 17.5 percent, which would require a reduction (from 1998 levels) of around 2.5 percentage points, mainly falling on social insurance. And, for good measure, it would require a concomitant reduction in state and local public spending by a quarter. These are strong recommendations to make on the strength of a statistical relationship; it's hard to see how anyone with a detached judgment of numerical economics could take them seriously. But their influence is enormous. The goal of sharply reducing government—and especially that of cutting Social Security and Medicare—has become a staple of economic policy goal setting in certain circles. Just before the Republican convention in 2012, David Malpass, an economist and adviser to Governor Mitt Romney, told Bloomberg News that the size of government was the single key issue in the campaign.

It falls to Alan Greenspan, an enduring figure with the merit of being able to express himself in precise technical prose—unusual for a former central banker—to bring the Cole-Ohanian argument about recovery and the Vedder-Gallaway argument about government together into a single extended statement of the crackpot worldview. Greenspan achieved this in an essay titled simply, "Activism," and published in *International Finance* in 2011.

The premise of Greenspan's argument is set out in his opening sentence: "The US recovery from the 2008 financial and economic crisis has been disappointingly tepid." The problem, therefore, is how to account for the failure of the economy to rebound to the output and employment achieved before the crisis. This is exactly the same question that Cole and Ohanian specify with respect to the New Deal. Greenspan then points to a key fact of the postcrisis period, "the unusually low level of corporate illiquid long-term fixed asset investment," which he says, "as a share of corporate liquid cash flow, is at its lowest level since 1940." Now this is not quite what it seems, since "corporate liquid cash flow" is a fluid term, influenced in part by actual sales and in part by the stance of monetary policy. Quantitative easing has pumped the liquid cash flow to the ceiling. Still, what Greenspan is saying is correct: companies are swimming in cash but they do not wish to build factories or buy equipment with it, and the question to ask is, why not?

Greenspan next draws on his perception[*] of the business mood: "While most in the business community attribute the massive rise in their fear and uncertainty to the collapse of economic activity, they judge its continuance since the recovery took hold in early 2009 to the widespread activism of government, in its all-embracing attempt to accelerate the path of economic recovery" (Greenspan 2011, 6). He then goes on to provide what he considers evidence. For, as he writes, "[T]he presumption that intervention can substitute for market flaws, engendered by the foibles of human na-

---

[*] The perception is unsourced and undocumented, but not for that reason necessarily invalid.

ture, is itself highly doubtful. Much intervention turns out to hobble markets rather than enhancing them" (Greenspan 2011, 7).

Several types of activism other than the ARRA of early 2009 appear in this story to have had this effect. These include the formalization of too-big-to-fail status for certain firms, something that Greenspan describes as having been "unthinkable" before the Lehman Brothers crisis. (Prior bailouts of, for instance, Citigroup, or the Chrysler Corporation, for that matter, have been forgotten.) A second area is more intense financial regulation, thanks to Dodd-Frank, which Greenspan judges substantial but "too amorphous to measure. It is impossible to judge the full consequences of the many hundreds of mandated rulemakings required of financial regulators in the years ahead by the Dodd-Frank Act" (Greenspan 2011, 9).

And then he turns—surprise, surprise—to the New Deal. Citing Cole and Ohanian, Greenspan treats the restrictive effect of the NIRA as now-established fact, supported by the assertion that "from 1932 to 1940, the unemployment rate averaged 19 percent and never fell below 11 percent." We have seen, however, that this claim is false: the unemployment rate, correctly measured, was near 9 percent by 1936.

Finally, Greenspan turns to his statistical analysis, which amounts to an effort to explain the variation in capital expenditure over four decades, and the large departure of business fixed investment from past norms. He finds—in an exact parallel to the Cole-Ohanian New Deal thesis—that in the past crisis years 55 percent of the variation cannot be explained by his model. And then he reaches for the factor that is new and different: "I judge that a minimum of half the postcrisis shortfall in capital investment, and possibly as much as three quarters, can be explained by the shock of vastly greater government-created uncertainties embedded in the competitive, regulatory and financial environments faced by businesses since the collapse of Lehman Brothers" (Greenspan 2011, 14).

President Obama and his administration are accordingly indicted and convicted. On what evidence? None at all. None is required. Entirely consistent with economic logic, the shortfall from the baseline growth rate *must* be the fault of the current policy maker. In this way, former chairman Greenspan of the Federal Reserve has a thesis with two effects. First, it treats his own tenure as having determined what is the "normal" behavior of the US economy. The Greenspan years, we may now infer, were not a bubble after all. They were the prosperity you get when you pursue a policy of hands-off deregulation and desupervision, letting the market rule. Second, the thesis exonerates the great man himself from any responsibility for the events that followed his departure. In this way, Mr. Greenspan assumes a new mantle: crackpot-in-chief.

Let us take further examples from the top tiers of modern mainstream economics. The work of the Harvard economist Alberto Alesina and his associates (Silvia Ardagna of Harvard, Roberto Perotti of Columbia, and others) is methodical and reliable so far as it goes, and it surfaces (at least initially) in the sober working papers of the National Bureau of Economic Research. What is interesting about this body of work are the questions that it chooses to explore, the methods by which it addresses those questions, and the uses to which the work is put, as the scholarly foundation of a body of economic policy belief.

In a paper circulated in October 2009, titled "Large Changes in Fiscal Policy: Taxes Versus Spending," Alesina and Ardagna examine large changes in fiscal policy, which can be of two types: large stimuli (the purpose of which must be to restore growth following a downturn) or large "adjustments" (relied upon usually to reduce public deficits and debt). Each of these can be driven mainly by spending or by taxes. They then ask about the consequences, in terms of later economic growth, of each of these four possible policy interventions. The universe of observations is the member-countries of the Organisation for Economic Co-operation and Development (OECD, the association of developed countries), and the time frame is 1970 to 2007. These definitions give them just over a hundred observations of substantial changes in policy. While Alesina and Ardagna discuss theoretical considerations—the various reasons why, under differing theories, one might expect one effect or another—their own analysis is almost entirely atheoretic. They simply list the episodes that meet their definitions and ask, what happened next?

The results are again of two types. First, Alesina and Ardagna find that successful fiscal stimuli are due more frequently to tax cuts than to spending increases. Successful adjustments—that effectively reduce budget deficits—are, on the other hand, due more frequently to spending cuts. In particular, they report: "[T]he most striking comparison is given by the transfers item. In successful adjustments transfers fall by 0.83 percent of GDP, while in unsuccessful adjustments they grow by about 0.4 percent . . . This comparison points in a clear direction: it is very difficult if not impossible to fix public finances when in trouble without solving the question of automatic increases in entitlements" (Alesina and Ardagna 2009, 13).

It is not difficult to see where this leads. In their conclusion, Alesina and Ardagna make (an entirely gratuitous, since the issue is not otherwise raised or investigated) reference to "the issue of Social Security, [which] has been in the background, but it has not disappeared" (Alesina and Ardagna 2009, 15). Is a pattern beginning to emerge?

Second, Alesina and Ardagna examine whether stimulus and adjustment are normally followed by increases in economic growth. Here they advance evidence that has come to stand at the wellspring of the backlash against the Keynesian revival and the ARRA. That is, in the modern experience of the OECD, they find there are significant cases where a fiscal policy that normally would be thought *contractionary*—that is, a policy of spending cuts and tax increases, but especially of deep cuts in public spending—is followed by a higher rate of economic growth. They call these episodes "expansionary fiscal adjustments" and find twenty-six of them in their sample.* Turning to the United States, they conclude with this verdict on the ARRA: "According to our results fiscal stimuli based on tax cuts are

---

* This is actually more than the (merely twenty) episodes of "expansionary fiscal stimuli": those moments when a policy intended to promote growth by cutting taxes or increasing spending actually worked.

much more likely to be growth enhancing than those on the spending side" (Alesina and Ardagna 2009, 15). An even more sensational conclusion occurs earlier on: *"[F]iscal adjustments occurring on the spending side have superior effects on growth than those based upon increases in tax revenues"* (Alesina and Ardagna 2009, 12, emphasis added). In short, if you want to stimulate, cut taxes. If you need to cut deficits, cut spending—and you may get growth.

The simplicity and clarity of the analysis, especially in comparison with much of academic economics, telegraphs that the intended audience is not restricted to specialists. Still, there are some regressions in the paper, and one may ask, to what extent does the empirical work meet the standards that a statistician might normally employ? In particular, is the sample of events reasonably composed of independent observations, each of them worthy of inclusion in the data at equal weight? For if it is not, then perhaps the statistical conclusions are not as "robust" as the authors claim them to be.

As noted, Alesina and Ardagna report twenty-six instances of "expansionary fiscal adjustment." Of these, three occur in consecutive years—1987, 1988, 1989—in one country. Four more are consecutive years in New Zealand (1993, 1994) and Norway (1979, 1980). And four more are overlapping or near-consecutive years—1986, 1987, 1988—in Portugal and Spain, two countries that lie side by side on the Iberian Peninsula. Were each of these independent events producing its own consequences for economic growth? Or were they perhaps linked by common circumstance? It would be quite easy to reduce the number of independent "expansionary adjustments" from twenty-six to nineteen, just by inspecting the data.

But there is a more telling point. Consider the full list of OECD countries that have experienced strong economic growth at any time since 1970 following the implementation of policies aimed at reducing their fiscal deficits. Here it is: Finland, Greece, Ireland, Netherlands, New Zealand, Norway, Portugal, Spain, Sweden. What do these countries have in common? The answer, of course, is that they are all *small*. The largest of the lot is Spain, with forty-six million people. And the rest are tiny countries with populations between four million and eleven million—small boats on the vast economic sea of Europe and the wider world. All of them (except Spain) have economies smaller than the standard metropolitan statistical area of, for example, Los Angeles.

Now, suppose that someone did a study of the budget practices of Los Angeles and other American cities. Suppose this found that, from time to time, the city engaged in budget cutting, and that following this painful exercise, the urban economy improved. Would anyone think to argue that the budget cuts *caused* the economy to improve? Of course not. The standard view would be: the city was forced to cut its budget owing to a shortfall of tax revenues in a downturn, and then it benefited from the forces of economic growth in the national economy at large in the ensuing upturn. No one would treat Los Angeles as a separate and independent economic observation from, say, San Diego. And no one would treat the urban budget of Los Angeles as a decisive force in its own later economic growth (even though it is true that lower tax rates might give the city an advantage, relative to its peers, in attracting new investments when the recovery comes). But that is the practice, hiding in plain view, in a paper like Alesina and Ardagna's. With an appealing conclusion, they could be sure that their paper would be cited abundantly and taken as an authority by those for whom the prospect of "expansionary fiscal adjustment" or "expansionary austerity" is deeply attractive.

It is not as though expansionary austerity doesn't happen. In the strict sense of "first one thing, then the other," it does happen. Indeed, when you think of the parallel to cities, it's *normal*: one cuts spending when tax revenues fall, and one increases it again when they rise. New cases are to be found quite often. In the early part of the 2010s, the tiny Baltic countries of Latvia and Estonia were frequently cited. But the fact remains: big countries aren't on the list. Alesina and Ardagna give no examples of expansionary austerity in Britain, France, Germany, Japan, Italy, or the

United States.* Meanwhile, their work fuels the belief that less government and especially less social insurance yield higher growth—quite the same as the claim made by the New Deal deniers, by the Armey curve theorists, and by the other high priests of the crackpot counterrevolution.

A final example of the general method was made famous by Carmen Reinhart and Kenneth Rogoff, author of a useful 2009 book on the history of financial crises titled *This Time Is Different*. Their book is primarily a work of descriptive statistics, a compilation and summary of domestic public debt crises, external debt crises, and inflations in sixty-six countries over eight hundred years. From this bare fact, we learn that financial crises are commonplace. We also learn, for example, that external debt defaults are more frequent than internal debt defaults: countries hit the foreigners when they can. We learn that although inflations tend to disappear from national histories, banking crises do not. We learn that in eighteen of twenty-six banking crises, "the financial sector had been liberalized within the previous five years, usually less" (Reinhart and Rogoff 2009, 155). On a question of considerable controversy in the history of economic thought, the authors write: "[T]here is indeed significant theoretical and empirical support for the view that a collapse in a country's banking system can have huge implications for its growth trajectory" (147).†

As it happened, *This Time Is Different* had practically nothing to say that was relevant to America's (or any other country's) public policy in the

_____

* On the other hand, the United Kingdom, Italy, and Japan are on their list of expansionary fiscal *stimuli*.

† This is a point that may seem obvious to lay readers, who have not immersed themselves in the arcane ways that economists enjoy obscuring the obvious. By showing that debt crises, inflations, and banking failures are endemic—and that they have consequences— Reinhart and Rogoff make the New Classical macroeconomics of Robert Lucas and his followers (which just ignores the financial instability problem) look silly, even though they don't say as much. Likewise, their facts expose the celebration of the Great Moderation as foolish. But, they write, "It remains to be seen how economists will assess the Great Moderation and its causes after the crisis recedes" (Reinhart and Rogoff 2009, 256).

wake of the Great Financial Crisis—in particular because that crisis was not a crisis of United States public debt. So in a 2010 working paper and article titled "Growth in a Time of Debt," Reinhart and Rogoff tried their hand at converting statistical regularities into policy prescription. The result was the famous Reinhart-Rogoff threshold, according to which a ratio of public debt to GDP above 90 percent was said to be associated with a sharp reduction in the rate of economic growth. This finding, it turned out, was based on a number of errors and indefensible judgments, including the use of one very bad year—minus 7.6 percent growth—in one very small country, New Zealand, in 1951. That was a year when there were over 150 days of strikes, not plausibly related to the debt ratio.

A graduate student at the University of Massachusetts Amherst, Thomas Herndon, eventually gained access to the Reinhart-Rogoff data set in a usable format, and discovered the flaws in their empirical argument, which were summarized in an article that he coauthored with Michael Ash and Robert Pollin (Herndon, Ash, and Pollin, 2013). With that, the Reinhart-Rogoff threshold disappeared from history. But the method did not disappear, and the exposure of numerical errors, while useful in this instance, had the ambiguous effect of leaving the underlying questions of method unexamined.

What Reinhart-Rogoff, Alesina-Ardagna, Vedder-Gallaway, Cole-Ohanian, the Congressional Budget Office, and Alan Greenspan have in common is, above all, their assertion of a universal standard of normality. This normality is given concrete measure by economic statistics. Debt ratios, budget adjustments, government share measures, and projections of the natural rate of unemployment and the growth of potential GDP are the various decorations of this underlying view. The problem is that while economic statistics are—one may argue—our only reliable way to assess the past, they do not lend themselves to the creation of universal standards for the future. You cannot do without theoretical interpretation tailored to the conditions of the moment. In one of his once-famous essays on the state of economic science, Tjalling Koopmans made this point many years ago:

"My first argument, then, is that even for the purpose of systematic and large scale observation of such a many-sided phenomenon, theoretical preconceptions about its nature cannot be dispensed with, and the authors do so only to the detriment of the analysis" (Koopmans 1947, 163).

The fact is, turning points sometimes happen. Big events may signal a new environment going forward. This time may be different, after all. And if the end of the information-technology boom in 2000 and the financial calamity of 2008 signal such a turning point, then the curtain will have to be drawn over the historical period that began in 1980—let alone the one that began in 1945. In which case, *all* analyses that operate by assuming the return of conditions that prevailed on average over the first six decades following World War II will be proven wrong.

Twelve

The Pivot, the Cliff, and the Brink of Default

The crackpot counterrevolution—the notion that the economy will naturally regain its previous growth path unless *actively* prevented from doing so by acts of government—is the logical end point of the equilibrium worldview. The cult of zero, in deficits and trade, is its bookkeeping offshoot. This is the notion that balance is the natural state of budget and trade relationships. Therefore *imbalances*—sustained departures from a net of zero, with associated increases in public and in national debts—are supposed to be the source of grave problems.

Like many modern ideas, the concept of imbalances has deep roots. It is not a new error but an old truth, superseded by events. Adam Smith's eighteenth-century contemporary and friend the Scottish philosopher David Hume is credited with originating the "specie-flow" view of international trade. Hume's argument was that the flow of money between countries would serve to rectify trade imbalance: a country running a surplus of exports over imports would see an influx of gold and silver coins, experience inflation, and lose its competitive advantage; meanwhile, a country running a deficit would lose its specie, experience deflation, and again return to trade balance. For this reason, the mercantilist goal of persistent trade surplus—with its objective of accumulating gold and silver "treasure"—was beyond reach. Hume's crucial point was that trade "balance" is normal, and imbalance an unsustainable state.

The particulars of this idea have changed with time and the evolution of economic theory, but the hold of the underlying notion remains strong. An example is the "savings glut" view of recent low interest rates and their effect on risk taking—an argument advanced by Ben Bernanke on numerous occasions and summarized in his 2009 testimony to the Financial Crisis Inquiry Commission:

> [T]he idea here basically is that after the Asian crisis in the nineties, many developing emerging-market economies became capital exporters rather than capital importers. That was because they either had large savings and investment differentials, as in China, for example; or they had lots of revenue from commodities, like the oil producers; or they were acquiring large amounts of foreign exchange reserves, which was a lesson of the nineties, that that was supposedly a way to protect themselves against the exchange rate problems. All those things created large capital inflow into the Western industrial countries, notably the United States. (Bernanke 2009, 4)

In this narrative, the channels are quite different from those of the eighteenth century—not a big surprise, given the invention since then of international money markets. Instead of precious metals flowing in to raise the price of goods, we now have electronic cash flowing in to raise the price of bonds, thus depressing interest rates, making borrowing inexpensive, and so stimulating risk taking among financial players. Yet it's basically the same story, except that instead of inflation, the consequence is risk; ultimately a crash, by depressing activity and imports, rectifies the imbalance. Continuing along this line, Bernanke finds here an explanation for the credit debacle: "[O]nce there became a sort of shortage of Treasuries, that there was [sic] strong incentives to US financial institutions to create, quote, 'safe assets.' *And that's where the securitized AAA credit assets came from*" (Bernanke 2009, 5, emphasis added).

Thus with breathtaking ease, the chairman of the Federal Reserve Board managed to suggest that the pensioners and municipalities of Europe, and the People's Bank of China, were the true villains of the great American mortgage meltdown. Imbalances, you see.

The notion that *balance* means *sustainability* pervades political discussion. One might therefore suppose that if economics presupposes a return to normal at high employment equilibrium, it must also expect a return to balance in the financial accounts. It is, after all, a bit difficult to see how one might have full normality in the real functioning of the economy over a long period of time, and something other than stable and sustainable financial relationships. But the accepted discourse takes the opposite view. On one side, there is a firm belief that "the economy will recover." And on the other, there is an equally firm belief that the finances of the public sector are on a path toward disaster.

The fear of an impending national financial crisis is the foundation of budget policy, the basis of discussions about the financial status of Social Security and Medicare, the underpinning of exercises that assess the "net present value" of the liabilities of the government of the United States, associated with the concept of "intergenerational accounting."* It is, above all, rooted in the long-term budget projections and the forecasts for deficits and public debt. In all cases, the idea behind the argument is that debt (of any type) cannot grow forever; that if it does, interest rates will rise, and investment and growth will be choked off; and that in some final analysis, the tax revenues associated with the government (and with specific pro-

---

* Intergenerational accounting is an invention of the economist Laurence Kotlikoff of Boston University. For a critique see http://tinyurl.com/m4s6ysj.

grams for which projections are made over long horizons) must be made to match the projected outlays. The 2013 Nobel laureate in economics, Eugene Fama, has given a succinct summary of this belief:

> *The problem is simple: bailouts and stimulus plans are funded by issuing more government debt. . . . The added debt absorbs savings that would otherwise go to private investment. . . . [G]overnment infrastructure investments must be financed—more government debt. The new government debt absorbs private and corporate savings, which means private investment goes down by the same amount. . . . Suppose the stimulus plan takes the form of lower taxes. . . . [L]ower tax receipts must be financed dollar for dollar by more government borrowing. The government gives with one hand but takes them back with the other, with no net effect on current incomes.* [*]

And as a matter of accounting as well as economics, it—all of it—is unfounded.

In real countries, and especially the United States, public debt can *and does* grow forever. In the American case, the public debt has been growing, with only minor interruptions, since the start of the republic under the Constitution in 1789. It will continue to grow until the end. Public budget deficits are normal in all large countries. Surpluses are typically possible only in countries small and rich enough to live on their endowment of natural resources. And the public debt is exactly the equal, in every country, of the net financial wealth [†] of the private parties who hold the debt—mostly the private citizens of the country in question.

---

[*] From Eugene F. Fama, "Bailouts and Stimulus Plans," January 13, 2009. I thank Warren Mosler for the reference, www.dimensional.com/famafrench/2009/01/bailouts-and-stimulus-plans.html.

[†] *Net* is an important qualification here. It reflects the fact that private financial assets held by some parties are (identically) the private liabilities of other parties.

It is true that books balance. That is what double-entry bookkeeping is all about. But they don't have to balance just between taxes and spending, or between exports and imports. Instead, they balance over the full range of parties and instruments. The incomes of one set are the expenses of another, and the liabilities of one side are the assets of the other. Thus public debt is private wealth, and the net contingent liabilities of a social insurance system such as Social Security are simply the net contingent assets of the people who will, at some point, receive benefits from the system. Moreover, the people who owe the liabilities as taxpayers are mostly the same people who hold the assets as beneficiaries in the future.

The United States also is in a special position in the world: a condition known as asymmetry, or sometimes, "privilege." America possesses the world's largest economy, the most liquid money market, and the most financially reliable government (the efforts of the Tea Party in the House of Representatives notwithstanding). For these reasons—and also to a degree, now fading away, because of the role of the American military in the world security system—most of the world has chosen to denominate trade in the US dollar and to hold financial assets in the form of Treasury bonds and bills. Thus almost uniquely in the world, the United States supplies an asset to its customers that costs it nothing in terms of resources, labor, and even transportation costs to produce. The United States merely sets up computer accounts for its foreign clients, and changes the numbers in those accounts to keep a record of the value of real goods and services that they ship to American shores. The United States may be the "global Minotaur" of Yanis Varoufakis's coinage, but unlike the Minotaur, the United States keeps books. Balance is provided by the external debt.

The consequence of producing a reliable financial asset for world use in the post–Cold War era is that the United States *must* run a trade deficit and (other things equal) a corresponding deficit in its budget. Why? Because the United States must produce the bonds and bills that others wish to hold. It has no choice in the matter, so long as the dollar has a price set on worldwide money markets. For if the deficit is not large enough to meet the demand, the price of the dollar will rise, imports will increase, and exports diminish—and as a result, taxes will fall and public expenditures will rise—until the supply of new debt instruments (the budget deficit) just equals the demand for them. The same is true of domestic asset holders as it is of foreign asset holders. So long as they wish to hold US government bonds, the price will rise, interest rates will fall, and activity and taxes will decline by enough to give them the assets that they seek. To use a technical term, for a country at the heart of the global credit system, the economy and the budget deficit are *endogenous* to the behavior of the financial markets.

A most vivid example of this occurred in late 2008 and early 2009. At that moment, with private financial markets in freefall, it became very difficult for those outside the United States who had borrowed dollars at low interest rates in the expansion to find the dollars with which to pay their debts when due. There was, accordingly, a sharp increase in the demand for dollars, as these players sought to dump other assets in order to raise the cash. And the consequence, in spite of the fact that US banks instigated the financial crisis, was that the price of the dollar *rose*. The effect, among other things, was to depress economic activity in the United States, increase the size of the US budget deficit, and so expand the universe of US dollar–based assets. Many of these were then bought by the US Federal Reserve System, flooding the world economy with dollar cash. And since that effect was probably going to be too slow to prevent a massive sell-off of nondollar assets, and also too damaging to economic activity in America, the Federal Reserve made some $600 billion in US currency directly available to foreign central banks to cover the worldwide surge in demand for dollars. These "swaps" were later unwound when the crisis eased.

In this situation, the question of imbalance arose only because some adjustment—a vast run-up in the price of the dollar, or (what would be the same thing) a panicked run on nondollar-based assets—was not tolerable to policy makers. So they mitigated the adjustment in some other way. Apart from that, there's no imbalance. So long as the central banks of

Asia and the oil producers of the Middle East want to hold financial assets denominated in dollars, and so long as they consider US government bonds and bills the safest and best choice for them, the books balance perfectly. On the one side, oil and goods flow into the United States. On the other, Treasury bills and bonds (and cash) are added to the accounts of those who sell them. The two sides match, in principle, to the penny.

Under what conditions is it fair to say that the public debt (and therefore deficit) of a country is "unsustainable"?* Some people fear that there may come a moment when the government's bond markets would close, forcing a default or even a "bankruptcy." But this betrays little understanding both of public finances and of debt markets. The government controls the legal tender currency in which its bonds are issued and can always pay its bills with cash. And if market participants thought otherwise, they would already have reacted with higher interest rates on long-term Treasury bonds. Apart (possibly) from the self-imposed politics of debt ceilings,† a US government default on dollar bonds is impossible, and the word *bankruptcy*—which is a court proceeding to protect *private* debtors from their creditors—also does not apply.

A more plausible worry is inflation, alongside depreciation of the dollar, either of which would reduce the real return on government bonds.‡

---

* I treated the issue in a Levy Institute paper in 2011; the next section is an adaptation. Those seeking math and graphs may find them at www.levyinstitute.org/pubs/pn_11_02 .pdf.

† In the debt-ceiling "crisis" of October 2013, the Obama administration deliberately rejected actions that would have deflated the crisis, including insisting on an overdraft at the Federal Reserve or issuing a high-denomination platinum coin to reduce the debt subject to ceiling. This set up the confrontation from which Republicans in Congress eventually retreated. Had the debt ceiling been breached, it is not clear what exactly would have happened, but everyone would have realized that the underlying securities would be paid eventually and that their ultimate value was not at risk.

‡ When Standard & Poor's issued its "downgrade" against US government debt in September 2011, many people assumed that the warning referred to inflation or devaluation risk. Logically, though, this cannot be the case. Inflation and a falling dollar would affect the

There are reasons to fear inflation. Most notably, there is a threat of rising energy prices in an oil-short world. And a lower dollar has been actual US government policy, at least with respect to one major currency, the Chinese RMB, or renminbi. But neither oil-price inflation nor dollar devaluation constitute default, and neither would be intrinsically "unsustainable."

Runaway inflation generated by the budget deficits is even harder to worry about in an economy that remains depressed. So far as one can tell, the scenario is based on a fringe fear: that the money deficits create will translate magically into price increases without first having any effect on real activity. Or perhaps that the world will someday suddenly panic and dump the dollar for the euro, yen, or renminbi. That would mean selling US bonds en masse to buy (say) Italian bonds. It seems . . . unlikely at best. The gold enthusiasts have thought otherwise, but fortunately their influence is limited to one thin and volatile market, deflating quickly at present writing.

A more prosaic problem with the runaway-inflation scenario is that the economic forecasters of the Congressional Budget Office, whose work is often cited as the benchmark proof of an "unsustainable path," do not expect it to happen. The CBO baseline resolutely asserts that inflation will stay where it is now: around 2 percent. CBO could be wrong, of course. But one can't logically cite an inflation threat and the CBO baseline at the same time.*

What CBO did warn, is that under its assumptions, *the ratio of US federal debt (held by the public) to GDP would rise relentlessly*, passing 300 percent by midcentury. And according to Budget Office analysts, net interest payments on that debt would rise to exceed 20 percent of GDP. With

---

real return not only on US government bonds but also on every long-dated asset issued in dollars: corporate bonds, municipals, and even bonds issued in dollars by foreign governments and firms. A downgrade warning due to these causes should have applied equally to all (rated) dollar bonds, regardless of who issued them or their default risk. But S&P mentioned only US government bonds.

* So far as I know, CBO does not attempt to model the exchange value of the dollar.

this forecast on the record, the projected ratio of the public debt to the national income has become the accepted benchmark of the debate over financial sustainability.

In a 2010 paper for Citigroup, the economist (and former Bank of England adviser) Willem Buiter spelled out the arithmetic of a rising debt-to-GDP ratio. His formula permits us to put the discussion of debt sustainability on a clear foundation. We can say that a path that leads to uncontrolled and explosive increases in the ratio of debt to GDP is "unsustainable"—in the precise sense that the path will have to be changed to prevent the explosion from occurring.* (We can say this without having to specify what the bad consequences actually are, as these may vary according to institutional context, the country involved, and its position in the world economy.)

A commonsense definition of an "unsustainable [policy] path" would be: one that must be changed eventually. An unsustainable path is not necessarily bad policy. In a crisis, you take temporary measures (stimulus programs, tax cuts, quantitative easing) that you would not wish to keep up forever. Conversely, a sustainable policy is not necessarily desirable. Our concern, for the moment, is simply to define in a sensible way when a "path" for the ratio of public debt to GDP is "sustainable"—and when it is not. By the same definition, *anything* that can be reproduced from one year to the next, indefinitely, is sustainable. Therefore, *any path that eventually stabilizes* is sustainable, even if the resulting debt-to-GDP ratio seems high to us.† Again, we can say this without being forced to specify the economic conditions that would pertain.

Applying the formula to Greece in 2009 gives an example of an unsus-

---

* The Buiter formula is the following: $\Delta d = -s + d^*\{(r - g)/(1 + g)\}$. Here d is the starting ratio of debt to GDP; s is the "primary surplus," or government budget surplus after deducting net interest payments (as shares of GDP); r is the real interest rate; and g is the real rate of GDP growth.

† We have already dismissed the Reinhart-Rogoff notion that there is a threshold for the debt-to-GDP ratio that interferes with economic growth. For a comprehensive treatment of these issues, including the full literature, see Fullwiler 2007.

tainable dynamic. Greece had a debt-to-GDP ratio of .86 in 2009. It faced a real interest rate on public debt of 4 percent, and a growth rate of minus 2 percent. Buiter's formula stipulates that Greece would have had to shift a large primary deficit to a primary surplus of more than 5 percent of GDP simply in order to keep the debt-to-GDP ratio stable. This was impossible, especially since austerity would bring on a further decline in real GDP and therefore tax revenues. The Greek public debt rose by 15 percent of GDP in 2010.[*]

Next, let's apply the same analysis to the United States. In 2011 CBO projected the real interest rate on US public debt to rise from negative values to around 3 percent after five years. A real growth rate of around 2.5 percent was also expected, though we can modify that to 3 percent to match the long-term average from 1962 through 2010. The starting point is a debt-to-GDP ratio of 0.74 percent; let's assume the primary deficit is about 5 percent of GDP (and that it stays at that high level, indefinitely).

The resulting path is plainly unsustainable, though (by a factor of 100!) not so dire as that of Greece. The projected debt-to-GDP ratio rises steadily, reaching about 300 percent at midcentury, which is about what the CBO itself projected. It continues rising thereafter.

However, the big, primary deficit was not the dominant source of "unsustainability." If we lower the primary deficit to any value greater than zero, the path remains unsustainable. Because the growth rate and the real interest rate are assumed to be about equal, the baseline requires a primary budget balance for sustainability.

But are the assumptions reasonable? In particular, is that interest rate assumption reasonable? In his paper, Buiter just asserts that governments in the advanced countries will face positive real interest rates on their public debts. He does not explain why this should be so—especially for the United States.

----

[*] In my Levy paper, I predicted, "Greece will default or restructure soon." And, of course, it did.

In economic terms, it normally should *not* be so for a sovereign borrower that controls its own currency and therefore cannot default. Why not? Because to an investor, safety is valuable, and because, under capitalism, making money ought to require taking risk. There is no reason why a 100 percent safe borrower should pay a positive real rate of return on a liquid borrowing. The federal government doesn't need to compensate for risk. It usually isn't trying to kill off inflation. It also doesn't need to lock in borrowing over time. Moreover, the Federal Reserve controls both the short-term rate and the maturity structure of the public debt and so the Treasury can issue as much short debt at a near-zero rate as it needs to.

Average real returns on the public debt were *negative* in eighteen of thirty-six years from 1945 through 1980 (measuring against the realized inflation rate). They were slightly negative on average over that entire period, even if one excludes the postwar inflation of 1946–47. They became highly positive only in the 1980s and 1990s, first because of the Volcker anti-inflation campaign in 1981 and later because long rates stayed high long after inflation disappeared. By the mid-2000s, average real rates on public debt were back below 2 percent and even below 1 percent in some years.

Simply put: poisonous assumptions generate ludicrous results. In its baseline forecasts, the Congressional Budget Office assumes that short-term interest rates will rise to around 4.5 percent nominal—or 2.5 percent real, given its low-inflation forecast—within five years. (Long-term rates rise to higher values.) This by itself makes the CBO debt-to-GDP path unsustainable. But the assumption is contradicted repeatedly by the policy statements of the Federal Reserve itself, which have been lengthening the time into the future that it expects to keep the short-term interest rate at zero. It would also be economically disastrous, since rising rates would clobber the stock, bond, and what remains of the housing markets. CBO assumes that disaster wouldn't happen. Obviously it would.[*]

* In its 2012 projections, CBO deferred to 2016 and beyond the moment when higher interest rates are expected, and reduced the expected average interest rate to roughly

What happens if instead we keep the average nominal interest rate on the public debt at its current, post-crisis value of around 1 percent? Then real rates are modestly negative: minus 1 percent. And even if the primary deficit stays at a "shockingly" high 5 percent of GDP every year *forever*, the debt-to-GDP ratio no longer rises without limit!* Instead, it stabilizes below 130 percent of GDP. This is not far above the highest historical value, 122 percent, reached in 1946. That's a high value. It may be unattractive, though it is not entirely clear why. But it is *stable*—that's the point of the calculation. And therefore, by definition, it is not unsustainable.†

The significant conclusion is that there is a devil in the interest rate assumption. If the real interest rate on the public debt is assumed to be greater than the real growth rate, unstable debt dynamics are likely. The offsetting primary surplus that is required for stability is onerous for most

---

match expected growth of nominal GDP, with the result that the debt-to-GDP ratio appears to stabilize in the medium term. Moreover, in the summer of 2013, the Federal Reserve discussed ending its policy of low long-term interest rates and retreated quickly when the market reaction was adverse. It is therefore not clear that there is any "looming crisis," even in the CBO projections, anymore. But the idea that there is remains firmly entrenched.

* CBO's baseline showed a declining primary deficit over five years, but then it pushed it back up with a series of ad hoc policy and economic assumptions, such as extension of the Bush tax cuts and runaway health care costs, calling this the "alternative fiscal scenario." The Bush tax cuts were extended, health care costs have not exploded, so their score on these suppositions is mixed. For simplicity, I ignore the compositional details and assume a constant, continuing high primary deficit indefinitely. Note that the assumption is not realistic: actual budget deficits have declined sharply, due mainly to rising revenue from capital gains and other asset-market-related taxes.

† If the primary deficit is larger, or the growth rate a bit lower, the path still stabilizes eventually. For example, a growth rate of 2.5 percent (CBO's own value) yields a stable debt-to-GDP ratio under 150 percent. The logic is that with the real interest rate below real growth, the primary deficit that is consistent with stability slowly gets larger with time, until eventually it equals the actual primary deficit. At that point, and thereafter, the debt-to-GDP ratio is stable.

countries, and to achieve it in the United States would be practically impossible, since the required cuts would undermine GDP growth and tax revenues. However, where the real interest rate can be below the growth rate or even slightly negative, the fiscal balance required for stability is a *primary deficit*, and the sustainable deficit gets larger as the debt "burden" grows. This is why big countries with big public debts can run big deficits and get away with it, as the United States has done almost without interruption since the 1930s.

Compared with other large industrial countries, the position of the United States is even better, because of the global role held by the dollar. America finds it possible to run a low, and even modestly negative, real interest rate on the public debt at a *low* rate of inflation, and therefore to sustain quite a large primary deficit essentially trouble free indefinitely—so long as we provide a liquid, safe market for the world's monetary assets. Exorbitant privilege that may be, but there are reasons why the United States is not Greece.

At a reasonable interest rate for risk-free liquid bonds, the present debt-to-GDP path of the United States is (or would be) sustainable, especially following modest economic recovery. CBO's assumption, which is that the United States must offer a real interest rate on the public debt higher than the real growth rate, by itself created an unsustainability that is not otherwise there. It is also against economic logic and belied by history. Changing that one assumption reverses the long-term dynamic of the public debt. By the terms of the CBO's own model, a low interest rate erases the notion that the US debt-to-GDP ratio is on an unsustainable path.

There is no need for radical reductions in future spending plans to achieve sustainability. If America were to follow the present fiscal *and monetary* path for fifteen or twenty years—and if that path achieves a positive rate of growth, with positive but low inflation—then the debt-to-GDP ratio will be higher than now but still within the postwar experience and that of other wealthy, stable, prosperous countries. Then the ratio of debt to GDP, having risen, will start a gradual decline, as it did consistently from 1946 to 1980.

The next issue, then, is, what determines the government's interest rate? Is it a number determined in the private financial markets? Or is it a *policy* over which the central bank has essentially arbitrary control? This question continues to bedevil policy discussion in the United States, even at the highest levels. As Noam Scheiber tells in *The Escape Artists,* Lawrence Summers rejected the large stimulus package proposed by Christina Romer in part because he felt that the numbers would scare the financial markets, drive up interest rates, and prove self-defeating. According to Scheiber, Summers was convinced that the economic effects sought by those who favored a more massive program *could not* be achieved: the markets were in ultimate control and would not permit it.[*]

An alternative view begins by pointing out that the Federal Reserve has full control over the short-term interest rate, specifically the overnight rate on interbank lending, known as the federal funds rate. As Chairman Bernanke put it during the 2011 Federal Reserve Labor Day meeting: "When we convened in Jackson Hole in August 2007, the Federal Open Market Committee's [FOMC] target for the federal funds rate was 5.25 percent. Sixteen months later, with the financial crisis in full swing, the FOMC had lowered the target for the federal funds rate to nearly zero." More than five years later, there it remained.

We may infer that markets will drive up long-term rates *only if they think the Federal Reserve will raise short-term rates in the future.* This is a fear that is almost entirely under the control of the Federal Reserve itself. Crowding out of private demand for borrowings has nothing to do with it, and inflation affects the issue only to the extent that the Federal Reserve is expected to start fighting inflation. Moreover, even if long-term rates did start to rise, the federal government can always issue its bonds to the Federal Reserve at the near-zero short rate. It may not choose to do so for various reasons, but it always can, so long as the central bank is playing

---

[*] In correspondence, Summers disputes this account, arguing that his position was governed mainly by the political context, including the strong prior beliefs of the president.

ball. In the financial crisis, the central bank played ball to the full extent of its powers.

It is not true that the federal government needs to balance its books, now or in the future. It is not even true that it could if it wanted to. It is not true that the United States must repay, at some time in the future, what is has "borrowed" from Japan or China. Those countries (and all the others that hold our bonds) buy at any given time exactly what they want and require; they do not change that on the mere basis of their dollar holdings. What is true is that the world financial position of the United States requires that the US government run a substantial budget deficit and a growing national debt in order to supply the rest of the world with the dollar-based assets that it wishes to hold. And that the interest rate that the US government will pay on its debts remains substantially and effectively under the control of our own central bank. So that the debt dynamics, as described above, will never get out of control so long as the central bank does not behave in a foolish and destructive way.

Mercifully, the triumph of the crackpot counterrevolution is not yet complete. Not every political figure believes that the United States is heading toward some sort of financial Armageddon. And even those who do feel sometimes obliged to lay aside that concern in order to deal with more immediate problems. Keynesian common sense and practical reality, if nothing else, warn them not to curtail the support brought by public debt to private wealth too soon. But even those who sense that the deficit and debt hysterics have sold them a bill of goods have a hard time coming to a clear and clean break with the crackpot position. The rhetoric of responsibility and the aesthetics of balance are strong. The cult of zero really is a cult.

Overall, the effect has been to establish the "pivot" as the moderate pole of the debt-deficit debate. According to the doctrine of a pivot, the middle, moderate, and sensible position is to stimulate in the near term but then turn toward austerity once the recovery is firmly under way. Given the rise of the ultracrackpot view that budget cutting should be undertaken immediately, this becomes the respectable *liberal* pole of the debate. It

221

is the apparently reasonable thing for humane (yet responsible) political figures to say.

But it is not a reasonable position. It presumes that recovery and "return to normal" will occur, and asks us to focus our attention past the immediate challenges of stabilizing the system. And the pivot position once again focuses our attention on legislating cuts in social insurance programs—in Social Security, Medicare, and Medicaid—only because they are the sole federal programs for which expenditures depend on formulas and not on annual appropriations, and therefore the only federal programs that can be cut years in advance.

What is the reason for this focus on "entitlement reform"? It cannot be because cutting Social Security, Medicare, and Medicaid would have any particularly useful effects on resource allocation, slaking the thirst of conservatives to cut government and release resources to the private sector. Transfer programs do not appropriate private resources for public use. They do not deprive the private sector as a whole of resources. Transfer programs simply reshuffle income in the *private sector*. Much of the critique of these programs is based on a confusion (possibly willful) between these programs and other programs such as defense procurement, which do use resources that the private sector might have access to otherwise.

Similarly, the notion that these programs face "deficits" of economic consequence is based on a confusion between private business practice and a public fund, which is part of the larger government and has no meaningful deficit of its own. After sorting through these confusions, one is left with a single conclusion: those who would cut Social Security, Medicare, and Medicaid simply do not like the public provision of insurance.

Guided by prognoses of budget and debt disaster, in 2011 Congress and the White House agreed on a draconian program of spending cuts to take effect in January 2013 unless rescinded as part of a larger postelection bargain. Thus the "fiscal cliff" was born. This was a deal to cripple the federal government in order to oblige Congress to enact long-term cuts in Social Security, Medicare, and Medicaid (among other programs). The fiscal cliff gave rise to the sequester, which at present writing is turning the fiscal stance toward austerity and restriction—a result that is slowing growth and once again causing the economy to rely on its automatic mechanisms for stabilization. Mercifully, an effort to use the debt ceiling to destroy the Affordable Care Act failed in the fall of 2013, but the campaign against Social Security, Medicare, and Medicaid is not over. So long as unrealistic, gloom-and-doom financial forecasts driven entirely by bad assumptions are allowed to frame the debate, the pressures continue.

Thirteen

Is There a European Crisis?

The economic crisis in Europe has been separated from that in the United States from the start by choices of language and framing. In Greece and in reference to Greece, one hears of a "Greek crisis." The phrase suggests that the crisis concerned mainly the financial condition of that country and the conduct of its government. Similarly for Ireland, Spain, Portugal, and Italy. Thus instead of one crisis, one has five, each with its own specific causes. Thus—it is widely agreed—Greece has a bloated public sector, a defective tax system, a politics of cronyism, and a culture of indolence. Ireland allowed commercial real estate speculation to get out hand and then made a regrettable decision to guarantee all deposits in its bloated banks. In Spain, there was a massive residential real estate bubble. Portugal has an uncompetitive industrial sector. And so forth.

None of this is false, of course. But it is not the only framing we observe, even in conventional circles. For example, taking all of the crisis

225

countries together, one hears the acronym PIGS* or sometimes PIIGS. Now, the effect is to suggest a common set of traits of the Mediterranean periphery of Europe. Exactly what these common traits are is left mostly unsaid, but the effect of the acronym is plain. It is to replace a set of crises specific to each affected country with the common affliction of an ethnic type. Those who remember racial stereotyping in the United States—not so long ago and not entirely repressed even today—will find this familiar. Of course, none of it is true: Greeks work longer hours than Germans, just for instance. And how the Irish are supposed to fit within the paradigm of shiftless sun worshippers is not entirely transparent. Perhaps it is the music.

If the relevant frame for the crisis is a country (or a racial type) damaged by its own institutional weaknesses and policy errors (or by defects of character and culture), then the remedy for the crisis is clear. It is reform. National institutions must change. National policy must change. Personal habits must change. Culture must change. Spending must fall, taxes must rise. Labor markets must be made flexible. Industry must become competitive. Regulation must be suspended. Public assets must be sold. People must accustom themselves to hard work. The reward for successful reform will be a return of confidence. Confidence is the gift of the credit markets; it is their seal of approval. When it is withdrawn, interest rates rise. When it is restored, they fall again.† This is the logical consequence of working with a national—or a racial—model of crises.

Yet the ethno-racial typecasting of the sun-loving southerner is not exactly a novelty in Northern Europe. Nor were the weaknesses of the Greek

---

* At a meeting in Lisbon in 2011, with the prime minister of Portugal in the audience, I suggested that the true meaning of PIGS was "Principal Instigator, Goldman Sachs." This brought cheers.

† At a seminar on the island of Poros in the summer of 2010, the Greek finance minister of the day, George Papaconstantinou, assured me that given resolute reform, within six months, Greek bonds would again be the darling of European credit markets. I bet fifty euro cents against that prediction.

state or the excesses of Spanish home building first discovered in 2009. So the attempt to explain *an event*—the financial crisis—by an ongoing and stable *state of affairs* is bound to be unsatisfactory. It cannot explain why the crisis hit when it did or why (in the case of the country models) why it hit all of the initially very different crisis countries at approximately the same time.

The answer to that question must be that the countries are linked. And, of course, they are: they are all in Europe, all members of the European Union and of the Eurozone. So switch the analytical frame to Europe; now other issues come to the fore. In particular: Why did the crisis hit countries inside the Eurozone and not (say) Poland—a member of the European Union but not an adopter of the euro? To raise this question is to ask, what's wrong with the Eurozone?

Those who study the European crisis from a pan-European standpoint have an answer. The problem of the Eurozone is a massive trade imbalance, favoring Germany, which has led to an accumulation of debt in the rest of the zone and an inability to adjust, thanks to the unique inflexibility of the euro.

Trade imbalances emerge in a unified economy when relative costs are fixed and one region—the center—has competitive advantages over the others. In continental Europe, the center is Germany and has been since the start of the industrial age. And the advantages of being at or near the center are not restricted to industry proper. They extend even to agriculture, where northern Europe has gained an edge over the South, in spite of inferior climate, thanks to superior industrial power. Thus Belgium exports lettuce, and Holland flowers, among many other products.* A growing cost differential favoring the center in many branches of traded production is the result of cumulating superiority in technology and organization.

But that is not all. In Germany, there have been major changes in the

---

* The Italian economist Bruno Amoroso first called this point to my attention.

labor markets, known as the Hartz reforms, and a growing fraction of German labor now works for very low wages by past standards.* This amplifies the German advantage in unit labor costs. Meanwhile, in the peripheral countries during the years before the crisis, unit labor costs rose as boom times generated wage gains. So it is not unusual for the German advantage to have grown by 20 or more percentage points compared with Italy, Greece, or Spain since the euro was born.† Given that European trade with the rest of the world is roughly in balance, the large and growing German trade surplus had as its inevitable counterpart large and growing trade deficits in southern Europe.

In the construction of the Eurozone, this development was foreseen. To counter it, Europe's architects created institutions that were to supply funds to the periphery, fostering development there. These included the structural funds, for infrastructure investment, and the creation of the European Investment Bank and the European Investment Fund, with a wide variety of mandates. However, none of these institutions could operate on the scale required to offset the German competitive juggernaut. And then matching fund requirements (which counterpart governments could not meet) worked to sideline these devices, so that in the crisis, when they were needed most, they became ineffective.

Initially, the peripheral deficits could be either public or private. That would depend on whether the active agent was (say) the Greek navy, buying German submarines, or (say) Spanish construction firms buying German equipment. Either way, interest obligations built up. These were unproblematic so long as interest rates remained low in the European periphery. But when trouble hit, the debts became unpayable. In order to save the banks, which had made the loans and stood to take the losses, those debts that had been private were quickly refinanced (in effect) with

---

* Many of the actual workers taking those jobs are not Germans but immigrants from lower-wage regions of the EU, such as Poland and Romania.

† I owe much of this argument to Heiner Flassbeck.

loans funneled through governments, converting the private debt into national liabilities. Thus the disparate problems of the Eurozone's periphery became a single crisis of the peripheral states.

How does this story differ from the previous one? Most important, it calls attention to the role played by German industry and policy in creating the conditions at the heart of the European crisis. Now, it's not only bad behavior—profligate borrowing and buying and building—that is at fault. We see that also "good" behavior, in the form of competitive industrial development, low wage growth, and restrictive macroeconomic policies, played a decisive role. Second, this view calls attention to the role played by German (and French) banks, which fueled the southern debt by making loans. Since banks are exposed to default risk, it also calls attention to the German (and French) policy makers' concern that any measures to deal with the crisis must first and foremost be tolerable to their own big banks.

If the European crisis is a crisis of trade competitiveness, then the fact that a common currency cannot be devalued in turn motivates a critique of the program of debtor-country "reforms." That program, of spending cuts and wage cuts, is (said to be) intended to foster "internal devaluation" and therefore to restore competitiveness by adjusting relative prices and wages. The idea is that German technical superiority can be offset with lower wage costs in Italy or Spain. But having multiple currencies (and devaluing one of them) would accomplish the same general objective at a stroke, and without any need to break unions, labor contracts, or labor codes. It seems that the "reform" strategy is just an inefficient and painful device, not to restore credit-market confidence (as in the first version of the story) but to make up for the (evidently unfortunate) fact that the Eurozone has locked itself into a rigid monetary framework.* At the same time, it con-

---

* Many people who take this view also now argue that the euro was a mistake, and there is an American "I told you so" chorus on the point. However, that is an irrelevance, since there is no easy way for the monetary union to be undone.

cedes that if a policy of reform could work, it would do the trick. Germans would start buying more Spanish goods, the imbalances would decline, and the crisis would be over. The problem is only that without the possibility of devaluation, the course is too long and too painful.

For this reason, Keynesian critics of European policy are drawn to the competitiveness view of the Eurozone crisis. To them, it suggests that the effective and efficient remedy is not pain but pleasure. Imbalances, after all, can be fixed with expansion just as easily—actually, more easily— than with repression. Let Germany abandon its policies of austerity and discipline and adopt an expansionist policy and mood, raising wages and growing employment. Then (the argument goes) the German consumer will open her wallet, German imports will rise, the German trade surplus will shrink, and competitive balance will be restored. Problem solved, the easy way.

Of course, if this argument is correct for Europe, it would also be correct for the United States. And in that case, one needn't worry about unstable energy prices, a fragile world order, labor-saving technical change, and a collapsed financial system. Conversely, if one accepts that these obstacles exist, then they exist equally for a policy of outright expansion in Germany and Europe. And in that case, it becomes necessary to move the analytical framework up yet another level: this time from the continental to the intercontinental plane.

Like the Eurozone, the United States is also vast, diverse, and continental in scale, with a single, inflexible currency. So a European frame for the crisis makes it possible to raise the question, how does the European experience differ from that of the United States? In particular, why did the US economy stabilize in the five years following the crisis, while the European economy did not?

An easy answer to this question is that the US economy was able to run large and persistent budget deficits without any financial difficulties, and so to stabilize, to a large degree, the total purchasing power in the country and prevent a complete collapse of internal demand. The answer is easy, but it is also wrong. This is not a major difference between America and Europe. For most countries of Europe also ran large budget deficits and benefited from automatic stabilization of incomes to nearly the same degree as the United States. This was true especially of Germany and France, inside the Eurozone, and of the United Kingdom outside it, until the latter launched its own (destabilizing) austerity program. None of those three large economies suffered significant public credit problems.

What then? An answer with better logical power is that the Eurozone has imposed on itself a constraint that the United States does not have: namely, that all members of the zone are states that must, one way or another, survive with most of their populations "in situ." No one cares if some Californians fled a state budget crisis by moving to Colorado, but this is not true of Greeks moving to Germany.

And while the major European powers can run budget deficits to their hearts' content, the minor members of the zone cannot do this. Nor can they benefit from the stabilizing power of budget deficits in the large countries, except to a second-order degree. If Germany did expand, Greece would benefit only to the extent that German holiday makers choose to go there, while nothing prevents them from choosing Turkey or Spain instead. Nor can they default unilaterally, as Latin American countries have learned to do in similar situations, without putting themselves in violation of commitments to their European partners and at risk of being forced to exit the Euro. The European problem, in short, is that it lacks effective automatic stabilization for its weaker member states.

A second big difference concerns the nature of the debts behind the crises. In the United States, the problem loans were (and remain) *mainly* private, though with some emerging exceptions such as the bankruptcy of the city of Detroit. And they remained private; by and large, the state did not assume responsibility for mortgages. Private mortgage loans are either paid down over time or they default, in which case the home owners are eventually foreclosed. Either way, the debts are not permanent: even a foreclosed home owner has the benefit of escaping from debt. And while losing a house may be tragic, economically it's no great disadvantage if the house is worth less than the loan with which it was bought. Other debts* also can be wiped out—unpleasantly and with increasing difficulties, it is true—in bankruptcy court. The same is true for municipalities in the United States.

The European public debt situation is quite different. National debts are owed to large banks, to pension funds, and, to an increasing degree, to European partner institutions such as the European Central Bank. These cannot be defaulted on without common agreement. And so normally, the debtor governments are in the thrall of their creditors, constantly renegotiating terms and extensions, constantly obliged to agree to stringent austerity programs in order to avoid the obloquy of an outright default. This places the smaller countries on a path of decline, with the consequence that their ratios of debt to income continue to rise, and each new round of austerity makes the problem worse.†

Europe is a rich and still largely stable continent afflicted with a few relatively small countries—Greece, Ireland, Portugal—that are in states of ongoing collapse. These countries were never very wealthy or industrially developed (by European standards), and they always had relatively weak social institutions and relatively large emigrant populations. Austerity places the institutions they do have under constraints they cannot bear. Meanwhile, it impoverishes large parts of the population, making formal employment for young people a rarity.‡ It stokes emigration of trained

---

* Not including student debt, America's new form of indenture.

† The ECB's charter prohibits it from purchasing sovereign debt directly from governments, but it can and has purchased large amounts of that debt from outside investors. The 2012 crisis of the Cypriot banks happened in part because those banks had bought, with official encouragement, large volumes of Greek bonds that, they had been assured, would not have a "haircut." And then they did.

‡ In Greece, a rising neo-Nazi movement adds an ugly tinge to the social mix.

professionals, which in turn cripples prospects for efficient government or profitable foreign direct investment. These countries are helpless in the present situation. Meanwhile, two larger and more powerful countries, Spain and Italy, which are not helpless and where social conditions are not yet quite so stressed, remain trapped in economic stagnation.

Ultimately there will come a breaking point in one country or another, most likely taking the form of a political refusal by the population to take further directions from the European center. Such a moment came close in Greece in the early summer of 2013, when the government announced the immediate closure of state television and radio ERT. The journalists refused, the trade unions supported them by keeping power flowing to the buildings, and the population turned out to act as a buffer against possible attack by the police. This stalemate continued for several months. In the initial upheaval, the conservative government lost one of its two minor coalition partners, narrowing its majority to just three parliamentary seats. At present writing, the political situation in Greece represents the largest chance of a political revolt—long overdue—against the current direction of European leadership.

Thanks to the structure of Eurozone integration, the consequences of a political blowup are much more dramatic for Europe than they would be for the United States. Although Greece represents only 2 percent of Eurozone GDP, a political and financial crisis engulfing that country would force precedent-setting decisions on the European Union and the European Central Bank—decisions that would have immediate implications for the other beleaguered countries. It is difficult to imagine that policies adopted for Greece could be credibly denied to Italy, an economy ten times as large with a nearly equally obstreperous population. This gives the Greeks leverage that, say, Detroiters do not have. It is therefore also likely that significant concessions will be resisted, and Europe will then find itself on the opposite horn of the dilemma. For if Greece is forced into full-scale collapse, then the full force of speculation will fall on the remaining crisis countries in turn. Either way, it is difficult to see an alternative between full-scale change of policy overcoming all resistance from the European center and the eventual downfall of the Eurozone itself.*

To understand the European problem as one of European institutions—the traditional problems of a loose confederacy rather than a federal union—is helpful. But does it go far enough? It does not explain the timing of the crisis: neither the simultaneous near collapse of all the crisis countries nor the coincidence of emerging problems in Europe with the fall of Lehman Brothers and related events in the United States. Evidently there is a global dimension.

That global dimension is not far to seek. In the first place, the toxic American mortgage derivatives were heavily marketed in Europe, as was the debt of Lehman Brothers itself, which had both subsidiaries and counterparties all across Europe. Moreover, the European banks were players in the United States, just as the American banks and other investors were players in European markets. It is therefore no surprise at all that when the American mortgage-backed-securities markets collapsed, investors worldwide began a comprehensive flight to the safety of large-government bonds. They sold off Greece, Spain, Italy, and the others in order to buy US Treasuries, German bunds, and British gilts. The yields on the weak assets went up; those on the strong assets fell. And so matters remain.

Raising the analytical frame of the European problem to the world level clarifies things instantly. There has been a worldwide slump of private credit provision to weak and risky customers of all types—private and public. Thus the financial problems described in the earlier chapter for the United States are not confined to America. How could they be? Instead,

---

* There may be a general principle that economic unions do not easily survive the departure of even their smallest members. Yugoslavia fell apart after Slovenia left. The USSR fell apart after the departure of the Baltic states. Reaching a bit further back into history, the United States fell apart in 1860 following the secession of South Carolina, famously described by one native at the time as "too small for a republic, too large for an insane asylum."

they extend to every corner of world finance that was made, by policy and design, dependent on investor goodwill. A key feature of the Eurozone was its construction so as to be vulnerable in this way. The never-to-be-broken Eurozone had its desired effect, which was to attract nervous capital to the peripheral countries of Europe. But when the global credit markets failed, that capital fled, and the institutions providing it failed. It would never return, just as it has never returned to the US private-label mortgage business.

To recognize the global dimension of the credit debacle is also to recognize that national programs of economic reform cannot resolve any national economic or debt problem. The credit markets are linked. Every sovereign investor knows that every other sovereign investor is looking not at each country separately but at the likely behavior of every other investor. Even if conditions stabilize for a time or ease slightly, a disturbance anywhere in the crisis zone will be felt in all the countries of the zone—no matter how well behaved they may have been and no matter how faithful to austerity or tolerant of pain. There is no reward for virtue in a credit market that is in permanent search of safety.*

In simplest summary: there is just one crisis. It is a crisis of worldwide growth and finance, with institutional variations between North America and Europe that have made the European problem more serious and more unstable. But ultimately both regions face deep and even intractable obstacles to full recovery and rapid growth. It is a crisis that is ongoing, unresolved, and without facile solution. It is time to face this situation and to ask, what to do?

---

* There is also no reward for virtue in a credit market in the grip of irrational exuberance, which raises a question of whether virtue is ever to be rewarded.

Fourteen

Beyond Pangloss and Cassandra

The analysis of resource costs and rents was well known to classical political economy but obliterated by growth theory in the postwar era. It must return. We must also restore the understanding achieved by Keynes and Minsky, and under the New Deal, of unstable speculation and financial fraud, later effaced by the doctrine of efficient markets. A new economics must rest on a biophysical and institutional framework, recognizing that fixed capital and embedded technology are essential for efficient productive operations, but that resource costs can render any fixed system fragile, and that corruption can destroy any human institution.

This is the economics of organizations developed by John Kenneth Galbraith, modified to emphasize that large, complex systems are not only efficient but also rigid. They are bound by rules, operating procedures, technique, and the force of habit. And so they are prone to lose efficiency when conditions change. When weakened by adversity, they become prey to destabilization from within, to fraud, predation, and looting. In this way, from a standpoint of a pure economic theory, the question of resource costs and the question of legal integrity are linked within a single conceptual framework in which efficiency and fragility are two aspects of the same system.

The policy economist is often asked how to fix such problems. But some things are given by principles that we do not control. The relationships of resource use to fixed costs, and of organization to management, are among these. Given globalization of economic life, and the scale of modern economic operations, we now confront these issues on a world scale. We have become very large, very complex, very efficient—*and therefore we have become very fragile*. The question of what to do, of what might be done, can come only after we understand the limits on our margin of maneuver.

The position taken by modern avatars of Keynes—especially Paul Krugman but also Joseph Stiglitz and in recent writings Lawrence Summers and many others—is that the problem is simple, the solution known, and the missing ingredients are only economic understanding and political will. The problem is a shortage of effective aggregate demand. The cure is more spending by government, business, foreigners, and private households. This simple argument is aimed mostly at the deficit hawks and debt hysterics, stuck in the world of the gold standard, who confect constraints out of accounting relationships and financial statements and live in awe of the bond markets or in fear of the central bank. For this purpose, the Krugman-Stiglitz-Summers position is a useful one.

But the biophysical framework warns us: matters are not that simple. What worked under some past conditions may not work today. That is— and to summarize the argument made earlier in this book—even were the political and ideological barriers to stimulus swept away, even if the New Deal were reinvented at full scale and with all the same political momentum and esprit de corps, there would remain at least four obstacles to achieving high growth and full employment.

First, energy markets remain both high cost and uncertain. And energy prices determine the price of all other resources, including food. The age of growth was enabled by cheap oil (and coal, and later gas) at stable prices. It created a system of fixed technologies that make heavy use of energy. Under fixed technologies, there is a world of difference between oil at $30 a barrel and oil at $100 or more. It's the difference between a world of high profits and rapid growth, and a world where margins are thin, profits alternate with losses, and where growth is likely to be slow at best.

Further, and of nearly equal importance, the world no longer expects any price of oil to remain stable. If demand rises sharply, investors know that hoarding and speculation will drive up the energy price. When the price is rising, it always makes sense to hold the product and sell it just a bit later, when the price is higher still. Volatile resource prices strongly discourage private investment at both ends of the energy market. When the price is high, new energy-using investment becomes unprofitable, so less of that will be done. But while high prices encourage new high-cost energy production, those investments (including renewables) can be undermined by the ensuing price fall. In this way, cost uncertainty *as such* slows the pace of economic activity. To the choke chain of speculative energy prices, one must add a whiplash effect of rapid changes.

In North America today, there are many who believe that shale gas will solve this problem, providing a new source of cheap energy for the century ahead. There is no doubt that shale is having a strong effect on the American economic picture at present writing, both directly as the industry booms and indirectly because the cost of gas in North America is far below that supplied by Russia to Europe.* But the outlook for sustained shale gas production over a long time horizon remains uncertain, for a simple reason: the wells have not existed long enough for us to know with confidence how

* In mid-2013 the comparative prices were $3.35 per trillion cubic feet (tcf) for North American gas and about $13 per trillion cubic feet for Russian gas in Europe.

long they will last. We don't know that they won't; but also we don't know that they will.* Time will tell, but there is the unpleasant possibility that when it does, the shale gas miracle will end.

The second great obstacle to renewed growth is that the world economy is no longer under the effective financial and military control of the United States and its allies. Since the end of the Cold War, the American military machine has demonstrated its impotence, most starkly in two wars: Iraq and Afghanistan. Of the web of semiclandestine control that used to extend through Latin America, Africa, Asia, and the Middle East, not much remains. Rising economic powers, notably China and India, are independent in every practical sense of the term; their competition for scarce and expensive resources cannot be constrained by force or fraud. Likewise Russia. For the moment, thanks to inertia and the lack of a viable alternative in the Eurozone or anywhere else, the world financial position of the United States has survived this decline of raw power and remains intact. For the time being.

Third, we have entered an era of radical labor-saving technological change. Digital technology undermines the previous structures of information transfer, production, inventory management, distribution, and marketing. Encouraged by antilabor tax structures, the new technologies replace many fewer jobs than they destroy. The jobs they do create are often in low-wage occupations, regions, and countries; the creative boom in high-end technology employment (mainly in the United States) ended with the turn of the millennium. As we have seen, the new technologies also tend to reduce the scope of paid and profitable economic activity, reversing the effect that automotive and home technologies had on employment in the machine age. So economic opportunities (for new business formation, for example) shrink alongside the loss of jobs. With fewer jobs, fewer people have economic incomes at any wage level. And therefore it becomes more

---

* Research on this matter is presently under way, but the answer won't be known until time has passed and the data are richer than they presently are.

difficult for public spending programs to gain traction, unless they are designed to create jobs directly—a difficult task organizationally in the modern world—or to provide incomes precisely to people who *do not* work for a living.

Finally, the private financial sector has ceased to serve as a motor of growth. The model of activity driven by speculative finance ran for thirty years, from the mid-1970s until the mid-2000s. In the 1990s, venture capital, backed by banks, gave us the information-technology boom. What was possibly the last great credit-fueled business boom of our time ended in 2000. In the following decade, mortgage capital, meaning loans to households rather than to businesses, gave us a pseudoboom in real estate, new home construction, and debt-financed consumption. That ended in 2007, taking with it the vast accumulated equity of the American home-owning population.* Years later, the private credit markets remain stagnant, and neither business, nor construction, nor households have returned in force to the credit markets.

In short, public provision of demand has been stymied, while the private provision of demand via new credit has not occurred. Therefore there will be no full recovery of demand. And even if there were, price volatility in the resource markets and the deployment of yet more labor- and capital-saving technology would soon choke it off.

To some, these barriers to growth may appear as welcome news. Why not live in a no-growth world? We are a wealthy species; don't we have enough already?† Can we even afford to grow, given the carbon-loading and environmental damage?

The problem with the no-growth position is that private business works for money. Growth is what gives private business, in general, the chance

---

* Shortly after, as we have seen, the ripples from that crash ended the Eurozone credit boom and precipitated the European crisis.

† *How Much Is Enough?*, a 2012 book by Robert and Edward Skidelsky, explores this question.

for profit. Negative growth in money terms means money losses, on average, throughout the business world.* If there are no profits to be had in the aggregate, the economic game becomes zero-sum or worse, which means that the winners, who are likely to be few, come at the expense only of losers, who are likely to be many.

In such a world, predators dominate. And while it's possible for economic activity to continue, since people overestimate their chances of gaining big prizes, it's not a pleasant world and likely not a stable one. Without the prospect of generalized profits made possible by economic growth, there will be little private investment, the capital stock will age and deteriorate, and many technical improvements, including those that make more efficient use of resources, will not be made. In sum, speculative markets will tend to convert a zero-growth or negative-growth economy into a collapse.

Thus fast growth is self-limiting, while negative growth leads to disaster. There remains one alternative. It is to engineer the economy to grow at a low, stable, positive rate for a long time, and to adjust ourselves materially and psychologically to that prospect. It is to pursue *slow growth*: a rate above zero but below what cheap energy and climate indifference once made possible. Achieving that much will require major reforms, followed by careful investment and persistent regulation on many fronts. Threading the needle of a slow growth rate over many years is no simple task. It is not the outcome anyone would choose in a world with no constraints. But it is the hope for survival of a modified capitalist economy in the world in which we actually live. So let's ask, what does it mean?

First of all, when resources become costly, there are things one cannot afford. It will be necessary to reduce the scale of institutions that use material resources as part of their fixed cost of operations. This is the kernel of wisdom in austerity. The eighteenth-century French foreign minister

* Falling prices, another consequence of negative growth, comport badly with fixed debts, creating a world of bankruptcies and business failure.

Anne-Robert-Jacques Turgot was right to worry about the expense of Versailles. The Mogul emperor Aurangzeb was right enough to worry about the expense of the Taj Mahal. Two major examples in contemporary America, neither of them nearly so beautiful or so worth preserving, are the global military and the big banks.

Thinking expansively for the moment, why exactly does the United States need an air force? Apart from enforcing an occasional no-fly zone, jet fighters have no current function. The new ones under development—the F-22 and F-35—are ongoing technical, cost, and procurement nightmares, with maintenance requirements such that they may never be deployable in any forward position. Strategic bombers are part of a long history of military futility stretching from Germany to Vietnam. They continue to have advocates, but there is almost no prospect for their further use in conventional war. For accurate demolition of selected targets, still occasionally necessary or useful as a threat, the cruise missile is highly effective. For the nasty work of selective assassination of tribal militants—and their wedding parties—there is the drone. Land-based nuclear missiles have never been used and never will be; their *only* surviving purpose is as a bargaining chip in arms-reduction talks. Meanwhile, close air support—still a useful function in such combat as there is—belongs mainly to the army and the marines. What does that leave for the air force? Troop and cargo transport. Those can remain.

Then again, what is the use of an army? Land wars in eastern Asia fell out of fashion with the fall of Saigon in 1975. After Iraq, another American invasion of any significant country seems most unlikely. Tank divisions are unlikely to be used ever again. Europe and Japan no longer need our garrisons, though it is useful to keep one in Korea. The army has a peace-keeping mission in situations such as Bosnia, but much of that could be performed, on the rare future occasions when it may be needed, by the National Guard. Threats to the American land mass from Canada or Mexico seem to be limited for the near future. On a long strategic view, it's hard to see exactly why the United States might not now take the path of Costa

Rica, which abolished its army in 1948. A new one can be built later, if ever required.*

As for the navy, its surface ships project power and patrol sea lanes while its submarines provide the remaining remnant of strategic deterrence. Arguably, both missions could be performed without aircraft carriers, which would in any event not survive beyond the early stages of any future war. (One might keep a few in service, just in case.) The navy remains a global stabilizer, for the simple reason that if the United States has a big one, no one else need be bothered. It's a sacrifice that America can make, saving resources at the world level. But the navy too could be smaller than it is. The Marine Corps and the Coast Guard—small and sometimes useful forces—one might leave alone.

Turning to the financial sector, banks are intermediaries. They provide nothing that contributes directly to current consumption or business investment. They are useful only insofar as they support either household consumption or business investment—and then only so long as they do so in an effective, responsible, low-cost way. Business underwriting was once such a function, but it entered a deep decline during the mortgage boom, if not before. Otherwise banks serve mainly to consolidate control and power, and they support this by exacting tribute, in the form of interest, from their borrowers. Financial firms also employ a large share of the best software and mathematical talent, in an arms race for computational superiority in their markets. From a social standpoint, this is predation: no net benefit to anyone outside the banking sector comes from it.

Perhaps the country would be better off without its big banks. The basic functions of banking for most of the public—deposits, payments, credit and debit cards—could be handled by a low-cost public facility,

---

* These suggestions are (I trust obviously) meant to provoke. However, news at press time suggests that the army will soon shrink to 1930s' levels; it may be that my thinking and that of the high command are not so far apart.

perhaps run by cities or states at municipal pay scales, or by the postal service. Smaller and regional and cooperative banks could grow into the work of business lending and of sorting good from weak household risks. Since executives of small banks are paid on a less lavish scale, the reduced cost of the financial plutocracy would be a social savings. There is no guarantee that these changes would bring financial stability: small banks can run in herds, and given the experience that bankers have acquired in distributing and hiding risk and fraud, there may be no solution, in the computer age, to the dysfunctions of finance. But a decentralized system with smaller top-level units, less powerful bankers, and stronger controls could not be a worse bet than the system that exists now.

Should government in general be given similar treatment? In fact, it already has been: in the United States, the civilian government has been shrinking in terms of jobs and services for three decades, with many functions now automated and computerized, as well as outsourced. At present writing, sequestration is subtracting from government spending every day. But the difficulty with treating government as a single entity for this purpose is that it isn't: there is no single-purpose entity called "government" but, rather, a wide array of specific and diverse regulatory and judicial functions. Many of these are provided efficiently, a fact reflected by the disciplined scale of civil service salaries, as compared with those of bankers and the higher echelons of the financial world.

Income transfers and taxation are public functions, both of which represent very large numbers in the public budgets. But they absorb very few administrative, or "real," resources. It is an analytical mistake, much favored by debt hysterics, to treat a Social Security payment as having the same effect on real resource use as, say, a helicopter contract or a courthouse. The latter is a use of real resources that might be deployed elsewhere. The former is just a check-writing and taxing service. Its purpose is to redistribute private consumption power, reducing it for some families (via payroll taxation) and increasing it for others (via benefit checks). It costs the country very little to provide this service; the real cost is just that of the computerized record keeping, and (as a redistribution) the checks themselves cost the country, or the economy, nothing at all.

So we come again to the vexed question of "entitlements," or, more properly, to the role of social insurance in a time of slow growth. In the United States, these include the programs Social Security, Medicare, and Medicaid, alongside deposit insurance, unemployment insurance, and the Supplemental Nutritional Assistance Program (formerly called "food stamps"). These are programs that somehow *always* end up in the crosshairs of the austerity crusaders. It is not just that *some* of the arguments for cutting back on the role of the public sector bear on these programs. Every single argument, a bewildering array of them, from the question of "solvency" of the trust funds that support Social Security, narrowly speaking, to the notion of "intergenerational accounting," to the larger question of the future public budget deficit and scale of the national debt—*all of these* somehow lead to the conclusion that the "entitlements" are unsustainable and must be cut. When one such argument (say, the scale of the budget deficit) recedes with a change of economic conditions, then another (say, the alleged long-term imbalance between benefits and payroll taxes with the social security system) is duly brought to the fore. A cynic might suspect that something other than strict policy analysis is at work; perhaps the goal of some "austerians" is *primarily* to motivate the reduction and destruction of these social insurance programs.*

But in an age of slow growth, a country needs the opposite. It needs more, stronger, and stabler social insurance programs. Franklin Roosevelt did not wait for full-employment prosperity before setting up Social Security in the first place; he did it in 1935, at a time when full recovery from the Depression had not yet been achieved. Deposit insurance—an even more perilous venture—was introduced in the first days of the New Deal,

---

* Eric Laursen's excellent 2012 book *The People's Pension* documents the history of the political wars against Social Security.

in 1933. Social insurance is an antidote to economic risk; its presence encourages private initiative and makes excessively defensive economic behavior unnecessary. In a world where the potential for private gain is limited by conditions and circumstances, a robust program of universal insurance for the essentials of decent life—old age, survivorship, disability, health care, and a safe harbor for savings—becomes more vital, rather than less so.

Two further aspects of the world-to-come bear on the need for robust social insurance. One is the need to reduce the energy intensity of economic life, which is to say, to increase the human element, including leisure, and decrease the material element in consumption. The other is the effect of technology on the demand for routine information processing and communications services, which means that ordinary business will, for the foreseeable future, be adding fewer new workers, in relation to revenues, than it has done in the past half century. Together, resource costs and new technologies create a situation where dependency ratios are set to rise even more than they already have.

A rising dependency ratio is not a bad thing. The ratio of eaters to farmers is much higher than a century back; no one complains. The proportion of people required in production jobs has been falling since the late 1950s. If the proportion now required in service jobs—for instance, retail, communications, information management, accounting, and so forth—now falls, there is no reason to regret it. The problem that remains is to find new areas of useful paid work, and to expand the opportunities for useful, instructive, entertaining, and sociable activity outside of work. To maintain decent living standards with improving technology ought not to be that hard. It is a matter of ensuring that the "right" groups of people work—and don't work—at any given time, and that all households have means of support suited to their needs.

Many writers have broached this problem over the years. Milton Friedman, for instance, long ago advocated a guaranteed personal income, in unlikely alliance with liberals such as James Tobin and Senator George

McGovern. Others, and notably in recent years the Washington left-liberal economist Dean Baker, have taken up the call for shorter hours at undiminished pay, emulating the French move toward a thirty-five-hour workweek under the government of Lionel Jospin in 2000. The difficulty with a guaranteed income scheme is twofold: there is a question of who exactly qualifies for the benefit and a question of how the benefit would interact with the general social expectation that one should work in order to live. The problem with a thirty-five-hour (or, alternatively, a four-day, nine-hour-per-day) week, on the other hand, is that it would require a major revision of business practices, imposing either shorter hours or more complicated work schedules on employers, while leaving at least some workers with the option of taking multiple jobs. It's not an insuperable obstacle, but not a trivial one.

In the situation created by the aftermath of the Great Crisis, a simpler, effective approach would be to ease the conditions under which workers can gain access to early retirement under Social Security. The problem is in part that many older workers are holding on to hard jobs (or collecting unemployment and engaging in fruitless job searches) only because they cannot afford to retire, while many younger workers are searching fruitlessly for employment that older workers have not yet vacated. A temporary window—say, three years—for improved early-retirement benefits* could work to solve both problems. It would permit a voluntary, graceful exit for older workers, and would be taken up mainly by those already out of work or laboring in hard jobs that have taken their toll on body and spirit. Those jobs would then be open for younger workers who want and need them. There would be no need for employers, meanwhile, to alter their practices; employers are fully accustomed to replacing workers as they age.

---

* One might, for instance, permit, for three years, early retirement under Social Security at age fifty-nine, and full benefits by age sixty-two or sixty-three. After three years, the retirement age could gradually revert to previous levels, depending on conditions at that time. Recently, evidence suggests that the Affordable Care Act is already having a similar effect, permitting people to leave jobs they only stayed in for the sake of medical insurance.

The approach of working on the jobs question through social insurance thus makes effective use of existing institutional structures that are already known to function efficiently and at low social cost. It has, in addition, two further advantages. First, their criterion of eligibility are well known. One works for a certain time in qualified employment, and one is eligible to receive the insurance benefit at a later date. Considerations of citizenship or legal residence, which would bedevil a guaranteed income scheme, do not apply. And there is a clear requirement to work (for those who can) in order to benefit, so that the program does not encourage freeloading, as a guaranteed income program would. Second, the income streams flowing to retirees, dependents, survivors, and the disabled are themselves a major stabilizing force on the economy at large. The old and disabled require care; the young require instruction. All of these groups can contribute to employment by spending their incomes on themselves. Providing them with sufficient means to do so is not a burden on the larger economy; on the contrary, it is an efficient, decentralized, small-government means of ensuring that the entire population has a realistic way to earn the income it requires.

Next, there is a question of what working people earn. Since the US federal minimum wage peaked in real value in 1970, it has become an afterthought of economic policy. For long periods, it languishes, declining in real value and touching an increasingly small fraction of the workforce. Periodically it is raised, producing momentary benefits for a few million workers, especially women, in low-wage regions. And then the decline and neglect set in again. One consequence is that families find it necessary, or at least useful, to deploy spouses and children in low-wage jobs in order to piece together the resources required to live. Another is that employers find it advantageous to recruit low-skilled immigrants, often illegally, to fill low-wage jobs that Americans are unwilling to take. A third is that eligible workers draw heavily on the Earned Income Tax Credit, a federal rebate to low-income employees with families to support, and on food stamps, making up their incomes at taxpayer expense and with the likely result that low-wage employers do not come under as much pressure, as they might otherwise, to raise their wages. Thus the federal government effectively subsidizes predatory labor practices, especially in the American South.

Many of these pathologies would yield before a large increase in the federal minimum wage.* The effect would be to raise and stabilize the incomes of relatively low-income working families, mainly in low-wage regions of the country. Small and medium businesses would experience some increase in labor costs but would in many cases make this up through a stronger customer base. Some younger workers would find themselves unable to compete for jobs, but if their family incomes were nevertheless higher, they would generally find it advantageous to return to school. Employers and labor brokers would have less of an incentive to seek out illegal labor, since the minimum wage would have to be paid to such workers, as well as to any others. Border enforcement could therefore be cut back. The premium accruing to union membership would be less; employers would therefore also have less of an incentive to resist unions.

In a slow-growth world, combined with cheap digital technologies, private business investment necessarily forms a smaller share of economic activity than has been the case in the postwar years. This is not a bad thing: with slower growth, you require less investment, in order that the investment you do have should be profitable. Should a larger share of investment materialize under the circumstances, that would merely produce a boom-bust cycle and end in generalized losses. So the income share earned by capital should be encouraged to decline, and that earned by labor should increase—precisely the opposite of the redistributive policies of the past thirty years.

---

* Say, from the present $7.25 per hour to $12 per hour, as proposed by this author and the former publisher of the *American Conservative*, Ron Unz. A minimum wage of $13 per hour has been put on the table in California by Rep. Mark Leno. A minimum of $15 is the present demand of fast-food workers, bless them.

In addition to a higher minimum wage and stronger social insurance, tax policy can work toward this goal. Present tax burdens, especially the payroll tax and sales taxes (and in Europe, the value-added tax, or VAT), fall heavily on current labor and work to discourage employment. That is because labor-intensive production and services, or, more precisely, services with a high ratio of volume to capital, are delivered repeatedly and taxed each time, whereas machinery—whether a car, household appliances, computers, or business equipment—is taxed only once, at the point of sale. After that, they render their services tax free. Reducing this distortion would not end the labor-saving effect of technological changes and capital investments, but it would slow the pace of machine-for-labor substitution and so increase job creation in the services sector.[*]

The implication for this is that taxes on labor should be cut, especially payroll taxes and sales taxes. On whom should they be increased? The right theoretical answer is that they should fall so far as possible on *economic rents*—on that part of income that accrues to the ownership of scarce resources, especially land, minerals, and energy, but also patents and copyrights and (in general) the fruits of innovation. Since there is a competing interest in innovation per se, one way to achieve this result is to tax accumulations more heavily at death by strengthening the estate and gift tax, with a substantial exemption but a very high rate on the largest fortunes. There is nothing intrinsically wrong with large accumulations as the reward for talent or creative genius, but there is also no case for allowing that wealth to be passed along beyond the end of the human lifetime, leading to the creation of dynastic wealth. Accumulations based on the control of urban land or reservoirs of coal and oil are another matter— often serving no larger social goals even at the time—and if they escape heavy taxation and are not given away during the life of the owner, then

---

[*] On this point, the work of the Georgist economist Mason Gaffney is illuminating, and I'm grateful for correspondence with him and with the economist and blogger Polly Cleveland.

the case for taxing them away at the turn of generations is doubly strong. Similarly, the estate tax serves as a final line of defense against the perpetuation of wealth generated by force and fraud.

The function of the estate and gift tax—proven successful in America for a century—is not to fund the government. It does not matter whether or not the estate and gift tax collects money for the public purse. The important purpose is to encourage the recycling of passive accumulations into active expenditure and employment. It does this by catalyzing gifts to appropriately tax-exempt institutions, including universities, nonprofit hospitals, museums, theaters, research centers, and churches. In this way, America's wealthy have a way to remain socially engaged, contributing, and esteemed members of their communities—an opportunity largely denied to the comparable classes of modern Europe. A useful further step, given present social needs, would be to create new tax-favored, philanthropy-attracting institutions to serve the needs of the elderly population, including provision of home care services, assisted living, and long-term care. If these could be run roughly as universities now are, and if they could be made to attract prestigious donors as museums and libraries once did (and occasionally still do), it would make a significant contribution both to the health and welfare of the older population, and to job creation for younger people.

The thrust of this constellation of policies is straightforward. It is to create an institutional, tax, wage, credit, social insurance, and philanthropic framework that favors the absorption of the working population into stable paid employment, while providing modest comfort for those who meet clear criteria (age, disability, student status) for not being in the workforce. The underlying insight is that a high-growth economic strategy favors capital investment, substitution of capital and energy for labor, and fosters increased inequality in a winner-take-all system. A slow-growth system cannot be simply a slowed-down version of the same model. That would be unstable; it would fail. A slow-growth model should instead foster a qualitatively different form of capitalism: based on more decentralized economic units with relatively low fixed costs, relatively high use of labor compared with machinery and resources, relatively low expected rates of return, but mutually supported by a framework of labor standards and social protections. Much of what a high-income, prosperous society values—education, health care, elder care, art, and sport—meet these criteria. The trick is to make them viable on sustainable terms.

And then, finally, there is the question of climate change.

Epilogue

When Homer Returns

In the summer of 2009, I attended a seminar sponsored by the Gorbachev Foundation and held in a small hotel in the hills of Umbria, near the town of Perugia, Italy. I was the only American present. There was one Italian and the rest—about a dozen—were friends and colleagues from the Russian Academy of Sciences and the Moscow School of Economics. When the moment came for my remarks, I addressed President Mikhail Sergeyevich Gorbachev—the last president of a disappeared country—directly:

"Mr. President, when Homer returns to write the history of our epoch, he will say that the Russian mathematicians swept out of Muscovy in 1991 and presented themselves before the gates of Wall Street, bearing the gift of quantitative risk management models. They were received with joy, set to work, and in twenty years had destroyed the place entirely. It was, he will say, the greatest Trojan horse operation since Troy."

Gorbachev responded: "I've been accused of worse."

The collapse of the Union of Soviet Socialist Republics, now two decades back, is a distant event to most Americans. Most decided long ago that it was the inevitable failure of an inferior system, forgetting (if they ever knew) just how much fear that system had instilled in us only a few decades before. Or they remember it as the triumph of Reaganism: the great success of an arms race that somehow broke the Soviet bank. In either case, the moral of the episode is reassuring. To American minds, it demonstrates the superiority of capitalism as we know it.

This is a fairy tale for children. In reality, at its peak, the real Soviet Union was a superpower like modern Europe and in some ways like the United States. It had been the world's "first successful developmental dictatorship"—in the phrase of Adam Tooze, a premier scholar of the Nazi war economy—having built an entire industrial heartland beyond the reach of the German army in 1941. In the 1980s, the USSR was the world's largest producer of (among other things) steel, nickel, wheat, cotton, and natural gas. It was (and its successor states remain) highly urbanized. It had its own aviation industry, space program, and a vast nuclear industry and arsenal with secret cities to support them, not to mention trains, subways, health care, universities, and high culture. "Upper Volta with nuclear weapons"—a common postcollapse gibe—it was not.

When seen as a physical system, the Soviet economy was like any other: it extracted resources from nature, converted them into usable products—alongside a great many unusable products and much waste. At the physical level, the Soviet economy was set up as a gigantic machine, designed by engineers and mathematicians, governed by a plan. It was intended to exploit increasing returns to scale, to invest (and therefore to grow) at the highest possible rate. Soviet factories were huge, high-volume affairs; the steel facility at Magnitogorsk, for instance, was the largest in the world—a scaled-up version of the US Steel works at Gary, Indiana, on which its design was based. It was a full-employment economy, built on the idea that everyone should work—but with notoriously weak incentives for workers to actually put effort into their work, especially once the spur of the gulags was removed in the 1950s and 1960s. It was a welfare state, run through state enterprises, with kindergartens, resorts, and clinics tied to factories.

The Soviet economy was a deeply integrated system, with little redundancy, little internal competition, weak capacity for introducing new technologies, and vulnerable to breakdowns in transportation and distribution. This did not matter all that much for bulk items such as oil or steel, but it was a serious problem for perishables like food. Fresh produce usually did not survive the trip from farm to market, which is why Russia's urbanites so prized their dachas. The postcommunist mayor of Moscow, Yury Luzhkov, made his reputation by attempting to reform the catastrophic food warehousing system in late-Soviet Moscow.

One way to sum up the Soviet system is to say that it operated with very high fixed costs. It had high overheads. To produce anything at all (or, for that matter, even to produce nothing), those fixed costs had to be paid. And they had to be paid whether or not output reached the consumer, and whether or not the consumer wanted that output when it did.

This was not a defect, it was a matter of design. Fixed costs are a key to efficiency, the mark of an advanced system. You make investments that enable you to take advantage of scale, technology, and interdependence. (Adam Smith wrote about this: "The division of labor depends on the extent of the market.") Efficiency is high especially at first, when the design of the system is in line with the cost of resources; resource use is optimized for the conditions that prevail when the system is first designed. It will make use of what is available most cheaply (placing electric power generators close to coal fields, for instance, or steel mills near iron ore deposits), and it will use the most efficient process designs at that moment (bringing automotive technology from Italy, for instance, to create the Soviet car industry in the 1960s).

If the system then runs at a high operating rate, the costs are spread over many units of output, and unit costs are low. So the system returns high value for its costs of production, especially (once again) at first, when the engineering is fresh and all those location decisions are well adapted to the geography of resources and markets. A newly built industry springs to the front line in technology and onto the world stage. This helps to explain the success of the Soviet industrial and therefore military response to Hitler—as good as the American or British, and under much tougher conditions since part of the country was being overrun. Something similar would also happen again after World War II in Germany and Japan, then Korea, and most recently in China.

For the Soviets, low resource costs continued into the postwar period, as the USSR developed its oil and gas reserves, and eventually became a lead supplier to Western Europe. This prompted American strategists to worry that political influence would follow, as sunflowers track the sun, and as the brutal Stalinist years faded in memory. And this in turn motivated the confrontational posture adopted by America and its dominant hard-line faction toward the USSR in the 1970s and 1980s—for instance, over cruise missiles, gas pipelines, and Afghanistan. The economic threat from the Soviet Union, in that time, seemed real because it was real.

But when conditions change, the advantage of a particular set of industrial choices tends to erode, for a simple reason: the design, which was adapted to the initial conditions, is no longer what you would have chosen under the new ones. Someone else, with newer technology or better access to some newly discovered resource, will have lower costs. And when waste and inefficiencies magnify these effects, a system built in this rigid way becomes fragile. The return on energy extracted starts to fall. The available surplus is less and less. Eventually the costs of production eat up the surplus, and in its final phase the system can continue to operate only at a loss. When this happens, economists start to speak of "negative value-added."

What does a country do when it starts to operate at a loss? Pretty much the same as a household or a firm: it carries on and hopes for the best. And for some time, the losses can be transferred to other parties—by deferring payment. This is done via external debts, contracted under the pretext that things will get better. And in the case of communist countries, it could also be done by forcing citizens to hold money for which they had no real use, because the goods they want are not available at the prevailing prices. This is called "suppressed inflation." The Soviets tried both expedients. Both worked for a while. And then they didn't work anymore.

Collapse happens in a rush. In the Soviet case, a major source of the collapse was the diversion of natural resources (oil and gas, especially) to external markets in order to pay down bank debt. This hurt domestic production, making the pressure to buy imports irresistible. And when the borders opened to external trade, no one wished to buy homemade products (textiles, appliances, even food) anymore. Demand for Soviet-made goods collapsed, just as domestic demand had collapsed in Eastern Europe when the Iron Curtain came down. Under the new private-economy rules, goods that couldn't be sold were not made. Output collapsed, and employment, and incomes.

More deeply, the political division of the country into fifteen successor states crippled industrial cooperation across what now became international borders. Industrial networks became even more fragile, unstable, and inefficient, or stopped functioning altogether. (The same happened in Yugoslavia.) And privatization created a crazy quilt of enterprises with essentially arbitrary structures of prices and costs. When one factory in a chain of suppliers could not earn enough to stay in business, the entire chain would, likely as not, fall apart.

In the collapse of the early 1990s, industrial production in the former Soviet Union dropped by around 40 percent. Factories closed, workers were not paid, systems of health care and education stopped working, and basic investments in housing and infrastructure ended. Living standards plummeted, and death rates—especially from violence and alcohol abuse—soared. The male life expectancy declined from around seventy-two years to fifty-eight. Anyone who could take money out of the country did so. The government was unable to tax, so it issued debt, internal and external, until the day in 1998 when it made the decision to cease paying on those debts. At that point, the ruble collapsed, and the destruction of the old order was complete. A new society—poorer, much more unequal, dependent on effective exploitation of the remaining natural resource base—had been born.

If this version of the story is about right, then we can ask: Could something similar happen in the United States? Or in Europe, for that matter? Or in Japan?

The United States is also an advanced society with very high fixed costs. We pay a high, fixed price for defense, education, health care, and transportation, and for public services of all types, including safety and environmental protection. We pay a high fixed cost for banking, whether or not the banks contribute anything to the goods and services we actually consume. We were once endowed with cheap energy and abundant raw materials at home, and we built our industrial capacity (near the Great Lakes, for instance) to take advantage of that. No longer. We pump our domestic energy these days from the ocean floor, in the Gulf of Mexico, from Alaska, and by fracking at high cost in hard rock.

Today we also buy oil abroad: from Canada, for example, where it is extracted from tar sands at a high cost. It is true that we pay for this, and everything else, with dollars that cost us nothing to create; in the short run, they remain unused claims on future production, stored up as Treasury bills and bonds. This is much better, for us, than the situation that faced the Soviets or the Yugoslavs, who had to borrow in a "hard" currency: namely, dollars. And it may go on for a long time. Whether it will depends on the continued willingness of the larger world to accept our payments. Should that ever stop, or even diminish in comparison to our appetite for the world's resources, we will have no escape from their rising real cost. Our ability to cope with that eventuality depends on our ability to think and plan ahead—a function for which we rely not on a planning agency but on Congress, the White House, and Wall Street. Enough said. Planning may be a deeply defective business, but the substitution of politics and financial arbitrage for planning does not guarantee a better result.

It's true that we are more efficient than the Soviets were—but by how much, especially recently? We have the virtue of business competition, and therefore some redundancy that the Soviets did not enjoy, but, again, by how much? Energy resources are dominated by small numbers of large and single-minded firms. And many of our most advanced sectors, such as aerospace, microchips, and computer operating systems, are dominated by near monopolies. If they fail at what they do—such as producing new aircraft safe enough to fly—then the American world position could be threatened quite quickly.

True, we have fostered and enjoyed technological change—most recently in the transformation of our communications technologies—and these reduce business costs. But are these gains sufficient, and particular enough to the United States, to offset the rise in resource costs and the squeeze on profits? If the answer is no, then how far are we, as an entire national economy, from running at a loss? Some of the same things that happened to the Soviet Union could happen to us. In fact, they may be happening now already—or would be, if the United States did not enjoy its natural gas boom and unique dispensation as the center of global finance. Except for that, we're not that different from any large industrial system faced with outmoded technologies, rigid enterprises, and rising external costs.

In truth, this analysis is simple. It is rooted in ideas that were explored fully in the theory of the business firm developed by Alfred Marshall, the great English economist and author of the first widely used economics textbook, *Principles of Economics*, first published in 1890. The key ideas—fixed and variable costs, increasing returns and monopolistic enterprise, the effects of confidence and uncertainty about costs on investment—are elementary. But for some reason, these ideas don't usually come up when leading economists, policy advisers, and politicians think and talk about economic issues.

This is a puzzle. It could be a fatal puzzle. Understanding what is happening to us—what could be happening to us—is a first step toward being able to change it, or, for that matter, to cope with it, if it cannot be changed. That is what the economics profession should be about. And sadly isn't.

The economists Axel Leijonhufvud and Earlene Craver wrote some of the most insightful contemporary papers on the Russian collapse. Their summary work was prepared for the World Bank in the mid-1990s, but the bank did not publish it. The authors were eventually able to publish it under other auspices in 2001. The opening lines of their summary read eerily at the present remove:

> At century's end, the real GNP of Russia was roughly half of what it had been in the last days of communism a decade earlier. In his inaugural address, President Putin would report that the Russian population had been shrinking at the rate of 700,000 per year. Numerous accounts spoke of the conspicuous consumption of the new rich contrasting garishly with the poverty of many Russians, and drew vivid pictures of the deterioration of education, health care and social security systems . . . No one among the Russian reformers or their foreign advisors or Western observers seems to have anticipated in 1990 the depth and duration of the unprecedented depression that Russia was about to undergo. The literature of the time generally conveys confidence that the Soviet system of central planning was well understood and, of course, that the capitalist market system was perfectly well understood. A good command of general economic principles, therefore, should suffice in order to chart a rational trajectory from one to the other.

Yet a good command of economic principles was not sufficient to foresee the Soviet collapse. And two decades later, we discovered that a good command of economic principles did not help foresee the world financial crisis either. Perhaps the problem lies with the economic principles or the way they have been understood.

And that's the reason for this book.

Acknowledgments

My greatest debt is to all those who have written on the crisis and whose work I've cited, often critically. Some may feel I have not done justice to their ideas. I am sure this is true.

This is a fairly gloomy work, and a departure, for me, from the optimistic Keynesianism I have expressed in the past. For bringing me to these dire straits I thank, in particular, Jing Chen of the University of Northern British Columbia. These pages contain many of his ideas, expressed as clearly I could manage without any mathematics.

Bill Black of the University of Missouri–Kansas City is our leading student of the economics of financial fraud. He will recognize his influence. Michael Marder and Charles Hall have helped educate me on energy. Paul Krugman and Joe Stiglitz have been admired friends for decades, notwithstanding differences expressed here.

My colleagues at Economists for Peace and Security, especially Richard Kaufman, Richard Parker, Linda Bilmes, Allen Sinai, Mike Intriligator, and Mike Lind, alongside the executive director Thea Harvey-Barrett, have kept me engaged with the problems of national security economics for many years.

263

Acknowledgments

Karel von Wolferen, Bruno Amoroso, Aurore Lalucq, Bertrand de Largentaye, Yanis Varoufakis, and Ping Chen have given me friendship and many conversations. With academic Post Keynesians, institutionalists, Marxians and modem monetary theorists, there have been too many meetings to recount. These pages bear the mark of long-ago friendships with Wynne Godley and Hyman Minsky.

My student colleagues at the University of Texas Inequality Project have been a source of encouragement, reflection, insight, and help—Wenjie Zhang especially, but also Beatrice Halbach, Aleks Malinowska, and Jaehee Choi. I am grateful for the backing of my dean, Robert Hutchings of the LBJ School of Public Affairs, for discussions with my other University of Texas at Austin students, and for the tireless work of my assistant, Lisa Johnson.

This book has not needed outside financial support, but it was helped indirectly by the backing given to EPS by Bernard L. Schwartz, and by that given to UTIP by the Institute for New Economic Thinking. I am deeply grateful to the sponsors of the Lloyd M. Bentsen Jr. Chair in Government/ Business Relations, and to the Bentsen family, for their support and also encouragement through the years.

The Washington Monthly gave me space, in early 2009, to surface the kernel of these ideas. *Ideas & Action*, the *Journal of Economic Issues*, and the *Cambridge Journal of Economics* have since allowed me to float a few more. The presidency of the Association for Evolutionary Economics, in 2012, was an honor that comes with the chance to give a well-attended speech. Lecture and seminar audiences all across the United States and in Copenhagen, Moscow, Brae, Pula, Rome, Paris, Seville, and many other places have helped me rethink these issues. Thank you all.

My agent, Wendy Strothman, has navigated me through many shoals. My editor, Ben Loehnen, displayed his talents and also his patience, while enduring a difficult moment in his own life. Simon & Schuster copyeditors Phil Bashe, James Walsh, and Nancy Sullivan, and designer Aline Pace were beyond superb.

Acknowledgments

I thank my remaining resident children, Eve and Emma, for filling our home with music while I wrote. And I thank Ying, for everything always.

From time to time I have wondered whether the pall on these pages is analytical, as it should be, or the fruit of a sour frame of mind. So far I've always concluded that, yes, this is what I do think. Tough luck.

Errors however are my own, and in this case, if History proves me wrong, I will be happy for that.

James K. Galbraith
April 20, 2014
Austin, Texas

Bibliography

Akerlof, George A., and Paul M. Romer. "Looting: The Economic Underworld of Bankruptcy for Profit." *Brookings Papers on Economic Activity* 24, no. 2 (1993): 1–74.

Akerlof, George A., and Robert J. Shiller. *Animal Spirits: How Human Psychology Drives the Economy and Why It Matters for Global Capitalism.* Princeton, NJ: Princeton University Press, 2010.

Albin, Peter S. *Barriers and Bounds to Rationality.* Edited by Duncan K. Foley. Princeton Studies in Complexity. Princeton, NJ: Princeton University Press, 1998.

Alesina, Alberto, and Silvia Ardagna. "Large Changes in Fiscal Policy: Taxes Versus Spending." NBER Working Paper 15438, National Bureau of Economic Research, Cambridge, MA, October 2009. Published later in *Tax Policy and the Economy.*Vol. 24. Edited by Jeffrey R. Brown. Chicago: University of Chicago Press, 2010.

Arrighi, Giovanni. "The Social and Political Economy of Global Turbulence." *New Left Review* 20 (March/April 2003).

Bibliography

Auerback, Marshall. "Time for a New 'New Deal.'" http://tinyurl.com/kg2gvpu, December 2008.

Bair, Sheila. *Bull by the Horns: Fighting to Save Main Street from Wall Street and Wall Street from Itself.* New York: Free Press, 2012.

Baker, Dean. *The Run-Up in Home Prices: Is It Real or Is It Another Bubble?* Washington, DC: Center for Economic Policy and Research, August 2002. www.cepr.net/documents/publications/housing_2002_08.htm.

Barofsky, Neil. *Bailout: An Inside Account of How Washington Abandoned Main Street While Rescuing Wall Street.* New York: Free Press, 2012.

Bernanke, Benjamin S. "The Great Moderation." Remarks at the meetings of the Eastern Economic Association, Washington, DC, February 20, 2004.

————. "Opening remarks." In *Achieving Maximum Long-Run Growth: A Symposium Sponsored by the Federal Reserve Bank of Kansas City.* Kansas City, MO, 2012.

Bilmes, Linda, and Joseph E. Stiglitz. *The Three Trillion Dollar War: The True Cost of the Iraq Conflict.* New York: W. W. Norton, 2008.

Black, William K. *The Best Way to Rob a Bank Is to Own One: How Corporate Executives and Politicians Looted the S&L Industry.* Austin: University of Texas Press, 2005.

Blinder, Alan S., and Ricardo Reis. "Understanding the Greenspan Standard." Presented at The Greenspan Era: Lessons for the Future. A Symposium Sponsored by the Federal Reserve Bank of Kansas City, Jackson Hole, WY, August 25–27, 2005.

Blinder, Alan, and Janet Yellen. *The Fabulous Decade: Macroeconomic Lessons from the 1990s—A Century Foundation Report.* New York: Century Foundation, July 1, 2001. http://tinyurl.com/mat25ua.

Bond, Patrick. "Crunch Time for US Capitalism?" *Z-Net Commentary.* December 4, 2004.

Brenner, Robert. *The Boom and the Bubble: The US in the World Economy.* New York: Verso, 2003.

Bibliography

———. "What Is Good for Goldman Sachs Is Good for America: The Origins of the Current Crisis." Center for Social Theory and Comparative History, UCLA, Los Angeles, April 18, 2009. www.sscnet.ucla.edu/issr/cstch/papers/Brenner CrisisTodayOctober2009.pdf.

Brynjolfsson, Erik, and Andrew McAfee. *Race Against the Machine: How the Digital Revolution Is Accelerating Innovation, Driving Productivity and Irreversibly Transforming Employment and the Economy.* Lexington, MA: Digital Frontiers Press, 2011.

Caballero, Ricardo J. "Macroeconomics After the Crisis: Time to Deal with the Pretense-of-Knowledge Syndrome." *Journal of Economic Perspectives* 24, no. 4 (Fall 2010): 85–102.

Carter, Susan B., et al., ed. *Historical Statistics of the United States.* Millennial ed. Cambridge: Cambridge University Press, 2006.

Chen, Jing, and James K. Galbraith. "Institutional Structures and Policies in an Environment of Increasingly Scarce and Expensive Resources: A Fixed Cost Perspective." *Journal of Economic Issues* 45, no. 2 (June 2011): 301–9. doi:10.2753/JEI0021-3624450206.

———. "Austerity and Fraud Under Different Structures of Technology and Resource Abundance." *Cambridge Journal of Economics* 36, no. 1 (January 2012): 335–43, doi:10.1093/cje/ber027.

Chen, Ping. *Economic Complexity and Equilibrium Illusion: Essays on Market Instability and Macro Vitality.* London: Routledge, 2010.

Churchill, Winston S. *My Early Life: A Roving Commission.* New York: Charles Scribner's Sons, 1930.

Cole, Harold L., and Lee E. Ohanian. "The Great Depression in the United States from a Neoclassical Perspective." *Federal Reserve Bank of Minneapolis Quarterly Review* 23, no. 1 (Winter 1999): 2–24.

———. "How Government Prolonged the Depression." *Wall Street Journal*, February 2, 2009.

Costofwar.com. Accessed April 13, 2013.

D'Arista, Jane. "The Overheated Mortgage Machine." *Flow of Funds Review & Analysis* (3rd quarter, 2002), 1–6.

Davidson, Paul. *Financial Markets, Money and the Real World.* London: Edward Elgar, 2003.

————. *The Keynes Solution: The Path to Global Economic Prosperity.* New York: Palgrave Macmillan, 2009.

Deffeyes, Kenneth S. *Hubbert's Peak: The Impending World Oil Shortage.* Princeton, NJ: Princeton University Press, 2001.

Dymski, Gary A. "Financial Globalization, Social Exclusion and Financial Crisis." *International Review of Applied Economics* 19, no. 4 (October 2005): 439–57.

Engel, Kathleen C., and Patricia A. McCoy. *The Subprime Virus: Reckless Credit, Regulatory Failure, and Next Steps.* New York: Oxford University Press, 2011.

Ferguson, Niall. *Colossus: The Price of America's Empire.* New York: Penguin Press, 2004.

Ferguson, Thomas, and Robert Johnson. "Too Big to Bail: The 'Paulson Put,' Presidential Politics, and the Global Financial Meltdown." *International Journal of Political Economy* 38, no. 1 (Spring 2009): 3–34.

Financial Crisis Inquiry Commission. *The Financial Crisis Inquiry Report: Final Report of the National Commission on the Causes of the Financial and Economic Crisis in the United States.* Washington, DC: US Government Printing Office, 2011.

Financial Crisis Inquiry Commission. Closed Session. Ben Bernanke, Chairman of the Federal Reserve. November 19, 2009. Confidential.

Foster, John Bellamy, and Robert W. McChesney. *The Endless Crisis: How Monopoly-Finance Capital Produces Stagnation and Upheaval from the USA to China.* New York: Monthly Review Press, 2012.

Frank, Jerome. *Save America First: How to Make Our Democracy Work.* New York, Harper, 1938.

Frank, Robert H. *Luxury Fever: Weighing the Cost of Excess.* New York: Free Press, 1999. Paperback ed. Princeton, NJ: Princeton University Press, 2010.

Bibliography

Friedman, Milton. *The Optimum Quantity of Money and Other Essays*. Chicago: Aldine, 1969.

Fullwiler, Scott. "Interest Rates and Fiscal Sustainability." *Journal of Economic Issues* 16, no. 4, December 2007.

Galbraith, James K. *Balancing Acts: Technology, Finance and the American Future*. New York: Basic Books, 1989.

———. "How the Economists Got It Wrong." *American Prospect*, February 6, 2000.

———. *The Predator State: How Conservatives Abandoned the Free Market and Why Liberals Should Too*. New York: Free Press, 2008.

———. "Is the Federal Debt Unsustainable?" Levy Economics Institute of Bard College *Policy Note*, 2011/2.

———. *Inequality and Instability: A Study of the World Economy Just Before the Great Crisis*. New York: Oxford University Press, 2012.

Galbraith, John Kenneth. *The Great Crash 1929*. Boston: Houghton Mifflin, 1954.

———. *The Affluent Society*. Boston: Houghton Mifflin, 1958.

———. *The New Industrial State*. Boston: Houghton Mifflin, 1967.

Gallegati, Mauro, Antonio Palestrini, and J. Barkley Rosser Jr. "The Period of Financial Distress in Speculative Markets: Interacting Heterogeneous Agents and Financial Constraints." *Macroeconomic Dynamics* 15, no. 1 (February 2011): 60–79.

Georgescu-Roegen, Nicholas. *The Entropy Law and the Economic Process*. Cambridge, MA: Harvard University Press, 1971.

Glassman, James K., and Kevin A. Hassett. *Dow 36,000: The New Strategy for Profiting from the Coming Rise in the Stock Market*. New York: Crown Business, 1999.

Godley, Wynne, Dimitri B. Papadimitriou, and Gennaro Zezza. "Prospects for the United States and the World: A Crisis That Conventional Remedies Cannot Resolve." Levy Economics Institute of Bard College. *Strategic Analysis*, December 2008.

Bibliography

Gordon, Robert J. "Is U.S. Economic Growth Over? Faltering Innovation Confronts the Six Headwinds" (working paper 18315, National Bureau of Economic Research, Cambridge, MA, August 2012).

Greenspan, Alan. *The Age of Turbulence: Adventures in a New World*. New York: Penguin Press, 2007.

———. "Activism." *International Finance* 14, no. 1 (Spring 2011): 165–82. doi:10.1111/j.1468-2362.2011.01277.x

Grunwald, Michael. *The New New Deal: The Hidden Story of Change in the Obama Era*. New York: Simon & Schuster, 2012.

Harcourt, Geoffrey C. *Some Cambridge Controversies in the Theory of Capital*. Cambridge: Cambridge University Press, 1972.

Harvey, David. *The New Imperialism*. New York: Oxford University Press, 2005.

Hayek, Friedrich von. *The Road to Serfdom*. Chicago: University of Chicago Press, 1944.

Herndon, Thomas, Michael Ash, and Robert Pollin. "Does High Public Debt Consistently Stifle Economic Growth? A Critique of Reinhart and Rogoff." *Cambridge Journal of Economics*, Advance Access, December 24, 2013.

Hobson, John A. *The Industrial System: An Inquiry into Earned and Unearned Income*. New York: Charles Scribner's Sons, 1910.

Jarsulic, Marc. *Anatomy of a Financial Crisis: A Real Estate Bubble, Runaway Credit Markets and Regulatory Failure*. New York: Palgrave Macmillan, 2010.

Keynes, John Maynard. *The Economic Consequences of the Peace*. New York: Harcourt Brace and Howe, 1920.

Koo, Richard C.. *Balance Sheet Recession: Japan's Struggle with Uncharted Economics and its Global Implications*. New York: Wiley, 2003.

Koopmans, Tjalling C. "Measurement Without Theory." *Review of Economics and Statistics* 29, no. 3 (August 1947): 161–72.

Krugman, Paul. "How Did the Economists Get It So Wrong?" *New York Times Sunday Magazine*, September 2009.

———. *End This Depression Now!* New York: W. W. Norton, 2012.

Kuznets, Simon. "Economic Growth and Income Inequality." *American Economic Review* 45, no. 1 (March 1955): 1–28.

Laursen, Eric. *The People's Pension: The Struggle to Defend Social Security Since Reagan.* Oakland: AK Press, 2012.

Leijonhufvud, Axel, and Earlene Craver. "Reform and the Fate of Russia." Document de travail de l'OFCE—OFCE Working Paper, No. 2001/3, Observatoire Français des Conjonctures Economiques (French Economic Observatory), Paris, May 2001.

Lewis, Michael. *The Big Short: Inside the Doomsday Machine.* New York: W. W. Norton, 2011.

Lomborg, Bjørn. "Environmental Alarmism, Then and Now: The Club of Rome's Problem—and Ours." *Foreign Affairs*, July/August 2012.

Lucas Jr., Robert E. "Macroeconomic Priorities." *American Economic Review* 93, no. 1 (March 2003): 1–14, doi:10.1257/000282803321455133

Mann, Michael. *Incoherent Empire.* London: Verso, 2003.

Marx, Karl. *Capital: A Critical Analysis of Capitalist Production.* London: Lawrence and Wishart, 1974.

McLean, Bethany, and Joseph Nocera. *All the Devils Are Here: The Hidden History of the Financial Crisis.* New York: Portfolio/Penguin, 2010.

Meadows, Donella H., Dennis L. Meadows, Jørgen Randers, and William W. Behrens III. *The Limits to Growth.* New York: Signet, 1972.

Meiksins Wood, Ellen. *Empire of Capital.* London: Verso, 2005.

Minsky, Hyman P. *Stabilizing an Unstable Economy.* New York: McGraw-Hill, 2008.

Mirowski, Philip. *More Heat Than Light: Economics as Social Physics, Physics as Nature's Economics.* New York: Cambridge University Press, 1991.

Mishel, Lawrence, Heidi Shierholz, and John Schmitt, "Assessing the Job Polarization Explanation of Growing Wage Inequality." Economic Policy Institute Working Paper, November 19, 2013.

Morgenson, Gretchen, and Joshua Rosner. *Reckless Endangerment: How Outsized Ambition, Greed, and Corruption Led to Economic Armageddon.* New York: Times Books, Henry Holt, 2011.

Orszag, Peter. "Estimated Costs of U.S. Operations in Iraq and Afghanistan and of Other Activities Related to the War on Terrorism." CBO Testimony: Statement of Peter Orszag, Director, Before the Committee on the Budget, U.S. House of Representatives, Washington, DC, October 24, 2007. Washington, DC: Congressional Budget Office.

Palley, Thomas I. *Plenty of Nothing: The Downsizing of the American Dream and the Case for Structural Keynesianism.* Princeton, NJ: Princeton University Press, 1998.

Paulson Jr., Henry M. *On the Brink: Inside the Race to Stop the Collapse of the Global Financial System.* New York: Business Plus, 2010.

Phelps, Edmund S. "The Golden Rule of Accumulation: A Fable for Growthmen." *American Economic Review* 51, no. 4 (September 1961): 638–43.

Raffer, Kunibert. *Unequal Exchange and the Evolution of the World System: Reconsidering the Impact of Trade on North-South Relations.* New York: St. Martin's Press, 1987.

Rajan, Raghuram G. *Fault Lines: How Hidden Fractures Still Threaten the World Economy.* Princeton, NJ: Princeton University Press, 2010.

Reinhart, Carmen M., and Kenneth S. Rogoff. *This Time Is Different: Eight Centuries of Financial Folly.* Princeton, NJ: Princeton University Press, 2009.

———. "Growth in a Time of Debt" (working paper 15639, National Bureau of Economic Research. Cambridge, MA, January 2010), www.nber.org/papers/w15639.

———. "Growth in a Time of Debt." *American Economic Review* 100, no. 2 (May 2010): 573–78. doi:10.1257/aer.100.2.573.

Rostow, W. W. *Stages of Economic Growth: A Non-Communist Manifesto.* 3rd ed. Cambridge: Cambridge University Press, 1991.

Roubini, Nouriel, and Stephen Mihm. *Crisis Economics: A Crash Course in the Future of Finance.* New York: Penguin Press, 2010.

Salter, W. E. B. *Productivity and Technical Change*. Cambridge: Cambridge University Press, 1969.

Samuelson, Robert J. *The Great Inflation and Its Aftermath: The Past and Future of American Affluence*. New York: Random House, 2008.

Sanders, Senator Bernie (D-VT). "Banks Play Shell Game with Taxpayer Dollars." Press release, April 26, 2011. http://tinyurl.com/3nant6c.

Scheiber, Noam. *The Escape Artists: How Obama's Team Fumbled the Recovery*. New York: Simon & Schuster, 2011.

Schumpeter, Joseph A. *Capitalism, Socialism and Democracy*. London: George Allen & Unwin, 1976 (1942).

Sen, Amartya, ed. *Growth Economics: Selected Readings*. Harmondsworth, UK: Penguin, 1970.

Shiller, Robert J. *Irrational Exuberance*. Princeton, NJ: Princeton University Press, 2005.

Shlaes, Amity. *The Forgotten Man: A New History of the Great Depression*. New York: HarperCollins, 2007.

Skidelsky, Robert. *Keynes: The Return of the Master*. New York: Public Affairs, 2009.

Skidelsky, Robert, and Edward Skidelsky. *How Much Is Enough? Money and the Good Life*. New York: Other Press, 2012.

Solow, Robert M. "A Contribution to the Theory of Economic Growth." *Quarterly Journal of Economics* 70, no. 1 (February 1956): 65–94.

———. *Growth Theory: An Exposition. The Radcliffe Lectures Delivered in the University of Warwick, 1969*. Oxford: Clarendon Press, 1970.

Sorkin, Andrew Ross. *Too Big to Fail: The Inside Story of How Wall Street and Washington Fought to Save the Financial System from Crisis—and Themselves*. New York: Viking, 2009.

Stiglitz, Joseph E. *Freefall: America, Free Markets and the Sinking of the World Economy*. New York: W. W. Norton, 2010.

———. *The Price of Inequality: How Today's Divided Society Endangers Our Future*. New York: W. W. Norton, 2012.

Bibliography

Suskind, Ron. *Confidence Men: Wall Street, Washington, and the Education of a President*. New York: HarperCollins, 2010.

Taibbi, Matt. *Griftopia: Bubble Machines, Vampire Squids, and the Long Con That Is Breaking America*. New York: Spiegel and Grau, 2010.

Taleb, Nassim Nicholas. *The Black Swan: The Impact of the Highly Improbable*. New York: Random House, 2007. 2nd ed., 2010.

Tirman, John. *Spoils of War: The Human Cost of America's Arms Trade*. New York: Free Press, 1997.

Tooze, Adam. *The Wages of Destruction: The Making and Breaking of the Nazi Economy*. Reprint ed. New York: Penguin Books, 2008.

United States Department of Agriculture, Report on Land Utilization, 1950.

Veblen, Thorstein, *Absentee Ownership and Business Enterprise in Recent Times: The Case of America*. New York: B. W. Huebsch, 1923.

———. *The Theory of the Leisure Class*. New York: Macmillan, 1899. Gutenberg e-book, 2008 (1899), http://www.gutenberg.org/ebooks/833

Vedder, Richard K., and Lowell E. Gallaway. *Government Size and Economic Growth*. Washington, DC: Congressional Joint Economic Committee, December 1998. www.house.gov/jec/growth/govtsize/govtsize.pdf.

Wedel, Janine R. 2001. *Collision and Collusion: The Strange Case of Western Aid to Eastern Europe*. New York: Palgrave Macmillan.

Wessel, David. *In Fed We Trust: Ben Bernanke's War on the Great Panic*. New York: Crown Business, 2010.

Yergin, Daniel. "There Will Be Oil." *Wall Street Journal*. The Saturday Essay. September 17, 2011. http://tinyurl.com/3tdsaau.

Index

Index

Chen, Ping, 89
Chicago economists, 47
"Chicago school," 65–66
China, 44, 54, 55, 56, 66, 77, 95,
    102–3, 108, 113, 119, 125,
    208, 214, 221, 240, 258
  as U.S. bond holder, 56
choke-chain effect, 95–111
Churchill, Winston, 116
Citigroup, 150
Citywide Builders, 151–52
civil service, 245
class struggle, 75–76
Cleveland, Ohio, 151–52
climate change, 28–29, 50, 109–10
Clinton, Bill, 57, 59, 85, 167
Club for Growth, 48
Club of Rome, 49–50
coal, 95, 96, 103, 136, 138, 239
Cold War, 25
Cole, Harold, 189–92, 194, 195,
    197, 198
colonialism, 115–16
colonies, 23
Colossus (Ferguson), 114–15
commodity dumping, 54
Commodity Futures Modernization
    Act (2000), 91
communism, 24, 25
Community Reinvestment Act of
    1977, 8–9
computers, 138–39
Confidence Men (Suskind), 1
Congress, U.S., 171, 173, 181,
    183–84, 222–23
Congressional Budget Office (CBO),
    173, 174, 175, 214, 217
Congressional Joint Economic
    Committee, 195
Congressional Oversight Panel, 2

conservation, 45–46
consols, 101
consumer culture, 136–37
consumption, 24, 27, 41
control fraud, 160–61
copyrights, 251
corporations:
  fixed costs of, 101
  resource scarcity and, 104
Costa Rica, 243–44
Council on Foreign Relations, 189–90
counterfeiting, 150
crackpot counterrevolution, 189–205,
    207, 221
Craver, Earlene, 262
creative destruction, 134–35, 137–38,
    140, 146
credit, 32, 184–85, 209
credit-default swaps, 91, 154, 155,
    182
credit markets, 235
"crowding out," 32
"Crunch Time for U.S. Capitalism"
    (Bond), 75
Cuba, 102
cult of zero, 207

D'Arista, Jane, 81*n*
Davidson, Paul, 157
debt, household, 12–13, 56, 77, 172
debt ceilings, 213, 213*n*, 223
debt-to-GDP ratio, 214–20
Deffeyes, Kenneth S., 40*n*
deficits, 36, 83–84, 85–87, 209–10
  budget, 186, 212, 213–14, 221,
    230–31
  trade, 41, 44, 56, 84–85, 105,
    211–12
deflation, 62
de Gaulle, Charles, 36, 37

government and, 194–95, 203
technical change and, 129–31,
132n, 133
"Growth in a Time of Debt" (Reinhart
and Rogoff), 204
Grunwald, Michael, 179
guaranteed personal income, 247–48,
249
Gulf of Mexico, 40
Gulf War (1991), 45, 113, 121

Haditha massacre, 123
Hansen, Alvin, 8n
Hartz reforms, 228
Harvard University, 74
Hassett, Kevin, 82n
Hayek, Friedrich von, 24
health, 25
hedge positions, 88
Herndon, Thomas, 204
Hitler, Adolf, 116, 258
Hobson, J. A., 11
Ho Chi Minh, 120
Holland, 108, 227
Home Affordable Modification
Program (HAMP), 182–83
home ownership rates, 160
home values, 172
House Appropriations Committee,
179
household debt, 12–13, 56, 77, 172
household spending, declines in, 172
housing, 25, 160
bubble in, 80–81
price/rental ratio in, 82
housing policy, 8–9, 10
"How Did Economists Get It So
Wrong?," 65–66
Hubbert, M. King, 40, 40n
Hubbert's peak, 40n

Hubbert's Peak: The Impending World
Oil Shortage (Deffeyes), 40n
Hume, David, 207–8
Hussein, Saddam, 45, 57, 122
hydroelectric dams, 102–3
hydrofracking, 103, 109

imbalances, concept of, 207–8
Impact of Poor Underwriting Practices
and Fraud in Subprime RMBS
Performance, The, 153–54
imperialism, 97
income inequality, see inequality,
income
income taxes, 187
index arbitrage, 105
India, 54, 116, 117–18, 123, 240
industrial age, 131
industrial organization, 30–31
industrial policy, 45n
industrial revolution, 113
inequality, income, 11–17, 30, 66, 77
effects of technology on, 130
information revolution and, 140–41
In Fed We Trust (Wessel), 1
inflation, 36, 39, 41, 42, 44, 46, 47,
57, 59, 61, 62, 111, 127, 176,
213–14
and budget deficits, 213–14
collapse of, 55–56
monetarist explanation for, 47
information revolution, 137–47
inequality and, 140–41
information-technology boom, 85
Inside Job, 149
interbank lending markets, 171, 220
interest rates, 32–33, 33n, 41, 46, 59,
103, 178, 181, 208
determinants of, 220–21
recession of 1970 and, 42

Index

mortgage-backed securities, 182*n*

mortgage capital, 241

mortgages, 150–55

Moscow School of Economics, 255

My Early Life (Churchill), 116

Naked Capitalism (blog), 80

Naked Keynesianism (blog), 80

Napoleon Bonaparte, 116

National Bureau of Economic Research, 199

National Guard, U.S., 243

National Income and Product Accounts, 83

national income identities, 83–87

national independence, 117–18

National Industrial Recovery Act (NIRA), 106*n*, 191, 198

nationalization, 182

natural gas, 103, 109, 136, 239

neutron loans, 149

New Classicals, 59–60, 203*n*

New Deal, 1, 11, 35, 106*n*, 143, 143*n*, 180*n*, 181, 187, 190–94, 197, 198, 238, 246

New Economics, 35, 42, 47

New Industrial State, The (Galbraith), 159*n*

New New Deal, The (Grunwald), 179

New Zealand, 204

ninja loans, 149

Nixon, Richard, 45, 46, 59

recession of 1970 and, 42–43

Nocera, Joe, 149, 152–53

nonaccelerating inflation rate of unemployment (NAIRU), 176–77

nonlinear financial dynamics, 87–92

North American Free Trade Agreement (NAFTA), 55

North Korea, 125

Norway, 108

nuclear power, 136

Obama, Barack, 1–2, 153, 175, 177, 179, 198

Obey, David, 179

Office of Management and Budget (OMB), 174, 175

Office of the Comptroller of the Currency, 167

Office of the Special Inspector General for the Truobled Asset Relief Program (SIGTARP), 2

Office of Thrift Supervision, 167

Ohanian, Lee, 189–92, 194, 195, 197, 198

oil, 43–44, 45–46, 49, 95–96, 100, 109, 110, 135–36, 138, 143, 239, 260

prices of, 31, 40, 41, 43–44, 54–55, 61

oil industry, 39–40

domestic peak oil in, 39–41

oil shocks, 43, 49, 108

Operation Desert Storm, 121

Organisation for Economic Co-operation and Development (OECD), 199, 201–2

organizational economics, 158–60, 237–38

Organization of Petroleum Exporting Countries (OPEC), 43, 47, 106

Ottomans, 113

output, 28, 30

outsourcing, 133

overcollateralization, 154

overnight banking loans, 33

Pakistan, 125

Palley, Thomas, 13